KILL THE KING

& Other Conspiracies

D. LAWRENCE-YOUNG

CRANTHORPE
—MILLNER—
PUBLISHERS

Copyright © David Lawrence-Young (2022)

The right of David Lawrence-Young to be identified as author of this work has been asserted by him in accordance with section 77 and 78 of the Copyright, Designs and Patents Act 1988.

All rights reserved. No part of this publication may be reproduced, stored in a retrieval system, or transmitted in any form or by any means, electronic, mechanical, photocopying, recording, or otherwise, without the prior permission of the publishers.

Any person who commits any unauthorized act in relation to this publication may be liable to criminal prosecution and civil claims for damages.

Many of the names, characters and incidents in this book are based on the truth. However, the conversations have been created by the author as he has imagined them to have taken place. Any resemblance to actual people, locales and events are as accurate as research has allowed and beyond the intent of the author or the publisher to be misleading or untruthful.

First published by Cranthorpe Millner Publishers (2022)

ISBN 978-1-80378-004-7 (Paperback)

www.cranthorpemillner.com

Cranthorpe Millner Publishers

Historical Novels by D. Lawrence Young

Fawkes and the Gunpowder Plot

Tolpuddle: A Novel of Heroism

Marlowe: Soul'd to the Devil

Will Shakespeare: Where was He?*

The Man Who Would be Shakespeare

Will the Real William Shakespeare Please Step Forward**

I, Master Shakespeare

Of Guns and Mules

Of Guns, Revenge and Hope

Arrows Over Agincourt

Away, Away from Botany Bay

Anne of Cleves: Unbeloved

Catherine Howard: Henry's Fifth Failure

Six Million Accusers: Catching Adolf Eichmann

Mary Norton: Soldier Girl

Two Bullets in Sarajevo

King John: Two-Time Loser

Go Spy Out the Land

Entrenched

Emma Hamilton: Mistress of Land and Sea

My Jerusalem Book (Editor)

Villains of Yore ***

Colonel Blood, Soldier, Robber, Trickster***

*Reissued as: Welcome to London, Mr. Shakespeare

**Reissued as: Who Really Wrote Shakespeare?

***Also published by Cranthorpe Millner

As: David L. Young

Of Plots and Passions

Communicating in English (Textbook)

The Jewish Emigrant from Britain: 1700-2000
(contrib. chapter)

Website: www.dly-books.weebly.com

Contents

Dedicated, and with apologies to my wife, Beverley, who has had to share our humble home with all sorts of nefarious and deadly characters, royal and otherwise.

Also to my mother, Leah Young, who first got me interested in the British royalty.

Preface

In the 1960s, when I should have been doing my homework, I was often to be found absorbed in Hugh Ross Williamson's riveting book, *Historical Whodunnits.* At that time, no-one - including me – could have guessed that one of the historical grains that would grow out of this 'illicit' reading would be the present book.

"Look into the seeds of time," Banquo commanded the witches in Shakespeare's *Macbeth*, "and say which grain will grow and which will not." For lovers of history, his command was as relevant then as it is today. This fascination with history expresses itself in our wanting to learn what happened in the past, who and what caused these actions and what happened as a result. Is there anything more intriguing than imagining the details, the sounds and the colours of the various conspiracies that are described on the following pages?

• How were the Princes in the Tower really murdered (if in fact they were?) Were they smothered to death, stabbed or poisoned?

• What happened to Amy Robsart, the wife of Queen Elizabeth I's favourite courtier? Was she pushed down the stairs to her death, or did she merely trip over the hem of her skirt in a fatal accident?

• Were the Gunpowder Plotters 'set up' and infiltrated by the authorities as a way of blackening the name of the English Catholic community?

• What did the Earl of Ruthven hope to gain by killing King James I in a back room of his Gowrie Castle?

• Who tried to kill Queen Elizabeth II in 1970 in Australia? What would they have gained from this alleged 'accident'?

I thoroughly enjoyed writing and researching this book and would like to thank my family and friends for their support and for hosting me on my regular trips back to Britain for research purposes: Derek Greenacre, Malcolm and Jean McCarthy, Carol and Joss Ollett, Patrick and Christine Nethercot, Reeva and Frank Godson, Rod Press and Marcia Feingold, Euan McPhee and Nona Wright, Colin and Shaney Wicks and Pat and Paul Zatz.

Even though *Kill the King & Other Conspiracies* has been written as a 'history is fun' book, I have tried hard to be as historically accurate as possible. However, if you find any mistakes, please write to me at: dlybooks15@gmail.com and accept my apologies.

D. Lawrence-Young,
November 2021,
Jerusalem, Israel

Introduction

The old man settled himself down comfortably in the old armchair. It was his favourite piece of furniture in that airy sitting room. The armchair was old and covered with some sort of pale brown, velvety floral material, which, to be honest, had looked browner and richer in the past. But this didn't concern Professor Warkworth. It was old, and he felt at home sitting in it. Sitting in this well-worn armchair next to the bay window overlooking the garden was like being with an old friend. Old, reliable and comfortable. In fact, the two of them had known each other for many years. They had both grown up and changed together over the past forty years – the professor, of course, more than the armchair.

But now the old man wasn't really thinking about his favourite piece of furniture. He was thinking about King Charles. King Charles II. Ah! there was a man, the old man thought, settling himself down to read about the 'Merry Monarch'. He knew how to live. At least, when he became king, that is. But life can't have been too much fun while he was on the run from Cromwell's troops or in exile in France. But he certainly made up for it afterwards, the old man thought, and smiled.

There he was, a young prince, brought up by an arrogant father and an extravagant mother. He had been forced to see his father lose his power, become a prisoner of the Scots, and finally end up as a royal prisoner who lost his head to Cromwell's executioner. Fortunately for Charles, these grim experiences didn't cause him to lose his love for life or women. When he became king on his return to England from his ten-year exile in France, his court became known as the bastion of licentiousness, the likes of which had never been seen or heard of before in the land.

Ah! there was a man, Warkworth repeated to himself. To survive a stuffy and suffocating childhood, civil war and exile and then bounce back to enjoy the favours of the most beautiful and vivacious ladies of his court. These included the beautiful, if somewhat imperious, Countess of Castlemaine, and the gorgeous Duchess of Richmond, to say nothing of course of Nell Gwynne, the actress and orange seller. Yes, he really must have been quite a fellow. Dark and swarthy, with long black curly hair reaching down to his shoulders, you couldn't have ignored him. 'Old Rowley' he was called. Now where did that nickname come from? Did it come from rolling from bed to bed, or am I just being crude? Yes, I must make the effort to find out.

He got up and walked over to the overcrowded bookshelves behind him to consult a heavy tome on the Stuart kings. As he pulled it off the shelf above his head, a dark green leather bookmark stamped in gold, 'Bosworth Battlefield Visitors' Centre, Leicester', fell out of the book. The professor placed it on a nearby coffee table. The bookmark had been a present from one of his students four years ago. It set his mind off once again, but this time about a different king and a different era. Richard III: 'A horse! A horse! My kingdom for a horse!'

22 August 1485, the Battle of Bosworth. The convenient event, that is, for historians that had settled the fate of the Plantagenet dynasty together with the personal destiny of Richard III. Now was this king really as evil and as devious as Shakespeare and countless history books had portrayed him? Was it Richard 'the Crouchback' who was responsible for the murder of the two young princes in the Tower of London? Was he really the forerunner of the 'wicked uncle'? Well, it was too late now. Prince Henry, the dashing Duke of Richmond may have sealed King Richard's fate on that Leicestershire battleground over five hundred years ago, but William Shakespeare had fixed Richard's place in history and the popular imagination more finally and effectively than any learned history book or Royal Commission could have done. The Bard had achieved

the most effective propaganda job on Richard that anyone could have done and he wasn't really a historian. Just a brilliant dramatist who had written great plays, putting bums on seats in the Globe theatre in which he had shares. But now it was up to the sceptics and the keen and earnest members of the Richard III Society to try and resurrect Richard's reputation as a good king, a king whose motto was *Loyaulte me lie* (Loyalty binds me).

Was he really worse than any of the other Plantagenet kings? Professor Warkworth wondered. Had he chopped off any more heads than the others? Had he flirted with more women than other kings? His older brother Edward IV was a greater womaniser, but most people today know nothing or little about him or his rapacious capacity for the fair sex. Edward IV didn't take up much room in the kids' history books. The professor knew that if you stopped the average 'man in the street,' this generic being wouldn't have the faintest idea about the dates of Edward's reign, let alone know any more details about his battlefield or bedroom exploits.

What a country we are, Professor Warkworth mused. We teach our history as if it all centred around our kings and queens. But I'm guilty too. I often did the same, especially when I was teaching at the local grammar school before I ended up lecturing at the university.

But what a terrible lot of monarchs we had. Most of them were completely unsuitable for the job. George I couldn't speak English and I don't think that his son, George II could, either – or not much better. Henry VI suffered several bouts of mental illness during his reign while the same could also be said for George III three hundred years later. Henry VIII was obsessed by having a son to reign after him, and George IV thought only about women and other worldly pleasures.

Well, I suppose that's a trifle better than the vain Edward II or Richard I. 'Lionheart' indeed! He spent most of his time either fighting in France and the Holy Land or thinking about young men and maybe horses instead. In addition, he bled the country financially dry with his Crusades while spending less than six months of his ten-year reign back here in England. And that's to say nothing about the huge ransom England had to pay in order to free him from the Holy Roman Emperor, Henry VI's grasping hands. As for being the perfect example of a model and merciful Christian king – well, wasn't this noble crusader the one who had nearly three thousand Moslem prisoners-of-war, men, women and children executed after he had captured the important city of Acre at the Massacre of Ayyadieh?

And what about Richard II? His only claim to fame was to confront the mob face-to-face during the Peasants' Revolt when he was only fourteen years old. And after that, it was downhill all the way. His only useful legacy to history was the use of the handkerchief, a device which caused his nobles to think that he was a useless and effeminate snob.

Now come to think of it, Warkworth asked himself, what am *I* going to leave to history? A generation of history students? Maybe they'll become history teachers of one sort or another like myself, or perhaps some will work in libraries or for organisations like English Heritage or the National Trust. Perhaps my books on King Stephen and King Edward III will become standard textbooks on those two medieval monarchs. Or, if I'm lucky, my latest book, *The Perennial Battle: King versus Church,* will become a bestseller. That is, in academic circles. Well, if not, it was fun to write anyway, beginning with all that research on William Rufus nine hundred years ago.

Suddenly Warkworth's thoughts were interrupted as the door opened and a young teenage girl came into the room.

"Grandpa," she said, "Granny wants to know if you want a cup of tea now. She said the kettle has just boiled and she'll make you a cuppa before she goes shopping."

The old man looked up at his sixteen-year-old granddaughter standing in front of him, hands on hips, waiting. Her parents, my daughter and her husband, have done a good job in bringing up my Sophie, he thought. And not only that, but she has also inherited my love of history as well. She's always asking me questions about this king or queen and why they did this, that and t'other.

"Yes, Sophie. Tell Granny I'd like a cuppa. And tell her not to forget the chocolate digestive biscuits this time."

"As if she would," Sophie replied, walking out of the room. "She's known you too long. And I suppose you want it in your coronation mug as usual?"

"Of course," Professor Warkworth replied. And he settled back once again in his favourite armchair to ponder on the legacy of history.

Chapter One
The Murderous Anglo-Saxon Monarchy

King Edward the Martyr   King Edmund Ironside

"Grandpa," Sophie asked as she munched on a chocolate digestive biscuit. "Did you know that Alfred the Great is the only English king who has been called the Great?"

"Yes Sophie. But you're both right and wrong at the same time."

"How so?"

"It's true that he is the only king who was called the Great, but strictly speaking, he wasn't English. He was actually the Anglo-Saxon king of Wessex, you know, Hampshire and Dorset and that area where we went on holiday last year. Wessex was one of the seven kingdoms that made up what we call England today, and he in fact called himself 'King of the English.' His faithful biographer, Asser, called him the 'Leader of the Christians'."

"And did he really burn the cakes, as he was supposed to have done?"

"Well, Sophie my dear, this is one of those stories in history that is hard to prove or disprove. But if he did, then Asser didn't mention it. I know that this story first appeared about a hundred years later. Now if you go over to the bookcase and take down that rather tatty looking brown book there… there… behind that photo of Winchester Cathedral, you'll find a poem about this cake-burning episode. How true it is I don't know, and the poem is anonymous anyway. Ah, here it is."

Putting on his reading glasses, Professor Warkworth read it out:

> *Where lying on the hearth to bake*
> *By chance the cake did burn:*
> *"What! Canst thou not, thou lout,"*
> *quoth she,*
> *"Take pains the same to turn?*
> *But serve me such another trick,*
> *I'll thwack thee on the snout."*
> *Which made the patient king,*

good man,
Of her to stand in doubt?

"But if this story is true or not, he was certainly a great king. He brought peace and quiet to that part of the land for a while and he also founded a Navy to patrol the coasts as well as being a good and just administrator. He also knew how to utilise other people's talents for the benefit of the country, so I think you can say that he really deserved the title 'Alfred the Great.' And this is, of course, in contrast to some of the other Anglo-Saxon kings who were to succeed him over the next one hundred and fifty years or so, until William the Conqueror came along."

"Like who?"

"Well, Edmund I or 'the Magnificent,' as he is sometimes called."

"Why? What dirty deeds did this magnificent man do?"

"Well, my dear Sophie, there's no need to be like that about him. As a king, he didn't do such a bad job. He was the grandson of Alfred the Great and successfully defeated the Danes who had become a real pain in the neck. Like Alfred, he brought peace and quiet to England, and he even gave Cumbria, the area around the Lake District, to the Scottish King Malcolm, but only on the condition that he should be his 'fellow worker by sea and land,' as the early *Chronicles* reported."

"So he was 'Magnificent' then?"

"Yes, but his luck ran out in May 946 when he was killed."

"How? Who by?"

"Oh, it was quite stupid really. The equivalent of a drunken brawl in a pub today. It was like this. Edmund was feasting at Pucklechurch in Gloucestershire. Come, picture the scene, King Edmund is sitting at the head of the table with his favourite lords, thanes and earls. They're all quaffing ale and mead and…"

"… and boasting to each other how many Danes they've killed in battle and how many women they've ravished."

"Exactly. Anyway, this scruffy looking robber called Leofa bursts into the celebration. It seems that he was, as the papers write today, already known to the authorities, and Edmund's guards tried to arrest him. And this, Sophie, is probably what happened:

Edmund: What's that noise by the door?
Cedric: It's someone who wants to come in and see
        you, sire. But the guards have told him you
        don't want to be disturbed.
Edmund: Who is it?
Cedric: Leofa, sire.
Edmund: The robber?
Cedric: Yes, sire.
Edmund: Hmm, the guards are right. Tell them to
        throw him out. I don't want to see him.
Cedric: Yes, sire. (Cedric gets up to carry out the

king's orders.)

Edmund: And Cedric, tell the guards that I don't want to see him now or even hear of him ever again.

Cedric: Yes, sire. (Cedric heads off in the direction of the noise and scuffling by the doorway.)

Edmund: (Lifting a large ruby-encrusted goblet) Come my friends. Let us ignore this Leofa ruffian and celebrate. You, boy, tell the cook to bring out some more venison.

And just as the king and his favourite earls were just about to tuck into a particularly juicy haunch of venison, the scruffy black-bearded Leofa burst through the assembled men and stood there facing the royal cupbearer.

"Out of my way, scum!" Leofa shouted, pushing the blond servant aside. The cupbearer did his best to stand his ground but it was to no avail. Leofa then drew his dagger, a particularly nasty looking weapon, and made stabbing motions towards the king's man. Suddenly he drew blood as a long bloody slash appeared down the length of the cupbearer's arm, who then fell aside.

Leofa faced his king. Edmund looked around for a sword or dagger as he was unarmed. A steward behind him thrust one over to him, over the king's shoulder. As Edmund turned to grab it, Leofa lunged at him. Edmund instinctively leaned to the side and seized a handful of the robber's long black greasy locks.

"Quick man! Stab him!" Edmund shouted to his

steward. But as he shouted, Leofa twisted himself round and plunged his dagger into the king's stomach. Edmund fell, clutching himself as the blood poured out over his fingers and down his leggings. He slumped forward, crashed onto a stool, his golden circlet crown hitting the table with a dull metallic clang as it rolled onto the rush-covered ground. It finally came to rest under a food-laden trestle table.

"The king's dead!' someone cried. And so he was.

"Edmund died almost immediately, his death putting paid to a promising reign. In fact, he ruled for only seven years, and the Church called him the 'Deed-doer' as well as 'the Magnificent'."

"So Grandpa, it was exactly as you said, a pub-brawl. And by the way, what happened to this Leofa thug?"

"Oh, I'm sure he didn't live long after that. Justice was pretty quick and nasty in those days. But whatever happened, you can't say that it was really a conspiracy, but this cannot be said for our next Anglo-Saxon hero, King Edward the Martyr."

"Well, there's another modest title for you."

"Oh, my dear. You are in a cynical mood today. But to be honest Sophie, this title was bestowed upon him after his death."

"Another violent death?"

"Oh, very. This is what happened and I think here you can certainly use the word plot or conspiracy. In fact, here you have all the ingredients of a good and bloody story: a king, unhappy relations, a wicked and hostile stepmother, lots of blood and a castle."

"Sounds like a typical Shakespearean plot."

"True, but the Bard tended to prefer writing about Roman rulers or medieval and Tudor kings. He left the Anglo-Saxon ones alone, apart from King Lear, and *he* never really existed in the way that Shakespeare described."

"So what happened to our martyred Edward? By the way, when was he king?"

"From 975 until 978."

"And then he was killed?"

"Exactly. First of all, he succeeded Edgar who was also known as 'the Glorious, by the Grace of Christ, Illustrious King of the English and of other people dwelling within the bounds of the island of Britain'."

"Wow! They really knew how to lay it on thick in those days."

"Not only then. Check out the titles belonging to the current Prince Charles. But anyway, let's get back to Edward the Martyr. First of all, he was the son of King Edgar's first wife, so of course he was the natural successor. However, his half-brother, Aethelred, King of Wessex, also had a lot of assistance – maybe because he was very young – and a gang of various earls and other nobles supported him. They knew that when the time came, they'd have their noses in the trough as well."

"Like the Seymour brothers and the young King

Edward VI?"

"Exactly. Some things never change. However, Edward the Martyr was an opinionated young man of about thirteen and he let it be known that no one, but no one, was going to take the throne away from him. And so, in 975, he did indeed become king as he had planned. But, because he kept having temper tantrums in council meetings, he began to lose much of his support, and soon he was encountering a growing opposition. And to cap it all, during this period of history many people were very superstitious."

"That's nothing new."

"True, but different periods have different superstitions. Soon, those who were against the king began to read all sorts of signs and prophecies into such things as comets in the sky and the famines which occurred at the time. Some people interpreted these as signs from God. They claimed that He was showing His dissatisfaction at how Edward's father, Edgar, had reformed the monasteries and how, within a year of becoming king, England had become a very unsafe and lawless country. In fact, the monasteries had been pillaged for their wealth and there was general chaos in the land."

"Sounds a bit like Henry VIII and the dissolution of the monasteries."

"True, but let's continue. The only one who seemed to support the king was Dunstan, the Archbishop of Canterbury. And now here's a really strange mystery about this fellow. In about the third year of Edward's reign, Dunstan called for a meeting of all the king's advisers at Calne, in Wiltshire, near Trowbridge. All of the men met in the upper room and suddenly, half-way through their deliberations, the floor gave way and many of the advisers were killed or injured.

"Only Dunstan remained unharmed. He just happened to be standing on a strong supporting beam at the time and so was saved. This was seen by all the superstitious people as a miracle, although the more cynical souls said that Dunstan had arranged this event. If so, it paid off. But personally, I find it hard to believe that this old Archbishop could plan such an event so meticulously. Anyway, he lived on for another ten years and was later canonised, but this is something that could not be said for his master, King Edward."

"But wasn't he King Edward the Martyr?"

"Well, we'll see how noble and holy he was. As I said before, young Edward was not very popular and one day, while he was hunting in the forest in Dorset, he decided to visit his stepmother, Queen Elfrida, and his half-brother, Aethelred. According to some sources, he was aiming to patch up this long-simmering family quarrel and had in fact conferred all sorts of honours on Elfrida, including grants of land in Dorset. However, this didn't satisfy her. She had one dream, just like all good aristocratic Anglo-Saxon mothers, and that was to see her son on the throne. So according to various historians, when Edward drew up close to the family home at Corfe Castle in Dorset, she sent out some of her henchmen to greet him. And that's exactly what they did. They greeted him with axes and swords and chopped him up there and then, on the spot.

"Another version is that the lovely Elfrida invited the unsuspecting young man into the castle and, in the words of an early scribe, 'received him with demonstrations of affection' and then offered him a goodly drink, and you can be sure that it wasn't hot chocolate."

"Which all goes to show that you shouldn't drink and drive. Or at least, ride a horse while under the influence."

"Exactly, Sophie. And while he was supping his ale, mead or whatever, one of the wicked stepmother's underlings came along, probably when he heard a pre-arranged signal like a bell ringing and promptly stabbed the young king. Fortunately for Edward, he wasn't killed, but ran out of the castle and jumped onto his faithful horse. But at this point his luck ran out."

"What happened?"

"Well, Edward fell off his fleeing horse probably as he was feeling too weak, and was dragged along by the reins until he died. His foot had got caught in one of the stirrups."

"Ugh! What a way to die."

"I agree. But which version of the story is true, I can't tell you. All I can say is that he was buried at nearby Wareham and a few years later, at the beginning of the next century, he was being called 'Edward the Martyr.' Then several years later, the body, which had been buried 'with no royal honours' for some reason, was now reinterred in Shaftesbury Cathedral, but this time 'with great ceremony'. All of this, of course, contributed to his holy status and people soon began to associate his bones with various miracles…"

"In Shaftesbury."

"Maybe, but listen for now here comes the twist in this Anglo-Saxon tale. In 1931, some bones, which were believed to be those of Edward the Martyr were unearthed during an archaeological dig in Shaftesbury. Then forty years later, in 1970, a very late post-mortem claimed that Edward had indeed been stabbed and that his body had been dragged along the ground. But then this mucky plot becomes even muckier. For some reason, the bones were returned to Shaftesbury where they were stored for several years in a bank vault. Then in mid-September 1984, they were taken out and enshrined in St. Edward's Orthodox Church at Brookwood near Woking, Surrey. However, there was a dispute about this and they were transferred to the Midland Bank in Woking, Surrey. They remained there for four years, from 17 September until 21 December 1988 to rest among the share-certificates, heirlooms and trinkets of the local citizens. Then, in December 1988, the saintly bones of King Edward the Martyr were returned to St. Edward's Orthodox Church, Brookwood, and that is where they remain to this day."

"But didn't the papers have something to say about this? They normally do."

"Oh yes. In September 1984, *The Times* printed an article about it: 'No Saxon can have deserved that fate'."

"And what happened to Elfrida?"

"Well, it seems the wicked stepmother turned over a new leaf. She was so sorry for what she had done that she founded a Benedictine Priory in Hampshire, and spent the rest of her days there doing good and charitable deeds."

"Very noble. And what about Edward's half-brother, Aethelred?"

"Ah, Aethelred II or as he is more popularly known, Aethelred the Unready."

"Unready for what?"

"Unready for nothing. No, that's not his real name. Aethelred means 'noble counsel' and the 'Unready' bit was a pun on his name meaning 'red-less', or 'lacking counsel', as he was often said to change his mind. Anyway, after having got rid of Edward the Martyr, he became king, but was soon in trouble with the Danes and Norwegians who sailed up the Thames and besieged London. Aethelred paid them sixteen thousand pounds to go away, which it seems that they did. Then a few years later, in 1002, Aethelred ordered that all the Danes living in England should be murdered. This was not a very wise action, to say the least, as the sister of Sweyn Forkbeard, the King of Denmark, was among the victims of this massacre. He promptly returned to

England and started burning and pillaging, especially in and around Norwich and the south-east. This time Aethelred bought him off to the tune of thirty thousand pounds."

"This Aethelred sure had an expensive foreign policy."

"True. But then he was lucky, because Mother Nature took a hand. A great famine broke out and the Danes returned home. After all, there's no point in pillaging a country if there's nothing there to pillage, is there? But Sweyn returned in 1013 and beat Aethelred, who promptly took to his heels and fled to Normandy. Sweyn became king in his stead but died a year later. Aethelred then returned, and after some violent plotting and executions, reigned for another couple of years, and as *The Anglo-Saxon Chronicles* point out, he died 'after a life of much hardship and many difficulties'. He was succeeded by his second son, Edmund the Ironside, as his first son had been killed in battle two years beforehand."

"So, with a name like Ironside, was there peace and quiet?"

"No, no, Sophie. Just the opposite. This period of Anglo-Saxon history was rife with plots and conspiracies. Firstly, between the Anglo-Saxons themselves, and secondly between them and the Danes."

"Because of Sweyn Forkbeard?"

"Yes, because of him and his son, Cnut, or as we usually call him today, Canute."

"The one who commanded the waves to go back?"

"Yes, that's him. But more about that later. Now let me think what happened to Edmund Ironside, or Edmund II, to give him his numerical name. You know what? I'll tell you about him after I've had a rest."

An hour later, Sophie was back and rushed into the front room where her grandpa was just finishing off a letter.

"Grandpa look!" she said thrusting out the paper to him. "You now that big mafia-style crook the police were looking for? Well, he was shot in the toilet in his office!"

"Sophie, that really is a coincidence, because it ties up with what I was going to tell you next about Ironside and some of the other Anglo-Saxon kings. This Ironside fellow was a born fighter and he was pretty disgusted at the way his father, Aethelred, had surrendered to the Danes."

"So he plotted against them?"

"No, not quite, but almost. Immediately after his father died, he decided to have it out once and for all with the Danes, who were now being led by Canute. Unfortunately, it didn't work out that way as both the Danes and the Anglo-Saxons were pretty evenly matched. So after the last of a series of five battles, the final one being at Ashington, the two kings got together and signed a peace treaty, as they had both had had quite enough of fighting. You must remember, all this fighting had taken place in just a few weeks, and both of them must have been completely exhausted. The treaty said that England would be divided into two: Edmund would be King of Wessex in the south and Canute would rule the area stretching from the Welsh border and over the Midlands to Lincolnshire and East Anglia, in other words, Mercia."

"So they all lived in peace and quiet."

"Not quite. Unfortunately for Edmund, he wasn't allowed to enjoy the peace for very long, because at the age of twenty-three he 'shuffled off this mortal coil' as Shakespeare would say. And in doing so, he shares his throne and his place in history with King George II."

"The king who reigned about three hundred years ago?"

"That's right, but a different throne. I mean, you know how some people call the throne room…"

"… the toilet."

"Yes, well, according to the legend, Edmund Ironside died in the toilet, or rather he was murdered there."

"But George II wasn't murdered."

"True, but he died one morning in the toilet, but less violently than Edmund."

"So how did Edmund die?"

"So, as I was saying, and this story hasn't been disproved yet, but Edmund was relieving himself when one of his arch-rivals, Edric Streama, hid himself in the king's toilet and stabbed him twice from beneath. Edric escaped leaving his dagger sticking into Edmund's nether parts and rushed off to tell Canute the good news."

"Who, no doubt, was delighted?"

"I don't think so. Canute's reaction was to tell Edric that he was going to promote him higher than all his other nobles. And this he did. He promptly chopped off his head and stuck it on a tall pole so everyone could see how and why he had been promoted. It seems that Canute didn't really trust this Edric character and preferred him to be out of the way. I suppose that Canute thought that if he would kill one king, what was there to stop him from killing another?"

"And so Canute supplied an example of justice seeing to be done."

"Exactly. So now Canute became King of England and later of Denmark and Norway. He was a tough ruler who did not take kindly to potential rivals. He ordered the assassination of Eadwig, Edmund Ironside's brother, and it is possible that he wanted to get rid of Edmund's young sons as well, but they were whisked off out of harm's way to Hungary. However, despite this early violence, he seems to have been a good king and he brought law and order to the land. He divided up the country into five earldoms or provinces and sent the Danish armies back to Denmark."

"And what about him commanding the sea to retreat?"

"Well, this story was recorded by one of the most well-known chroniclers of the time, a Henry of

Huntingdon. According to him, Canute took his flattering courtiers to the beach, and when the sea surprisingly refused to obey his commands and began to soak the royal feet, Canute rebuked his courtiers and told them what he really thought of them. If you give me that hefty brown book again, we'll see what he said. Ah, here we are:

> *Let all men know how empty and worthless is the power of kings, for there is none worthy of the name, but He whom heaven, earth and sea obey by eternal laws.*

"Then, according to tradition, as a sign of humility, he stopped wearing his golden crown and he placed it upon a figure of Jesus Christ. Then in 1035 he suddenly died."

"Murdered?" Sophie asked, expecting a positive answer.

"Possibly, or maybe he died of natural causes because he had been suffering from some kind of illness for several months. However, when he did die, it was pretty sudden. He was succeeded by Harold I, alias Harold Harefoot, who grabbed the throne as quickly as possible, that is, before his half-brother Harthacanute could get to England from Denmark."

"Why was he called Harefoot?"

"Because he was said to be fleet of foot, and from the

way he treated people, he really needed to be able to make a quick getaway. First of all, to make sure that he was ruling all of England and not sharing it with his half-brother, he exiled his stepmother, Emma, to the Continent. Then when one of her younger sons, Prince Alfred, showed up to claim the throne, Harefoot imprisoned him and had him blinded so viciously that the prince died of his wounds."

"I'm sure that didn't make him very popular."

"I agree, especially when he went on to row with the Church about the ownership of lands at Sandwich. Then fortunately he died although, as the police would phrase it, foul play cannot be ruled out. He was succeeded by his equally obnoxious half-bother, Harthacanute, who had returned to England. One of the first things he did was to dig up Harold's body, behead it and then throw the whole lot into the marshes."

"Sounds like a real gentleman."

"Exactly, and that was just the beginning. Harthacanute needed a lot of money, since he had to defend Denmark as well. He hoped to collect this from his subjects in England who naturally were not pleased about this."

"Seems a bit like Richard the Lionheart milking England to pay for his Crusades and French wars."

"Exactly."

"But there wasn't much the English could do against Harthacanute, was there?"

"Well, some of them tried. The good citizens of

Worcester resisted and started a minor rebellion. Harthacanute, or Hardicanute as he is also known, suppressed this pretty viciously and in fact almost destroyed the town in doing so."

"Another example of justice being seen to be done?"

"Perhaps so. And now here comes the story of Lady Godiva."

"Who? The lady who rode naked through the streets of Coventry?"

"Yes. The same one. Her husband, Leofric, the Earl of Mercia, was forced to impose these heavy taxes and the people of Coventry couldn't pay up. Lady Godiva then came up with the following proposition: 'Leofric my love, if I ride naked through the city streets, will you reduce the taxes?' Leofric, who probably thought that his wife was just joking, agreed, and so she did exactly that: ride naked through the streets of Coventry."

"But is that really a true story?"

"Personally, Sophie, I'd put the whole thing down to folklore, especially as Leofric still had to come up with the money in the end. After all, I can't really imagine him saying to Harthacanute, who, let's face it, was not known for being a nice, kind and forgiving sort of ruler, 'I'm sorry Your Majesty' – or whatever they called the king in those days – 'I haven't been able to raise the taxes, or even half of them because my townspeople are a bit hard up. And in addition, my wife, Lady Godiva, you know, the one with the long blonde hair, was riding around the streets naked for a bet to ease their financial burden so they wouldn't have to pay up in the end'.

"True. As you describe it like that, it does sound a bit far-fetched to me as well."

"Fortunately, however, the country didn't have to suffer him for long, for in June 1042, while he was stuffing his face at a wedding feast in Lambeth, he suddenly had a fit. Here, let's see what *The Anglo-Saxon Chronicles* say about this one. Ah, here we are:

> *As he stood at his drink, he suddenly fell*
> *to the ground with a horrible convulsion;*
> *and those who were near thereto took*
> *hold of him, but he never spoke again,*
> *and passed away in June.*

"And was that a natural fit?"

"Well as I said before, foul play couldn't be ruled out. The question of a conspiracy was certainly a possibility here."

"You mean someone may have put some rat poison in his wine?" Sophie asked with relish.

"Yes, something like that. But if there was such a plot, it has never been proved."

"And was his successor any better? Were there any plots against him?"

"Who? Edward the Confessor? No, not really. I suppose that was because all he was really interested in was the Church. He spent most of his energy, especially towards the end of his life, building Westminster Abbey.

But I must add that one of his chief statesmen, to use a more modern term, was forever plotting, a gentleman called Godwin, the Earl of Wessex."

"Hey! Wasn't he related to Harold, you know, the king who was killed at Hastings?"

"Very good, Sophie. I am impressed. Yes, Godwin was Harold's father. And to make sure that he hobnobbed with royalty and moved in the best circles, he first married a lady named Gytha, a member of Canute's family. Godwin then sailed to Denmark with Canute to help him fight the Swedes and when they returned to England, Canute gave him a plot of land as a way of saying thank you very much. It was then that Godwin was made an earl."

"But I take it that that wasn't enough?"

"Oh no. Our Godwin was a very good speaker and soon was carrying a lot of clout at court. Then, when Canute died, Godwin first sided with Harthacanute, but then changed sides and supported Harold Harefoot. It was during this time that Godwin was suspected of being involved in the plot to blind Prince Alfred. However, when Harefoot died, Godwin swore an oath of allegiance and became one of Harthacanute's men again."

"A real politician!"

"Such cynicism, and in one so young, too! But to continue, this grasping Saxon really came into his own during the reign of Edward the Confessor. First of all, he married off his daughter, Edith, to the king himself.

This brought him even more land which he gave to his sons, Sweyn and Harold. But then his luck turned."

"Why? Had he climbed too high too fast?"

"Possibly. Such people always make enemies in their rush to the top. But I think the real reason was that our Godwin was first and foremost a Saxon, and Edward, who had been educated in France, preferred the Norman style of doing things. This meant that he tended to hand out the plum jobs at court to the Norman hangers-on. Godwin protested, and so he and all his family were banished from court. Off they went to Bruges, a city in today's Belgium and, in the meanwhile, the old rumour that Godwin had been involved in the blinding of Prince Alfred was raised once again.

"After a year on the Continent, Godwin had had enough, so he put together a fleet of ships and sailed back to England. When he heard that Edward had also called out his navy, Godwin turned tail…"

"… or turned sail…"

"… and returned to Bruges. This action confused the king's fleet, which didn't chase him, but sailed back to London. Then when Godwin heard this latest piece of news, he sailed again for England, met up with his son, Harold, and together with some more ships from his Irish supporters, they sailed to London where they threatened the king and his navy. Neither side really wanted a fight so they called it quits and…"

"… Godwin was once again in the king's good books."

"Exactly, but it didn't do him much good."

"Why not? Did the Normans at court start plotting against him again?"

"No. Mother Nature interfered again. The contemporary records state, rather sanctimoniously I think, that Godwin:

> … *was taken ill soon after he landed and afterwards recovered, but he made far too few amends regarding Church property which he had taken from many holy places.*

"And, of course," Sophie added, "it was the Church who wrote the records at the time."

"Exactly. He probably suffered a stroke of some sort, and during the following Easter he collapsed and died at a feast while he was celebrating with his sons, Harold and Tostig.

"Our friendly recorder of the time, Henry of Huntingdon, also noted another version of his death and this one is a bit more colourful and dramatic, although I don't really know which one is true. According to Henry, Godwin was indeed at the feast and denied that he'd ever plotted against the king. To prove his words, he stood up in front of all the assembled guests and said, and remember, this is in the presence of Edward the Confessor himself, 'May this morsel of bread choke me, if even in thought I have ever been false to you'. Then he put that morsel of bread into his mouth and choked to death on the spot."

"Some feast," Sophie commented, eating her biscuit somewhat more delicately than before.

"As you say, some feast," Professor Warkworth agreed. "Then after this, the last few years of Edward's reign were quite busy as he was full of plans about building his abbey in Westminster, while worrying about who would be his successor. He himself wanted William of Normandy, but the Saxons naturally favoured Godwin's son Harold."

"But hadn't Edward already promised the crown to William?"

"Yes, but in the meanwhile Godwin had been restored to favour and Edward's earlier promise seems to have been put on the back-burner. And also, when Edward heard that his nephew, Edward the Exile, was still alive and in exile in Hungary, he wanted him to be recalled to England."

"I bet Harold wasn't pleased with that one."

"I agree. However, by some coincidence, young Edward was killed soon after returning to England, but it was never proved that Harold had a hand in that. Since the only other remaining regal relative around was Edward the Exile's four-year-old son, Edgar, the king had to accept the fact that Harold would succeed him, especially as he was number one in the Saxon popularity stakes. Then, just to complicate matters, Harald Hadraada of Norway thought that *he* should rule

England. As a result, he got together with Harold's jealous brother, Tostig, and they decided to challenge Harold for the throne. Their plot failed as they were both killed fighting Harold at the Battle of Stamford Bridge in Yorkshire. This meant that Harold, that is, Harold II, had to hurry back to the south of England to meet the next challenger and invader, Duke William of Normandy."

"And that spelt the end of the Anglo-Saxon plots and conspiracies forever."

"Exactly."

Chapter Two
William II's hunting 'accident'(1100)

The death of King William II in the New Forest

"Grandpa, do you remember when we were talking about King Alfred the other day we said that he was the only king who was called 'the Great'?"

"Yes."

"Well, many of the others also had strange names, like George III was called 'Farmer George,' William IV was called 'Sailor Bill' and James I was referred to as 'the wisest fool in Christendom.'."

"True, and what about William II, alias William Rufus and also Bad King John?" Grandpa asked.

"Well, they were a pair of bad guys, weren't they? I mean, I guess their names haven't been blackened for nothing, have they?"

"Oh, haven't they just, my dear Sophie. Just think when they were living."

"William reigned about a thousand years ago, and John was king about a hundred years later, right?"

"Right. And who was writing the history books then, you know, *The Anglo-Saxon Chronicles*?"

"The Church I suppose. Those scribes with the tonsils."

"Tonsures, my dear Sophie, tonsures."

"Like Friar Tuck in the old Robin Hood films."

"Exactly. And what were the Church's criteria for being a good king?"

"Ah, Grandpa, I see what you're getting at. If the king acted in a way that the Church approved of, say like Richard the Lionheart going off on Crusades, then he was a good king, but if he didn't, then the Church and its scribes came down heavily on him like a ton of bricks."

"Exactly. You've hit the nail smack on the head. And by the way, despite his noble image, backed up by the Church of course, your precious Richard the Lionheart was a really bad king as far as England was concerned."

"Why?"

"Well, of the ten years he was King of England, he spent only six months in the country. And he used that time for raising money for the Crusades. He was supposed to have even said that he would sell London to pay for his precious Crusades. No, no, he wasn't interested at all in what happened in England, in fact, he was more interested in his French possessions and the Holy Land instead. Also, some people say that he was possibly interested in young men as well. But, my dear, let's leave him and get back to William II, alias William Rufus."

"So called because of his red hair and red face."

"Right, although some of the older history books say that his colour wasn't natural and was brought on by too much drinking."

"Church history books?"

"Probably."

"But Grandpa, was he really such a bad king?"

"Hmm, that depends on how you look at him. As we said, the Church said he was certainly a bad man, saying that he was debauched and that his behaviour was less than Christian. In fact, in their records they summed up his rule as 'very harsh and fierce' and said that he was 'hated by almost all his people and abhorrent to God'."

"Meaning the Church didn't always get what it wanted?"

"Sophie, you are growing up to be a regular cynic. Very useful for a historian. Keep it up. And yes, there's probably a lot in what you say. Actually, as a soldier he wasn't too bad and even had some military successes in Wales, putting down rebellions and things like that. But, in general, I would say that he must have been quite a devious character altogether. For instance, he managed to persuade his brother, Robert, to go on a Crusade and then when he returned home he found that William had taken over his lands in Normandy."

"Sounds like a really nice family."

"Well, our William wasn't much of a family man, and he never married."

"But I suppose he had a girlfriend or two, no?"

"No, not really. And that is what seems to be one of the major black marks against him. He wasn't your typical medieval family man, you know, wife, mother-in-law and fifteen kids, to say nothing of a wolfhound or two. In fact, he wasn't very interested in women at all and that is why the Church hinted that he was homosexual, although they didn't come out and say so in so many words. Just nasty innuendos. And on top of that, the Church claimed that he was so debauched that the Archbishop didn't want to crown him at first, but eventually he did. As I said, the Church wrote that William did 'everything that was hateful to God and to man'."

"Well, he certainly doesn't sound like Mr. Popular of the eleventh century."

"You're right there. Especially as he used the Church's funds for his own pleasures, to say nothing of the fact that some people claimed that our William even dabbled in the black arts."

"Witchcraft?"

"Yes."

"Oh, I can see the Church liking that one."

"Exactly. Especially in that superstitious day and age. When he was killed, or supposedly died in a hunting accident in the New Forest, no doubt all the churchmen tut-tutted and muttered things like, 'served him right', and 'good riddance'."

"Grandpa, you're becoming as cynical as me. But how did he die?"

"Strangely enough, it is his death and how it came about that is the most fascinating part of his career. So, my dear Sophie, cast your mind back nine hundred years to Ringwood in the New Forest. Picture the long great hall in a Norman castle, with its round-arched windows and doorways. The windows wouldn't have had any glass in them, but they would have had shutters to keep out the wind and the rain, as well as much of the light as well. The atmosphere to our modern super-sensitive twenty-first century eyes and noses would have been somewhat smoky, as there was no chimney for the great fire on the hearthstone, and the smoke would have only eventually found its way out through a covered hole in the roof.

"The atmosphere in this great hall would also have been pretty noisy as the king's friends and nobles, all seated at the top table on a raised platform, would have all been calling out for food and drink at the top of their voices. This was also true for the other souls who were sitting down both sides of the long hall at their long trestle tables. If all this friendly confusion weren't enough, there would also have been the constant movement of servants scurrying to and fro, carrying great trays of meat or flagons of mead and wine. They in their turn had to make sure that they didn't trip over the ever-present dogs which were forever on the lookout for tasty bones and scraps that had been carelessly dropped or thrown onto the crushed rush-covered floor. And then, just as a last point, you should remember, these castles were not noted for their noise absorbing acoustic properties. And of course, all this noise would have been reverberating off the stone walls echoing like crazy."

"Sounds like one of our local youth club's dances."

"Yes, it probably did, but then I suppose that sitting at the top table with the king was better than sitting at the other tables, for the food and drink were probably better and the service was faster. It didn't pay to keep the king waiting. And so, the conversation that particular day in the summer of 1100 probably went something like this:

William: So, my good Lord Dubois, what do you think of the chances of us having a good day's hunting tomorrow? Do you think these clouds will blow over and this drizzle disappear?

Dubois: Oh, it should do, sire. After all, tomorrow will be the second day of August and one of my most trusted servants has assured me that it will be a fine day tomorrow.

William: And how can he be so sure?

Dubois: Oh, he put his finger in his mouth and then held it up to the wind.

William: I see. (obviously not impressed)

Dubois: He also said something about how his cow and pigs were behaving.

William: Hmmm (continues to sink his teeth into a particularly juicy chunk of venison). By St. Luke's face! (William suddenly said aloud, quoting his favourite oath). If we come back tomorrow with more meat like this, it will be a good day. Yes, Master Tyrrelll, what did you wish to say? What are you giving me?

Tyrrell: Sire, please look at these arrows. One of the local fletchers gave me a quiver of them as a gift and he said that he would be honoured if I would try them out next time I go hunting with you. Would you like to inspect them, sire? The fletcher whose name is... oh, I've forgotten it, said these arrows were particularly deadly and would fell any stag or deer that crossed your bow.

William: Hmmm (runs his fingers appreciatively down the shafts and fingers the feathers carefully). They are certainly very fine arrows. I wouldn't like to fall prey to one of these. Here, you look after these until tomorrow. But I think they are best suited for your bow and not mine, which is longer. Don't you agree?

Tyrrell: Yes, sire. I was just thinking the same thing myself.

William: Good man. It always pays to agree with your king. (Looks along the top table to the other men who are inspecting the arrows while listening at the same time). But Master Tyrrell, let it not be said that your king is not of a generous nature. Tomorrow, when you give me these fine arrows, keep three of them for yourself and see if you too can't also bring down a goodly deer or stag. How's that for regal generosity, heh? (He claps the embarrassed Tyrrell on the back. Tyrrell then shows the arrows to William's brother, Henry, who has just entered the banqueting hall and is now standing next to the king at the top table).

Tyrrell: (Showing him the arrows) See, my lord Henry. See what your kind brother has given me for the hunt tomorrow.

Henry: Well, just you see you make good use of them. That's all I can say. It would be a shame to waste such good arrows by missing the target, eh? (He winks at Tyrrell in a friendly fashion and pats him on the shoulder).

William: (Now standing in front of the assembled men) So my friends, before we leave for the hunting lodge in the New Forest, let us drink a toast here tonight, to tomorrow's hunt and... wait for it... for remember, if you haven't done so already, that today is the first day of August, Lammas Day, and as my churchmen always tell me, and you know how much I always take heed of their wise sayings... (somebody belches loudly, others laugh)... and as I was saying, I always listen to them, so we must be especially joyful on this day as this day is for celebrating the wheat harvest, the Lord's own bountiful harvest. And so, my loyal friends and subjects, let us raise a toast to Lammas and tomorrow's hunt!

All:(Raising their goblets) To Lammas and tomorrow's hunt!

Lord Stephen: (Speaking to Cedric of Winchester) Since when has the king taken to quoting his churchmen?

Cedric: My lord, don't you know how much our king loves the Church?

Lord Stephen: Aye, he does that well enough. Especially its money and riches.

Cedric: Ah, but don't you remember when he became religious?

Lord Stephen: Yes. About seven years ago. But that was only because he fell ill and thought he was about to die. But then, my friend, if you do but remember, he made a great recovery and forgot the Church.

Cedric: Well, it didn't prevent him from appointing a new Archbishop of Canterbury.

Lord Stephen: Anselm of Bec.

Cedric: (Nods) You are right there. But tell me, where is the good prelate now, heh? Chased out by the king.

Lord Stephen: In exile. Somewhere over in France, I think.

Cedric: True. But do not let the king hear you prate of such matters. Mention the Church or its leaders to him and his red face grows even redder.

Lord Stephen: Aye, you are right there. Look, preparations are being made to leave. Let us join the others. (They drain the dregs of wine in their goblets and hurry out to the courtyard where horses and pack-animals are being loaded before moving out in a long cavalcade. The king has told them that he intends to reach the hunting lodge before nightfall.)

"That night the king hardly slept. As soon as his head touched the pillows, strange visions flooded into his mind. The main colour of these visions was red. 'My blood', William thought, as the red cloud rose unto the heavens. Tossing around in his bed, he pushed his fists into his eyes in an effort to exorcise these visions, but it did not work. Then he lay face down, his head buried deeply in the downy pillows, but neither did this succeed in dispersing the bright blood-red cloud.

"Suddenly, sitting bolt upright in bed, he opened his eyes and reached out for some wine. He gulped it down greedily, and, like a man whose life depends on every drop, drained the goblet before throwing himself back onto the bed. He lay there for a few minutes, motionless, in a drink befuddled state. But as the minutes passed, the blood red vision rose up yet once again before his eyes, and the king could not succeed in shaking himself free of it, try as he would.

"'Boy!' he shouted out at last into the night. 'Boy! Bring me a light and rid me of this cursed gloom! And be quick about it!' Within two minutes, two chamberlains came rushing into the room bearing flaming torches. 'I cannot sleep', called out the haggard looking king. 'Stay here in this chamber this night and keep those torches burning. If they go out, by St. Luke's face, you will pay for it! Now let me sleep'.

"And so the night slowly passed. Just as the king would begin to drift off to sleep, the red phantoms would reappear, only to disappear as the exhausted king forced himself to open his eyes and sit higher up in his bed. Then, as the sun broke through the grey clouds over the New Forest of Hampshire the next morning, King William II was to be found slumped over in his bed fitfully asleep. Somnus, the god of sleep, had finally triumphed over the red devils.

"Later that morning, after having dealt with several affairs of state, the king indicated that the royal hunting party would leave for the forest after a short midday meal. As they set out for the New Forest, all their talk was about the upcoming afternoon's sport. The atmosphere between the lords, knights and their king was friendly, and no one could have predicted the tragedy that was to befall one of their number. Only one or two of the assembled men knew of the king's troubled night:

Walter: Sire, it was a good thing that your father was so foresighted as to preserve the New Forest for our hunting.

Dubois: Mais oui. *Especially for the royal use.*

Lord Thomas: And what do you think we'll find today? Red deer? Fallow deer?

Dubois: Roe deer perhaps?

Walter: Or maybe a wild boar or two.

Henry (the king's brother): Or a hare for you, Walter.

William: And a fox for you, Henry! Let's see what you shoot, eh?

Tyrrell: Well, I for one want to try out one of these new arrows. If they're good, I will ask my fletcher to provide me with some more.

Henry: Well, just make sure you aim well, Master Tyrrell. I also want to see how good a shot you are.

Tyrrell: Fear not, my good prince. You'll be feasting well tonight. Have you no fear of that.

"In this jolly mood, the cavalcade cantered on into the forest. As they approached Cadnum from the west, one of the royal huntsmen drew his horse alongside that of his king's and leaned over to him. 'Sire, I suggest that we dismount here and spread out in this area of the forest. We should send the horses away with one or two of the servants, so that their noise will not disturb the deer. I also think that some of the others should go on ahead to persuade our prey to start moving in this direction'.

"William nodded in agreement, and several men left the party and headed even deeper into the forest. The king dismounted and, using hand-signals, indicated that the others do the same and spread out among the trees and the undergrowth. Pointing at himself, then Walter and Tyrrell, the king showed that he wanted his friend to remain nearby. Half-hidden, and crouching a few paces behind his king, Tyrrell prepared one of his new arrows and waited.

"Apart from the rustle of the wind in a few light branches, nothing could be heard. Nobody could guess, spread out in that royal forest, that Henry, William's aggressive brother, and a few friends, were also crouching low in the undergrowth similarly anxious to let their arrows fly at the target. All the men waited, their eyes and ears strained for the first signs of the deer which they knew would pass their way.

"Suddenly, the undergrowth was disturbed as a lone rabbit popped up from nowhere, rose up on its hind legs, sniffed the air, and then scampered away. The royal hunters were too well-trained in their art to waste their time and arrows on a rabbit, especially when they knew that better prey was on the way.

"They were not to be disappointed. Suddenly, with a great crashing noise of fast hooves on dry twigs and leaves, a magnificent dark brown stag burst into view, its antlers breaking off the lower branches of the oak and elm trees as it crashed its way through the forest. As the king rose to loosen his first arrow at this perfect target, he found that an overhanging branch was blocking his view. Immediately noticing that Tyrrell had a better view of the beast, William shouted, 'Shoot, Tyrrell! Shoot!'"

"And he did?"

Grandpa nodded. "Tyrrell hesitated for a split second, but the impatient king shouted again. 'Shoot in the Devil's name, or it'll be the worse for you!' Tyrrell let fly. But it was not the stag that fell. It was the king. King William Rufus. His body was bleeding from Tyrrell's new arrow which was now sticking out of his trunk at a grotesque angle.

"By the time Tyrrell had reached the fallen king, it was obvious that he was not long for this world. The bloodstain was visibly and rapidly spreading out over his pale brown tunic. A large pool of the royal blood could also be seen spreading out over the leaves and twigs that lay under the fallen body. The arrow sticking out of the body was quivering lightly, showing that the king was still breathing. But only just.

"Tyrrell clapped his hand over his mouth and half bent over his king in silence. It was hard to see his face or guess what thoughts were going through his mind.

Was he shocked that he had killed his king? Was he pleased that he had rid the country of a hated and despised ruler? We shall never know, for suddenly he shook himself, spun around and ran for the only horse that had been left behind. Without looking behind, he leapt onto the saddle, throwing aside his bow and quiver full of arrows, and charged noisily off into the forest to leave King William II, the son of William the Conqueror, to breathe his last.

"Raising his pale face surrounded by his red and shaggy locks, the dying king opened his eyes and tried to focus on the blue sky and green leaves above him, which were becoming increasingly blurred. Failing to make any sense of it all, and becoming even more aware of the pain, emanating from somewhere in the centre of his body, he sank back, blood now trickling out of his mouth onto the leaves which formed his pillow. His face rolled over to the side. He tried to open his eyes again but found he could not. A weird sort of deep darkness was closing in over him. His body gave a final shudder and a strange noise came out of his throat. That was it. The king was dead. Just then, a crumpled russet leaf fluttered down and settled on the king's face.

"Some time later when the rustling wind had grown into a minor storm, a party of the king's companions were chattering happily as they cantered towards the break in the forest where the king's bloody body lay:

Henry: What ho, Dubois! That was a good day's

hunting, was it not?

Dubois. Oh aye, my prince. It certainly was that.

Henry: Six stags and several other deer. What say you to that, Sir Robert?

Sir Robert: It has been an excellent day for sport, sire, I think...

Henry: You know what I think? I think we should go back and shoot some more. It's not every day we are so lucky.

Sir Giles: Sire, if you don't mind, I think it would be better if we come back tomorrow. After all, if we shoot everything today, what sport shall we have on the morrow, eh?

Henry: (Reluctantly) Perhaps you are right. So let's go back to the lodge. Come.

Dubois: My prince. If we... What ho! What's this? Sire! Sire! Come here quickly! It's your brother, the king! (Kneeling over the dead body). He's dead. Look! Look here! Here's the arrow that killed him. Look, it's sticking out of his gut. It looks like one of Tyrrell's new arrows. You know, the ones he was boasting about last night.

Henry: (Kneeling over the prostrate form of his older brother) Are you sure he's dead? Is he breathing?

Sir Giles: (Bending over the king's mouth) No, sire. He's not. He's dead. Look at all that blood he has lost. (Takes off his hat as the others do the same, that is, all except Henry, who remains standing).

Dubois: (Suddenly turning round and kneeling in front of Henry) I suppose that means you are the new king now, sire...

Sir Giles: (Now kneeling as well) ... unless your older brother, Prince Robert, claims the throne, sire. But isn't he away on a Crusade? Isn't he...? Sire! Sire! What are you doing? Where are you going? What are you doing on your horse?

Henry: Follow me! (Pointing at the body). Leave that alone!

Sir Giles: (Leaping into the saddle of his own horse) But where are we going?

Henry: To Winchester! To Winchester! To the treasury! And at full speed! Now come, man, if you wish to help your new king!

"Within a few minutes, the men had fled the scene and were galloping hard westwards to Winchester, England's ancient capital. After having seized the treasury, Henry, together with a band of devoted knights, then galloped to London. Three days later, Prince Henry, the youngest son of William the Conqueror, had himself crowned King Henry in Westminster Abbey. Although he was known to be a literate and educated man, hence his nickname 'Beauclerc', he also had a reputation for being a particularly nasty and vindictive ruler."

"Why, what did he do?"

"While it is true that he put down much of the lawlessness that was prevalent in England at the time, Sophie, he also himself took a strong hand in punishing wrong doers. This included personally pushing a prisoner, who had betrayed an oath of allegiance, off the ramparts of the castle at Rouen onto the rocks below. He also ordered all the money-makers in England to be mutilated as a way of discouraging their successors from damaging the coinage. And if these vicious deeds were not enough, he also ordered two young girls to be blinded as a punishment for their father's perceived anti-royalist behaviour.

"In 1106, after he had finally defeated his older brother, Robert, at the battle of Tinchebrai, Henry seized his duchy and imprisoned his unfortunate brother for life in Cardiff castle, where he died some thirty years later, aged eighty."

"But, Grandpa, what happened to the man who shot William?"

"Oh, Sir Walter Tyrrell? Well, naturally he fled the country and ended up on the Continent. Many years later, one Abbot Suger said that Tyrrell claimed that he had had no part in the king's death. However, it is recorded that Henry did look after Tyrrell's family later on."

"So was William's body just left to rot there in the New Forest?"

"No, not at all, Sophie. After several hours, a

charcoal-burner, one of the few people who were allowed to live and work in the royal forests, found his body, loaded it onto his cart and took it to Winchester."

"That doesn't sound a very honourable or respectable end for the King of England."

"True, but at least he was properly buried beneath the tower of Winchester Cathedral, that is, at least for a year."

"Why only for a year? Why not forever, or at least for a few centuries?"

"Well, a year later, the tower at the cathedral came crashing down and that was it."

"Why did it fall? Was there an earthquake?"

"I don't know about that, but many people at the time, naturally influenced by the Church, claimed that this was because the king had been such a bad man and not a true Christian, and that this was some kind of divine punishment. If you look in that maroon book over there, you'll find out what the Church wrote about him. Here we are. Look, it says that he 'died in the midst of his sins, without repentance'. In other words, to the superstitious people of the time, William Rufus got his just desserts, both in life, and also in death."

"Wasn't the Church prepared to forgive him at all, Grandpa? You know, real Christian charity?"

"No, Sophie. There was no Christian charity for William Rufus. In the eyes of the Church this man had been a real sinner. They even claimed that he had dabbled in black magic, and perhaps it was that, the black magic, that had caused his death."

"What do you mean?"

"Well, according to one historian, a Dr Margaret Murray, William II was a devil-worshipper, and we know that in those days all sorts of witchcraft were practised. People not only believed in Christianity, but also in Catharism, which was a sect that professed great purity. And this is in addition to various other non-Christian beliefs as well, like Paganism. Sometimes these ideas and cults overlapped, and one of the beliefs decreed that the god-king, William Rufus in this case, had to sacrifice his life for the benefit of his people. This belief was especially strong in the years that came at the end or beginning of a century and…"

"… and William was killed in the year 1100 exactly!"

"Exactly. So some people say that his death in the New Forest was no accident or political murder at all, but some kind of religious or mystical rite. The Church of course wanted him to be seen as a really wicked man and they wanted everyone else to believe this as well. And if that weren't enough, who was William II's grandfather?"

"You mean William the Conqueror's father?"

"Yes. He was none other than 'Robert the Devil,' also known as the 'Red King' – red being not only the colour of blood, but also the colour of witchcraft."

"I see. So, Grandpa, you could say that there were three possible reasons why William was killed. One, it was a genuine hunting accident, which I suppose happened then like car-crashes do today."

"Two?"

"As a result of some sort of witchcraft or black magic."

"And three?"

"He was killed by Tyrrell who was acting on instructions from Henry. Henry, we know, was very cruel and wouldn't have lost any sleep about killing his brother. Besides, he had to get William out of the way before Robert, who was really next in line, returned home from the Crusades."

"Very good. I'm impressed. And now, Sophie, which of these three reasons do you think explains the untimely demise of our ruddy faced William?"

"Number three."

"Why?"

"Well, Grandpa, I think this witchcraft thing is a bit far-fetched, and its relevance was probably pushed by the Church who really had it in for William. I'm also not too convinced about this hunting accident business, and I think that Henry had the greatest motive and most to gain by his brother's death."

"Fair enough, my dear. But can you prove any of this? Historians as well as lawyers should be able to back up their theories."

"Well, you said earlier that Henry was a tough and determined man, and that he looked after Tyrrell instead of hanging him for killing his brother. So, through

Tyrrell, Henry had both the means and the motive. *Quod erat demonstrandum.* Here is your proof."

"Very impressive. Now listen here to what it says in this book, *The Saxon and Norman Kings* by Christopher Brooke. Here, I'll summarise what it says: Tyrrell's wife and her family were leading figures of the time and they were well looked after by Henry. In fact, Henry made one of the family an abbot in Ely, while another became the Earl of Buckingham, and yet another became the Bishop of Winchester. Now, you wouldn't do all that to someone, or his family, who had killed your ever-loving brother unless you wanted to reward him, no? Brooke doesn't say that Tyrrell himself gained anything, except that he wasn't executed as a murderer, but that he may have been used as a tool by his powerful family to gain favour with the new king."

"In other words, my dear grandfather, it's not, as you often say, what you know, but who you know."

"Exactly. And I'm sure it was as true then as it is today. Whenever people want to succeed, then connections and the 'old school tie' certainly help."

"So it would seem that our William was wearing the wrong tie, no?"

"Well, I'm not sure about that. But it seems quite sure that he was wearing the crown, and that was what his younger brother really wanted. And, as you said, he seemed to have been prepared to commit murder to get it."

"True, Grandpa. And if we're talking about old

school ties and murders, I've got to go now and murder my biology homework. We've got to write up something about deadly nightshade and other poisonous plants."

"Now, do any of them grow in the New Forest by any chance?"

"I don't know, but after what you have just told me, I wouldn't be surprised."

Chapter Three
Richard III, the original
Wicked Uncle? (1483-85)

Killing the Princes in the Tower   *King Richard III*

"Grandpa?" Sophie asked, looking up from reading about the mysterious disappearance of some minor European royalty in the paper. "Of all the mysteries, plots and conspiracies that you can think of in English history, which one is the most mysterious?"

"Oh, that's easy. The mystery of the princes in the Tower."

"What? Those two little princes in the picture in your big maroon history book? You know, the one with the two murderers standing over them in the background holding a big pillow?"

"Yes. That's it."

"Why?"

"Well, Sophie, do you remember when we were talking about the who, why and how of a murder? Well, here you have it all. First of all, the who. Who did it? Richard III, as is often claimed, the princes' 'wicked uncle'? Or was it Henry VII, the cunning king who succeeded Richard? Or maybe it was Richard's one-time friend and accomplice, the Duke of Buckingham? And then, how? Tradition has it that they were smothered to death while sleeping in the Tower of London, but there's no real proof of this either. Then the motive, why? If it were Richard, Henry or the Duke of Buckingham, what did they have to gain by getting rid of the princes? What was in it for them?"

"Wow! That's a real mystery!"

"And then there's another theory. That they were never murdered at all, or maybe that only one of them was. And if so, what happened to the other one? Did he later resurface and claim to be a Pretender to the throne of Henry VII?"

"So, in other words, historians don't really know who did it, when or why, or if this or these murders were carried out at all. Now that really does sound like some mega-mystery. The Oscar prize for plots, mysteries and conspiracies all rolled into one. OK, Grandpa, let's hear what happened in those far off days of yore. Whodunnit?"

"Fair enough. But be ready for some complicated twists and turns. Ready?"

"Ready, steady, go!"

"So, my dear Sophie, cast your mind back over five hundred years, to April 1483 to be exact. At the beginning of this month, England is being ruled by Edward IV. England has had about twelve years of peace following the Battle of Tewkesbury which resulted in Edward IV getting rid of the weak and sometimes insane Henry VI. According to some historians, Edward's brother, Richard, the Duke of Gloucester, murdered or caused the gentle and academically minded Henry to be murdered. But whatever happened, this saintly soul was never seen alive again after he was taken to the Tower.

"Now, Edward IV was a really kingly fellow. He was over six foot tall, a natural leader, a great military commander, a clever statesman, and to top it all, he also had two sons and five daughters. So it seemed pretty sure that there would be no problems about the succession."

"The way you describe it, Grandpa, it sounds as if our Edward IV had it all."

"He did. And if all of the above weren't enough, he was very fair and handsome and all the ladies at court were really crazy over him. And Edward, being Edward, was also more than crazy over them. In fact, you could say that Edward of York was a terrific womaniser, the Casanova of England in the late Middle Ages."

"So what's the problem? A handsome king, lovely ladies throwing themselves at him and lots of kids. Sounds like a perfect situation."

"Well, it wasn't. In fact, it was Edward's non-stop womanising that lay at the root of the mystery of the princes in the Tower."

"How?"

"As I said, Edward IV loved women, all of them near enough, and then he died suddenly on 9 April 1483. This was probably due to pneumonia, though some people have hinted that he was poisoned or had overeaten. Naturally, his sudden demise led to a really problematic situation at court. His newly-widowed wife was Queen Elizabeth Woodville and she was a terrible trouble-maker."

"Why? What did she do?"

"She was extremely pleased to be queen, and even more so since she had fulfilled her royal duty by having seven kids. This meant that her eldest son, also called Edward, would succeed daddy and Elizabeth, now Queen Mother, would keep all her money, jewellery and power. But that was not the end of it. This ruthlessly ambitious lady had plans for all her Woodville family and other friendly hangers-on. She made sure that they all had good positions at court, in the Army, the Treasury and in the Council and at the Tower, which then served as a royal palace as well."

"She sounds like a really jumped up nouveau-riche type lady."

"Yes, she was definitely that all right. But meanwhile, Edward IV's Chief of Guard and Chamberlain, a very loyal chap called Lord Hastings, saw what was going on and passed on the message about what was happening at court to Edward's short and dark brother, Richard, Duke of Gloucester. And he wasn't slow either. Towards the end of April, about two weeks after Edward had died, Richard started heading south for London from York where he usually lived and guess whom he met on the way?"

"Lady Elizabeth and her bunch."

"Good guess and you're half right. He didn't actually meet Elizabeth, for she was in London, probably trying on all her new jewellery, etc. But there, north of London, at Stony Stratford in Northamptonshire, he bumped into two of her family, Lord Grey and Lord Rivers. They had been sent to escort the young prince Edward to London from where he was living in Ludlow, Shropshire to be crowned as Edward V. And of course, these two lords wanted to make sure that they too would benefit from the proceedings."

"I bet Richard wasn't very pleased about that."

"He wasn't, especially as he was the officially designated sole protector of the future king, that is, he had been personally appointed for the job by the dying Edward IV. Richard immediately seized control of the situation and took charge of the young prince. At the same time, he arrested Grey and Rivers on various charges. Very soon after that he had them, together with another member of the Woodville clan, Sir Thomas Vaughan, executed at Pontefract in Yorkshire, some two hundred miles north of London, well out of the way."

"That can't have kept Elizabeth Woodville very happy, knowing that her brother-in-law was chopping up her family."

"It didn't. In fact, the dear lady became so worried that she fled to Westminster Abbey and claimed sanctuary. She also took the future King Edward's younger brother, Richard, with her as well as her daughters and Thomas Grey, the Marquis of Dorset, another of the clan."

"By the way, Grandpa, have you noticed that during the Middle Ages all the kings and nobles are called Richard, Henry and Edward, while all the women are called Elizabeth, Anne or Mary?"

"I know. It makes life for us historians today very complicated. So I suppose that is why we usually refer to them as Richard or Elizabeth of somewhere or other, so we know who's who. But anyway, to get back to the mystery of the princes in the Tower, a few days after Richard had taken over, he escorted the young Prince Edward into London. According to the tradition of the time, he was placed in the Tower which also served as a palace. Richard then proceeded to start organising the coronation which was due to be held towards the end of June, some six weeks later. Meanwhile, the Council confirmed that Richard was to be the official Regent and Protector of Edward and of the country, that is until

Edward became of age and could become an independent ruler in his own right."

"So, no problems so far, except for the Woodvilles who must have felt that their noses, as well as some of their heads, had been pushed somewhat out of joint."

"Exactly. I mean, for them, this Richard, apart from being the dead king's brother, had hardly spent any time in London. He had spent the past few years being his brother Edward IV's very loyal and very efficient representative in the north of England. He had not made his presence felt much in court up to now, and yet here he was now telling the Woodvilles what to do and how to do it. So now the proceedings for the coronation were going ahead very smoothly, when on 8 June 1483, just two weeks before this happy event was to take place, Robert Stillington, the late King Edward IV's Lord Chancellor and the Bishop of Bath and Wells, set a cat among the pigeons."

"Why? What did he do, or say?"

"On 8 June, in a council meeting, he confessed that he had acted as a witness to a pre-marriage contract which was signed between the late King Edward IV and a Lady Eleanor Butler. And to make matters worse, this had happened before Edward had married Elizabeth Woodville."

"So, in other words, King Edward IV was a bigamist."

"Exactly, but not only that. It also meant that as his marriage to Elizabeth Woodville was not legal, Prince

Edward, now waiting to be crowned, to say nothing of his younger brother, Richard of York and his five sisters in sanctuary, were all illegitimate so…"

"… Prince Edward couldn't become King Edward V."

"Exactly, since the king…"

"… or the queen…"

"… must be legitimate. This meant that the only legitimate successor to Edward IV was…"

"… the one and only Duke Richard of Gloucester himself."

"Exactly."

"But Grandpa, Edward IV hadn't exactly been married to this Lady Butler, had he?"

"No. Not as we know it today. But in those days, such pre-nuptial contracts were considered to be just as binding."

"And where was this lady? Didn't she have something to say about all this?"

"She was dead. She had died, very conveniently it so happens, in a nunnery in Norwich in 1468. And then, just to rub some more salt into the very open and smarting Woodville wounds, Stillington repeated this story to the other lords in Parliament, so that it really became public knowledge.

"A few days later, Richard himself surprised everyone. He went to the Tower of London, unannounced as it were, and promptly arrested Lord Thomas Stanley, Cardinal John Morton and Lord

Hastings. Now this Lord Hastings had originally been on Richard's side, but when he thought that Richard wanted the throne for himself, he turned against him.

"Then, on 13 June, these three were sitting in the White Tower in the Tower of London, together with Thomas Rotherham, the Archbishop of York, probably discussing the latest political situation, when suddenly Richard entered and accused them of treason, the worst crime of all. There was a minor scuffle with some of Richard's guards and after a few minutes Morton and the Archbishop – probably because they were important churchmen – were taken to a special prison in the Tower, together with Stanley, and placed under house arrest. Hastings had no such luck. He was taken outside, allowed to say a quick prayer and then beheaded, a large block of wood or a tree trunk being used as a block.

"Unfortunately for Richard, he released Stanley and Morton soon after. These two were to cause him much trouble later, especially Morton, who told all sorts of anti-Richard stories to Sir Thomas More who later rewrote them up as a best-selling history book during the reign of Henry VIII."

"The son of the king who had killed Richard at Bosworth Field?"

"Exactly. But we're jumping the gun by about fifty years. But to get back to Richard. This rather hasty action of bumping off Lord Hastings without giving him anything resembling a trial got Richard some very bad publicity. The word got out very quickly, as it seems that

Hastings had been quite a popular fellow and that chopping off his head was not the best way of winning future friends or keeping the ones you already had."

"So now I'm beginning to see why Richard has such a lousy reputation."

"Wait a minute, Sophie, there's still a lot more to come. Three days later, on 16 June, a week before the planned coronation, Cardinal Bouchier, the Archbishop of Canterbury, the most important cleric in the land, persuaded Elizabeth Woodville to release young Richard, the younger prince, from sanctuary in Westminster and join his older brother in the Tower."

"So now both princes were in the Tower."

"Exactly. And under the direct authority of the official Protector, Richard, Duke of Gloucester. A week passed, and on 22 June Edward was supposed to be crowned, but he wasn't. In fact, he was never crowned. Instead, Dr Shaw, sometimes spelt S-h-a-a, who was the brother of the Lord Mayor of London, preached an open-air sermon in the centre of London and took as his theme, 'Bastard slips shall not take root'.

"What does that mean?"

"It means that the bastard sons of Edward IV, namely Edward and his brother, had no right to succeed their father as they were the result of a bigamous marriage. And then, to make sure that this message was even more clearly understood, Richard's friend, the Duke of Buckingham, repeated this sermon in the Guildhall the following day to the most influential citizens of the City of London.

"Two days later, Parliament reassembled and agreed with Richard that the two princes were illegitimate and so Richard should become the next king. And then, two weeks after that, Richard, Duke of Gloucester and Protector of the Kingdom officially became King Richard III, the most discussed king in English history and according to Shakespeare, the original 'wicked uncle.'"

"Even though he ruled for only two years."

"Exactly."

"And all this time, the princes were in the Tower."

"That's right. And now Richard carried out the traditional action that all newly-crowned kings did..."

"He chopped off some more heads?"

"No. Not quite. He set off on a royal progress, a journey around England, stopping off at various castles to see how everything was going. This meant three things: one, as there was no television then, this was a way of showing himself off to the people; two, his own castles were able to have a thorough spring cleaning, like changing the smelly rushes on the floors, and three, it also meant that the lords and nobles whose houses he stayed at had to pay for the honour of wining and dining the royal court instead of the king himself. Quite a system, eh?"

"But who was running the show in London while Richard was gallivanting around the countryside?"

"The Duke of Buckingham. Richard left his good

friend to hold the fort, which also meant that Buckingham was directly responsible for the Tower of London and all that it contained. This of course included the two sons of Edward IV and also the royal armoury. For you must remember, Sophie, the Tower was the country's central arms depot. Then, about three weeks later, the good duke met his king at Gloucester. At this point, the two friends fell out and there was a terrific argument, although about what we don't know. The writer of the most anti-Richard play, or any piece of writing about him..."

"Shakespeare and his *Richard III*?"

"Yes. Shakespeare claimed that Richard had promised Buckingham 'the Earldom of Hereford and moveables.' In other words, important titles and properties which Buckingham would get for his earlier support for Richard, but Richard did not deliver the goods to the duke's satisfaction. So about two months later, in September 1483, a very disgruntled Buckingham got together with some of the leading lights of the still frustrated Woodville clan and plotted to place Prince Edward on the throne. However, at the same time, a rumour had started circulating that Richard had already killed the princes."

"So, to start a revolution and place a non-existent prince on the throne didn't really make much sense, did it?"

"No. And that's one of the strange things about Buckingham's behaviour, and about how and when the princes were killed."

"If they were really killed."

"Exactly. In his classic study, *Richard III,* Professor Kendall puts forward the possibility that Buckingham had the princes killed after Richard had left London to start out on his progress, since he held complete power in London which included free entrance to the Tower of London. The killing of the princes would then be laid at Richard's door and this would definitely succeed in blackening the king's reputation.

"So, Buckingham and some other nobles planned their revolution, as some historians say, so that Buckingham, who was known to be ambitious, could exploit his own aristocratic background and connections to become king himself. But then, unfortunately for the plotters, in mid-October when Richard was at Lincoln, word got out and Richard then declared Buckingham to be a rebel.

"The duke started moving east from South Wales, but many of his officers and simple soldiers deserted him. By the time he arrived in Shropshire, he saw the game was up, so he disguised himself in rough peasant clothes and went into hiding. Unfortunately for him, his chief servant, Ralph Bannaster, handed him over to the king's men in Salisbury. Despite his pleas for mercy, he was found guilty and…"

"… beheaded."

"Exactly. So from now on, Richard was king without any rivals, at least in England. The princes were dead, or if not, they were not legally allowed to succeed Edward IV because of their illegitimacy. However, there is another theory about these two lads and it is this. They were still alive, but had been secretly smuggled out of the Tower and were now somewhere in the North, perhaps at Richard's favourite home at Middleham Castle in Yorkshire. But this, as with many other stories about the princes, cannot be proved. It's all speculation."

"Grandpa," Sophie said slowly after a long pause. "If what you have just told me is true, it doesn't seem right that Richard murdered the princes."

"Why?"

"Because he was the legal king. The top brass of the time accepted him and…"

"Wait a minute, Sophie. I must interrupt you here. Not everyone accepted him as king. Remember Buckingham wasn't the only one who had deserted him. There were others, you know."

"Such as?"

"For a start, there was Henry Tudor hanging around in the background, in the north of France, actually like a vulture hovering over the body. He kept himself well-informed about what was happening in England, and all the time he was waiting for Richard's position to become weaker so he could pounce."

"Yes, I know that, Grandpa, but I still don't see why Richard had any reason to murder the princes. After all, they had been declared illegitimate and therefore couldn't succeed him, could they?"

"No."

"And in any case, Richard had his own son, Edward, and a young wife to give him some more sons, no?"

"Yes, all this is true enough. But his son had died early soon after the beginning of Richard's reign. In addition, there were already rumours floating about that he had killed the princes in the Tower. And yes, there were other nasty rumours which claimed that he'd poisoned his wife who had died in the meanwhile – and whom he deeply loved by the way – so that he could marry Elizabeth of York…"

"But hadn't Henry Tudor promised to marry her?"

"Yes, but the rumours said that Richard was going to marry her, both to have an heir and also to keep the Woodville clan happy. This was even though Richard detested them, but the rumour mill claimed that he'd prefer to have them on his side rather than against him."

"But wait a minute, Grandpa. If, as you said, Richard may not have murdered the two princes, how is it that you hinted that Henry Tudor might have had a hand in their deaths instead? What would he have had to gain from such a dirty deed?"

"Plenty. First of all, if Henry Tudor had sworn to marry Edward IV's daughter, Elizabeth, then he first had to remove the label of illegitimacy that she and all her brothers and sisters carried. And then, if she were to be made legitimate, then so too were her brothers to be similarly legitimate."

"So?"

"So, Sophie – oh you are slow on this one. Don't you see, if Elizabeth of York was now legitimate…"

"Then so were her brothers, meaning that Prince Edward, the older of the two princes in the Tower, now has the strongest claim to the throne."

"Exactly. And Sophie, Henry wouldn't be pleased with that one, to say the least. So, if Henry wanted to be the strongest claimant to the throne, then he had vested interests that the two princes be completely removed out of the way."

"Exactly, as you would say, Grandpa. But tell me, who was this Henry Tudor who claimed that he had the right to be king?"

"Well, Sophie, it's like this. And try not to muddle up all the names and events. First of all, we have to go back over sixty-five years before Richard became king, that is, near the beginning of the 1400s. Henry V, the victor of Agincourt…"

"… and Shakespeare's hero."

"… married Catherine, the French princess, in 1420. But two years later, he died, leaving her with a baby son who became Henry VI. Catherine then married this Welsh fellow, Owen Tudor, who was later executed for treason in 1461. Owen Tudor had a son called Edmund who became the Earl of Richmond, and it is this man who became Henry Tudor's father. Get it?"

"So in other words, Henry Tudor was the direct grandson of Henry V's widow."

"Exactly. And in addition to all that, Henry Tudor said that, through his father and grandfather, he could claim descent from an ancient line of Celtic princes. To prove this, he named his first son Arthur."

"What? In memory of King Arthur and his knights of the Round Table?"

"That's right. And if that weren't enough, he also based his claim on the fact that he was a descendent of King Edward III's son, John of Gaunt. Now this man had a mistress called Katherine Swynford, and their son, John Beaufort, became the Duke of Somerset. Now, Somerset's granddaughter, Margaret, eventually became Henry Tudor's mother, giving birth to him when she was only thirteen years old."

"Grandpa, this sure is a complicated story. But all this meant that Henry could claim royalty through both of his parents."

"Exactly. But there's more to come."

"There always is. Go on."

"Then in 1406, Henry IV had declared that the House of Beaufort could not be used to make any claims to the throne."

"Because of Katherine Swynford?"

"I suppose so. It didn't pay to mix mistresses with the royal succession. But then the future Henry VII said that he was a legitimate successor. And in addition to all this, Henry Tudor was a Lancastrian, whose badge was a red rose, while Richard was a Yorkist with a white rose. So here again you have another cause for rivalry. And in fact, Henry had already tried to reinforce his claim to the throne."

"How? You said that he was in exile in France."

"Yes, but he'd returned to England with an invasion force later in 1483, just a few months after Richard had been crowned and had heard that there was still some opposition to him being the new king. However, when he heard that Buckingham's uprising had failed and that the Woodvilles wouldn't be there to support him, he returned to the north of France."

"But wait a minute, Grandpa. Didn't you say that the Duke of Buckingham himself also had some sort of claim to the throne?"

"Yes. And some historians say that Henry Stafford, the second Duke of Buckingham, had an even stronger claim than Henry Tudor, or the Earl of Richmond, to use his formal title. For a start, he was married to Elizabeth Woodville's sister, Katherine, and then he himself was a direct descendent of Edward III's seventh son, Thomas of Woodstock. This last-named man was also known as the Duke of Gloucester, but that was about fifty years before Richard was given that title."

"So that means that Buckingham, like Henry Tudor, could claim the succession from two angles; from his marriage to the queen's sister as well as through his own ancestors."

"Exactly. And that's what makes him yet another suspect in the 'Who Killed the Princes in the Tower' mystery. And this is especially true as Buckingham was known to be a ruthless and ambitious character who, because he had helped Richard gain the throne, was promoted to be the Lord High Constable of England. As I said before, this allowed him free entrance into the Tower and also allowed him to override the authority of the Lieutenant of the Tower, Sir Thomas Brackenbury. So all in all, like Henry Tudor, Buckingham also had vested interests in getting rid of the two princes, and as the police say today, he had the means as well as the motive."

"Well, Grandpa, he sounds like a really nasty piece of work."

"He was, as you phrase it so delicately, my dear. Then, in addition to all this, some historians have noted that when some of the dirty work was done at the beginning of Richard's reign, then it just so happens that Buckingham was hanging about ready to do it. This was actually quite clever on Buckingham's part, because it meant that Richard, as number one, carried the can. So, to sum up his career, it is very possible that he murdered or ordered the murder of the two princes, in order to remove the first obstacle on his own way to the top. The second stage, of course, was to defeat Richard in battle."

"But there he failed."

"Exactly. So now we have collected all or most of the evidence and motives for the murder, let us see if we can come to some conclusion regarding who really killed the princes in the Tower. However, I feel I must warn you, my dear Sophie and fellow sleuth, unless some very new and convincing evidence in the form of newly discovered documents or some sort of DNA proof comes to light, Richard III will remain the chief suspect for a long time to come. But you know, before we continue, I think we should take a break and have some tea. Besides, I want to watch the news on television. There'll be something about a *coup d'état* in one of the Balkan republics, though I can't remember in which one."

"What? The one we heard about on the radio this morning, when this exiled past prime-minister returned to the capital with loyalist troops and tanks, etc?"

"Yes."

"Sounds a bit like Richard III and Henry Tudor, no?"

"Exactly, except five hundred years later. So you see, my dear Sophie, some things never change."

Ten minutes later, after hearing that it was not sure whether the Balkan Prime Minister had succeeded or not, Grandpa switched the radio off.

"Come, Sophie, let's get back to our own mystery. At least this one happened in England and so any of the necessary documents are in English, Latin or French. So, let's see. What was the beginning of this mystery? I mean, where do we start reading about the 'wicked uncle' Richard, if indeed he was the 'wicked uncle'?"

"In some history book written at the time, I suppose."

"Exactly, Sophie. And one of the major historical records of the time was written by Sir Thomas More."

"The man who was friendly with Henry VIII, and

was then beheaded by him?"

Professor Warkworth nodded.

"So how was he involved in all of this? Didn't he live sometime after Richard was supposed to have killed the princes?"

"Out of the mouths of babes and sucklings…"

"Excuse me?"

"I'm just quoting the Psalms. But yes, you're right. Sir Thomas More wrote his history about Richard in 1513, and you don't have to be a great mathematician to see that this was thirty years after the event. In fact, when Richard was crowned, our saintly Thomas was a mere five years old."

"OK Grandpa. I understand that they weren't so fast in those days. You know, they didn't have the BBC or CNN, but he had to get his information from somewhere, no?"

"Of course. And Sir Thomas based his history on the oral and written word of John Morton, the Bishop of Ely, that is Henry VII's Archbishop of Canterbury."

"You mean the same Morton of 'Morton's Fork'?"

"Yes, the same ecclesiastical rogue."

"But why do you call him a rogue? What was his connection to this story?"

"Well, Sophie, it's like this. Morton was one of the quickest and luckiest changers-of-sides there ever was. First of all, he was a Lancastrian supporter under Henry VI. Then after the Yorkist Edward VI usurped Henry, Morton decided to work for him instead and became the

Bishop of Ely while accepting a bribe at the same time from the King of France for two thousand crowns a year to do some dirty deed. Then he began to work for the Woodville clan after the death of Edward IV and helped them to plan how to get the crown. Then he decided to throw in his lot with the Lancastrian Henry VII, and so became Richard's sworn enemy. Are you with me so far?"

"Yes. Just about, but carry on."

"Luckily for Morton and unluckily for Richard, Richard forgave him the first time for his treasonous activities, but then Morton fled to the Continent and allied himself with Henry Tudor who later made him first Lord Chancellor, then Archbishop of Canterbury and then, with the blessing of the Pope, a cardinal. And so, Sophie, you won't be surprised to learn that everyone feared and hated him, and it was this disgusting man who was the source of Sir Thomas More's history of Richard III."

"But what's the connection between Sir Thomas More and Morton?"

"Oh, that's an easy one. When Thomas More was a young lad, about eleven years old, he went to live in Morton's household, you know, as a student or page or something like that. Naturally, this way he heard all sorts of stories and gossip about Richard III and Henry VII directly from the horse's mouth, so to speak."

"Well, isn't that a good source of information?"

"No, not in this case. Because the Reverend

Archbishop Morton was now a yes-man for Henry VII and of course everything he said would be anti-Richard. This accounts for why various scholars say that Sir Thomas's account of the events is nothing in fact but a plagiarised copy of Morton's own distorted records. And if all that weren't enough, then guess who published More's history of Richard III."

"Henry VII?"

"No, but you're moving in the right direction. It was William Rastell, Sir Thomas' son-in-law. Now let's see if I can find More's description of the murder of the princes. I remember it being pretty grim and graphic. Ah, here it is, in *Richard III and the Princes in the Tower* by A.J. Pollard. Here we go. Chapter Five. And remember these are More's own words, not those of a latter-day historian:

> *Sir James Tyrrell devised that they should be murdered in their bed, to the execution wherof he appointed Miles Forest, one of the four that kept them, a fellow fleshed in murder before time. To him he joined one John Dighton, his own horse-keeper, a big, broad, square, strong knave. Then, all the other being removed from them, this Miles Forest and John Dighton about midnight the sely (*that is 'innocent', Sophie, not 'silly') *children lying in their beds came into the chamber and suddenly*

lapped them up among the clothes so bewrapped them and entangled them, keeping down by force the featherbed and pillows hard into their mouths, that within a while, smored and stifled, their breath failing, they gave up to God their innocent souls into the joys of heaven, leaving to their tormentors their bodies dead in the bed.

"Wow! Sir Thomas really knew how to lay it on, didn't he? All that 'big, broad, square, strong knave' bit stifling 'the innocent souls'. He sure knew how to use his adjectives. But my history teacher, Mrs Ingram, wouldn't have been impressed. 'Too melodramatic' would be her comment."

"Well, melodramatic or not, it was stuff like this that inspired Shakespeare to write his play and it formed the background to Polydore Vergil's history, *Anglica Historia.*"

"Who's this Vergil fellow? I thought Vergil was an ancient Greek."

"No, Sophie, not this one. Mr. Polydore Vergil was an Anglo-Italian historian who was commissioned by Henry VII to write a history of England. And naturally he wasn't going to write a book his employer wouldn't like, especially the parts concerning his enemy, Richard III?"

"No. I suppose not. And is that why Shakespeare

wrote his play as he did?"

"Of course. He wrote it while Elizabeth was on the throne, and who was her grandfather?"

"Henry VII."

"Exactly. And since I suppose the Bard of Avon wanted to keep his head on his shoulders, or at least, stay out of the Tower, he couldn't or wouldn't have written any pro-Richard stuff, now would he?"

"I suppose not. You know, Grandpa, it's a bit like someone today writing a book or play saying that Hitler was really a very funny man, you know, a variation of Charlie Chaplin. It's just not done."

"I agree. But today we have such a mass of evidence about Hitler and his regime. Newsreels, documents, live witnesses for a start, as well as lots of university and other research organisations and museums. But although it was different four hundred years ago, people also felt that they knew the truth, especially as such well-respected people as Sir Thomas More, Polydore Vergil and the writers of *The Crowland Chronicle* stated very clearly that Richard III was absolutely, definitely, and without a shadow of doubt the wicked murderer of the two innocent little princes in the Tower."

"And Shakespeare's play certainly reinforced that one."

"It certainly did. The imagery of Tyrrell, Forest and Dighton all working on behalf of Richard is so powerful that I doubt if it will ever be rubbed out. I would even go so far as to say that Shakespeare was the most effective spokesman or propagandist that the Tudors ever had – and that includes even Henry VII himself."

"How so?"

"Well, soon after Richard had been killed at Bosworth Field, the new King Henry drew up an Act of Attainder against Richard III. This was a legal document that basically allowed the king to forfeit the estates, properties, civil rights and titles of someone who had crossed the king's path, so to speak. In drawing up such an Act, Henry justified himself by saying that Richard had been wicked and cruel and all manner of nasty things, but the strange thing is that he never, and I repeat the word 'never', said that Richard actually murdered, or was directly responsible for the murder of the two princes in the Tower."

"That is really strange. That was his most important piece of ammunition, no? So what did he say?"

"Well funnily enough, he just accused Richard of the usual sort of crimes which were quoted in your run of the mill Act of Attainder."

"Such as?"

"Oh, tyranny, 'shedding of infants' blood', without stating specifically who the infants were, and all sorts of things like that. And there was absolutely no mention whatsoever of King Richard III's most well-known alleged crime: killing the princes in the Tower."

"You are right, Grandpa. That is really strange. So did Henry bring this up in another Act or something similar?"

"No, Sophie, he didn't. And what else is strange is that, according to Hugh Ross Williamson and other historians, as Henry was in possession of the Tower just a few days after the Battle of Bosworth, it can be concluded that the princes were still alive, otherwise he would have very happily stated that Richard had already killed them in the Act of Attainder."

"So in other words, the princes were still alive in August 1485."

"Exactly. Therefore, Richard couldn't have killed them…"

"And neither could Buckingham, as he had been executed by Richard two years earlier."

"Exactly. And in addition to all of this is the strange fact that Henry neither completely blackened Richard's name with the crime of regal infanticide, nor did he say anything about more direct heirs from the Yorkist line of Edward IV hanging about in the wings ready to usurp him…"

"… as a natural continuation of the Wars of the Roses."

"Right."

"But Grandpa, what about Edward's daughters? Didn't they count for anything?"

"No. People in those days were thinking in terms of kings ruling them, not queens. Remember, up to that point, there had only been one queen, that is, reigning in her own right and not just as wife of the king, and that had been Matilda in the twelfth century. And if you also remember, she had done such a terrible job that she had been forced to flee the country and ended up in Normandy."

"Well, what about Mary Tudor and Elizabeth? They were certainly queens who reigned in their own right."

"Yes, but they came nearly seventy later and they also ascended the throne probably because daddy, that is, Henry VIII, had made sure how and who was to succeed him. In fact, Edward VI, who was younger than his two sisters, came first, simply because he was a man, or rather a boy at the time of Henry's death, even though Mary, his first-born child was over thirty years old at the time."

"So, Grandpa, is there any other evidence that Henry VII bumped off the princes if, as you claim, Richard didn't?"

"Well, my dear, think about this one. In July 1486, that is, almost a year after Richard was killed at Bosworth, one of the aldermen of the City of London, a Robert Fabyan, wrote in his diary that 'common fame', meaning 'publicity' in modern English, was ordered to be spread about that Richard III had murdered the princes in the Tower 'to a secret death' as he recorded it."

"So why is that important?"

"Because it seems to show that if the princes had indeed been killed by Richard during his reign, there would have been no need to drag up this story again. Everyone would have known about it already, no?"

"So in other words, Grandpa, you are saying that because Henry VII ordered this new publicity in 1486, then it seems as if they'd have been alive up until then, more or less, and that they were killed after Henry had become king?"

"Exactly. It certainly seems like that if you read between the lines closely. And in addition, certain documents have been found, dated March 1485, saying that silk shirts should be delivered to Lord Edward, that is Edward V, and to the Lord Bastard, the younger Prince Richard. Now would anyone do that if the princes had been murdered two years earlier?"

"Well, Grandpa, that sounds pretty convincing evidence that they were alive at least until then."

"And if they were, I'm sure Richard didn't try and kill them then because he had too many other fish to fry. First he had to see about the question of who would succeed him, since his own only legitimate son, also called Edward, had died a year earlier in 1484, while another problem was what to do about his queen."

"Why? Didn't he get on with her?"

"Oh no. The opposite is true. It is well-recorded that he loved her very much. But the Lancastrian supporters of Henry VII claimed that he had poisoned her, but there was no proof of this. In fact, according to the records, gossip and other evidence, the poor Lady Anne had probably died of tuberculosis, and this had apparently devastated the king."

"So he certainly doesn't sound like a cold,

calculating murderer, when you describe him like that."

"No, Sophie, I don't think he was. And then, to cap all of this off, there's another part of this mystery that needs clearing up."

"I was afraid that you'd come up with something or someone else."

"Well, this someone is called Sir James Tyrrell."

"The man mentioned by Sir Thomas More?"

"Yes. The same man. Now, Sir James Tyrrell of Gipping had been a faithful servant of both Edward IV and Richard III and had even been promoted to become Lord High Constable as well as Master of the Horse. When Richard became king, he honoured Tyrrell with lands and titles. However, while Richard was fighting for his life at Bosworth, Tyrrell wasn't around as he was serving abroad as Governor of Guisnes, near Calais, England's last possession in France. After Henry became king, he pardoned Tyrrell for helping the Yorkists and so he continued living happily in his castle, or château, in France for the next sixteen years, without ever hitting the Tudor headlines."

"Nothing mysterious there. Sounds very generous on Henry's part, I would say."

"Ah, but wait a minute, Sophie. Then in 1502, a few years after Henry had finally rid himself of the last of the Yorkists, such as Lambert Simnel, Perkin Warbeck and the Earl of Warwick, Edward IV's remaining nephew, Henry suddenly ordered Tyrrell to be arrested and brought to London to be tried for treason. The charge: corresponding with the Yorkist Earl of Suffolk, the son of Edward IV and Richard III's sister, Elizabeth. At first, Tyrrell refused to budge, knowing that if he returned to London…"

"… he'd get the chop."

"Exactly. So he made preparations to defend himself in his castle at Guisnes, but then he relented and allowed himself to be persuaded to return to London. He went on board one of the king's ships with the idea of checking out the situation, and in fact, he was even issued with a safe conduct passage by the Lord Privy Seal, the Bishop of Winchester. So far so good. No one's going to argue with that one. But the whole thing blew up in his face and he was whisked over to England and locked up in the Tower of London. Then in May 1502, he was executed, as they recorded it at the time, 'in great haste and without trial'."

"But Grandpa, what about 'Magna Carta?' and the right to receive a trial, especially if you were a nobleman?"

The professor shrugged and continued. "Now what is strange here, is that Tyrrell, according to Sir Thomas More, and probably to Morton before him, was Richard III's buddy and was also supposed to have supervised the murder of the princes in the Tower. If that indeed were the case, why didn't Henry put him on trial for this and then get some extra publicity proving that it was Richard who had been responsible for the princes' untimely demise? Actually, it was reported that Tyrrell had confessed to the murders, but it was never *officially* recorded, meaning…"

"… that this confession was a put-up job."

"Exactly. And what also adds to this already mysterious situation is that it seems as if it was only Sir James Tyrrell who could have shed some real light on the whole scene."

"So Grandpa, in other words, Henry Tudor really wanted Tyrrell out of the way so that he wouldn't spill the beans about his, Henry VII's, part in the murder. 'This man knows too much' etc."

"Exactly. Tyrrell was officially executed for treason, not regicide."

"But Grandpa, surely Henry would have published the wicked Tyrrell's confession if he'd murdered, or supervised the murder, no?"

"Not in this case."

"But why not?"

"Because, my dear Sophie, Tyrrell probably wasn't responsible. But what Henry did was to let his court historian, Mr Vergil, write up some sort of account saying that Tyrrell was supposed to have done the dirty deed. In fact, by having Tyrrell executed, Henry was in a win-win situation. If Tyrrell had murdered the princes under Richard's authority, then the king was right to punish him. But if Henry had organised the murder himself, then he was covering himself up very well by getting rid of the chief witness."

"So our Henry sounds like a very cunning and

devious character."

"Oh he was certainly that. You know, he even had the beginning of his reign dated from the day before the Battle of Bosworth. That meant that anyone who fought against him could then be legally accused of treason. To sum it up: one, since Sir James Tyrrell was not publicly tried for murder, and two, since Henry never produced the dead bodies at the very beginning of his reign, and three, he never specifically charged Richard of murdering the princes, then I think we can deduce that our murderer was really Henry VII and not Richard III. And all of this is especially true if you take into account that the princes had already been declared illegitimate, that is, the sons of a bigamist, by a top cleric during Richard's reign. And of course, that meant that they wouldn't have been a threat to their 'wicked uncle' in any case. And just to make sure, the boys' mother, like everyone else connected with this mystery, was removed from the scene and isolated in a nunnery where she could do no harm as far as Henry was concerned."

"Hey, but wait a minute, Grandpa. Just before you wrap it all up, I've just had another idea. What if no one had murdered the princes and they had escaped or were allowed to escape from the Tower for whatever reason?"

"That point has also been written about by various historians, my dear. However, I think we can rule out the idea of the princes escaping. Here we are talking about the massive fortress called the Tower of London, not some tin-pot temporary structure. Number one is that they were only young boys, not hardened criminals, and number two is that to escape from the Tower is practically impossible. Only a few had tried it, and even fewer had succeeded. And even if you had succeeded, you probably wouldn't have stayed free for very long considering that the Tower was an integral part of the City of London. One poor fellow, Griffith, the last Welsh Prince of Wales, who was imprisoned by Henry III in the thirteenth century, managed to pull off the classic escape…"

"What? Using knotted sheets and curtains, etc.?"

"Yes, but either they weren't long enough or they ripped. Anyway, the end result was that he fell and broke his neck. So, my dear Sophie, I think we can forget about the idea of the two princes making a dare-devil escape from the Tower like that."

"And is there a possibility that they were allowed to escape, for any reason?"

"That possibility does exist, but I think it's a faint one. First of all, if it had happened, they would have been a threat to Henry VII in terms of the succession. However, despite this, there is a theory that they were smuggled out of the Tower, Edward becoming known as Sir Edward Guildford, while his younger brother Richard became a physician called Dr John Clement. And there are people who claim that this is the shadowy person in the background of Hans Holbein's portrait of Sir Thomas More's family. Other people claim that Henry VII organised this together with the princes' mother, Elizabeth Woodville, but this doesn't really make much sense, especially as Henry didn't want any possible claimants to the throne hanging about.

"There is also another theory which states that the murderers took pity on the younger prince and smuggled him out of the Tower, making him promise to keep mum for several years. Later, a young man appears on the scene called Perkin Warbeck and he claims he is Richard, son of Edward IV. Warbeck was supported, or exploited if you like, by the remaining Yorkists and duly crowned Richard IV, but in Dublin. Soon after, he comes to England, but is defeated by Henry's troops at the Battle of Stoke, which could be called the last battle of the Wars of the Roses."

"And what did Henry do to him?"

"Henry had him executed, together with Richard's last remaining nephew, the Earl of Warwick."

"And so, my dear grandpa, after all this, you claim that the murderer of the two princes in the Tower was Henry VII, as he had the most to gain and that he also had the means to do so. In other words, William Shakespeare and everyone else got it all wrong."

"Exactly."

Chapter Four
The Would-be King, Lambert Simnel, (1486-1487)

Lambert Simnel   *King Henry VII*

"Oh, Grandpa, you're not playing that 'Platters' CD again, are you?"

"Of course I am. Can't you let an old man enjoy his music in peace?"

"I know Grandpa, but you play it so often. Even I'm beginning to learn the words of that old song, *The Great Pretender*. It's from the forties, no?"

"Wrong. As far as I know, it was first recorded in 1955 and then the most recent recording was done in

1987 by Freddie Mercury."

"Wow Grandpa, I'm impressed. I see you're really up on this stuff and you don't just read history books for fun."

"And you, Miss Sophie are one cheeky young lady."

"No, not really. But actually, despite myself I quite like that *Old Pretender* song, but don't tell Harry when he comes over later, OK?"

"OK."

"By the way, Grandpa, weren't there quite a few Pretenders in English history?

"Oh yes. There were two Scottish ones, James Edward Stuart, the 'Old Pretender" and his son, Charles Edward Stuart, the 'Young Pretender', otherwise known as 'Bonnie Prince Charlie'."

"And were there any English Pretenders?"

Professor Warkworth nodded. "Yes there were, and the most amazing ones were Perkin Warbeck, who I have previously mentioned, and Lambert Simnel."

"Why, who did they pretend to be?"

"They pretended that they were the rightful Yorkist heirs to the throne at the end of the fifteenth century."

"You mean that they were against the Lancastrian Henry VII?"

"Exactly."

"But I thought that after he won the Battle of Bosworth Field he sat very firmly on the throne. I mean that the people had had enough of the fighting and the Wars of the Roses."

"Oh no. Not really, and certainly not at the beginning of his reign. I think that he was justifiably worried by the thought that some Yorkist would try and snatch the throne from him, in the same way that he'd done to Richard III. Why do you think that his son Henry VIII was so obsessed about having a son to succeed him? I'm sure it wasn't just an ego trip. It was because he believed that a son was the only way of making sure that the Tudor dynasty would continue. I'm not sure that he had much faith in women as successors."

"Well, he certainly believed in them as wives!"

"Maybe, maybe not. But don't ask Anne Boleyn or Catherine Howard about that. But to get back to Henry VII, he can't have been too pleased to hear that the first of these two Yorkist Pretenders, Lambert Simnel, was challenging him for the throne, and within a couple of years of him grabbing it from Richard III."

"So who was this Simnel character?"

"Well, my dear Sophie, this story is a bit strange because Lambert Simnel had absolutely no right and no legal claim to the throne at all. At least Henry VII had some tenuous claims through his grandfather's marriage to Henry V's widow, while his mother was the great-great-granddaughter of Edward III. But this Lambert Simnel was nothing but the son of a joiner, or some such trade, from Oxford.

"So, the traditional story goes like this: Once upon a time towards the end of the fifteenth century, there was an ambitious priest called Simonds. His first name we're not sure of but it was probably either Richard or William. He wanted to get on in the ecclesiastic world, but he wanted to do so quickly. So he thought of the following devious, if somewhat unbelievable, plot. He would train one of his young charges to impersonate a Yorkist prince and once this young man was accepted as such, Simonds would rise to priestly glory and the new ruler would make him a bishop or something like that, in return for his help."

"Wait a minute, Grandpa. You are telling me that an unknown priest decided to help an unknown boy to become the future King of England, so that the priest could then be promoted in the Church?"

"Exactly."

"Is this true, or is it just a folk-tale?"

"Oh no. It's very true. It was recorded by Henry VII's historian Polydore Vergil in his *Anglica Historia* which was written at the beginning of the 1500s. And what we do know is that the priest and Simnel were well into their plot at least by the summer of 1486 and…"

"But Grandpa, that would mean that Simonds would have to teach this young man how to act and talk like a prince and to teach him all sorts of things that a prince would know and that ordinary people wouldn't."

"Exactly."

"To me it sounds like an early version of Professor Higgins trying to teach Eliza Doolittle in *Pygmalion*, you know, passing a poor flower-girl off as a duchess or something like that."

"Exactly. And you know what, Sophie? Simonds succeeded, just as Higgins did with Eliza. He managed to convince people that this young Lambert Simnel, who was about twelve years old, was in fact the Yorkist prince, the Earl of Warwick."

"But wait a minute, Grandpa. Wasn't Warwick killed about fifteen years earlier fighting Edward IV?"

"No, my dear. That was a different Warwick. That was Warwick the Kingmaker. The one I'm talking about now was the son of Edward IV's brother, Clarence."

"Clarence? Who was drowned in a butt of Malmsey?"

"Right. And this Warwick probably had more right as Richard III's nephew to inherit the throne than Henry VII. Hence Henry was less than happy to say the least when he first heard about this plot."

"So what did he do?"

"He… wait a minute. Wasn't that the front door?"

"Yes. It must be Harry. I'll just go and let him in… Here Harry, here's my grandpa."

"I know, Sophie. I met him when he came to give a talk at our school."

"Anyway, he's busy telling me about some weirdo priest who wanted one of his pupils or choirboys to be king so he could then become a bishop in return."

"Do you mean Lambert Simnel?"

"You mean you've heard of him?"

"Sure. He's mentioned in that book *1066 & All That*. Him and Perkin Warbeck."

"Ah, very good Harry. I'm glad someone else has heard of these two Pretenders. I was just telling Sophie about Edward IV's nephew, the Earl of Warwick."

"I see."

"So, Sophie, when Henry heard that Simonds and others were claiming that they had the real Earl of Warwick, he decided to call their bluff and so he released the *real* Earl of Warwick from the Tower where he had been keeping him and paraded him around London so the people would know that the other one was an impostor."

"So that must have foiled the plotters."

"It didn't. By now Lambert Simnel was in Ireland and was being supported by the pro-Yorkist Irish, and by some influential lords such as the Earl of Lincoln, Sir John de la Pole, who was another nephew of Edward IV and of Richard III, as well as Viscount Francis Lovell and a Captain Thomas David. What these men did was to say that the Warwick whom Henry was parading around was a fake and that they had the *real* Warwick with them in Ireland."

"But Professor Warkworth, why did these aristocrats support this anti-Henry plot? What did they hope to gain out of it?"

"Well Harry, as I was telling Sophie, Henry didn't feel too secure on the throne, so one of the first things he did was to stick young Perkin Warwick in the Tower and…"

"Why didn't he just chop off his head and be done

with it?"

"My dear Sophie, although Henry VII has gone down in history as a miser – which he wasn't – he was certainly not a bloodthirsty ruler. In fact, when he took over, he chopped off very few heads. He preferred to silence the opposition by making them pay heavy fines instead. In that way, he looked good and he also made a lot of money in the bargain. But to return to the spring of 1486, that is, after he had been ruling for just over six months, Henry decided to leave London and do a public relations tour around the country and set out on a royal progress, and it was then that his reign was first challenged."

"By unhappy Yorkists?"

"Exactly. By our friend Viscount Lovell and the Stafford brothers, Sir Thomas and Sir Humphrey. The Staffords raised an army in Worcestershire and Lovell did the same in North Yorkshire. Fortunately for the king, neither army attracted the number of people that looked like a threat, so Henry as usual settled the problem with words rather than with the sword. He offered pardons to all those who would surrender. Most of the troops did so and, as a result, Lovell fled north to Lancashire."

"Sounds like our Henry was quite a devious character."

"Yes, Harry, he certainly was. But he wasn't finished with the Yorkist plotters yet. First of all, he still had to deal with the Stafford brothers."

"Heads or cash?"

"Both. They were both tried and found guilty. Sir Humphrey was hanged, drawn and quartered, but his brother was pardoned."

"And paid a huge fine."

"Probably. And meanwhile, Lovell fled abroad and ended up at the court of Richard III and Edward IV's sister, Margaret, who was by now the Dowager Duchess of Burgundy. Now, this lady's court became the focus of pro-Yorkist plots. It was here that Lovell met Captain Thomas David. This stalwart fellow was a fighter with a chip on his shoulder. He'd been fined and fired by Henry for refusing to swear an oath of loyalty while he was serving at the garrison at Calais. These malcontents were also joined by Margaret's nephew, the Earl of Lincoln, another prominent pro-Yorkist."

"So Professor Warkworth, where does Lambert Simnel fit in all this?"

"That's just what I was coming to, Harry. While all these discontented sons of York, to misquote the Bard, were sitting around grumbling and plotting, someone – and we don't know who – suggested that they should exploit their new 'Warwick' figurehead."

"But Grandpa, wouldn't they need a lot of money for all this plotting?"

"That doesn't seem to have been a problem, Sophie. Simnel's new 'Auntie Margaret' seems to have supplied the cash and yes, I think that they must have needed quite a lot of it, because when this band of Yorkists set sail for Ireland, which was to serve as a springboard for their *coup*, they took, in addition to themselves, some two thousand German mercenaries under the leadership of Captain Martin Schwarz."

"What did he have against Henry VII?"

"Probably nothing, Sophie. He was a mercenary and was in it purely for the money."

"Exactly, Harry. And this Schwarz character had fought for Burgundy before and was known as a pretty brutal character."

"And what did Henry do when he heard about this possible invasion?"

"Ironically enough, he acted in a way that was similar to Richard III when he, Henry, invaded England from the west coast. He moved his army north out of London and established his base at Kenilworth Castle near Coventry. In the meanwhile, Lambert Simnel, Lovell and Co. had arrived in Ireland, and in May 1487 Lambert Simnel, now as the Earl of Warwick, was crowned King Edward VI of England at Christ Church, Dublin. They were joined by other Yorkists such as the ex-Governor of Jersey, Richard Harleston, some knights from Cornwall and a band of Irish soldiers. Then about ten days after the coronation, Simnel and his supporters landed on the north-west coast in Cumbria."

"But Professor Warkworth, isn't that a long way north? Wouldn't they have had to do a lot of fighting before they reached London?"

"Yes, Harry, you're right there. However, the rebels

chose this site deliberately because this area was owned by Sir Thomas Broughton who had been a fellow plotter with Lovell a year earlier. From here they all moved south, together with Broughton's men as well. All in all, they now numbered about four to five thousand men."

"And Grandpa, did Henry know all about this activity?"

"Oh, he knew about it all right. Our devious king had his spies everywhere, and besides, you couldn't exactly move five thousand soldiers around quietly without attracting some sort of attention."

"So what did Henry do about it? I mean, five thousand men are just too many to pay off or just hope that they'll surrender without a fight, no?"

"True, so Henry decided to march north with some of his most trusted men under the command of Viscount Lisle, Sir Edward Grey and Lord Scales. He also took his uncle, Jasper Tudor, the Duke of Bedford and various other lords and knights who had fought with him at Bosworth Field."

"So the rebels moved south and Henry moved north," Sophie concluded. "So Grandpa, where did they meet?"

"They met at East Stoke, which is just south of Newark in Nottinghamshire. The rebels had crossed the Pennines in North Yorkshire and had then marched south via Boroughbridge, Tadcaster and Rotherham. They had hoped the people of York would support them, but that didn't happen, so they just carried on south. In the meanwhile, Henry's army was reinforced in

Nottinghamshire by about six thousand men led by Lord Strange.

"The question now was where exactly they would meet and who would fix the site of the battle so that they'd have the advantage in terms of terrain, you know, sun behind their backs, use of any woodland or pasture, etc. These were the sorts of traditional questions commanders in those days asked themselves before going into battle.

"And if you ask me, I think the following thoughts must have been going through Lovell's head the night before the battle, which would be known later by historians as the Battle of Stoke – the battle that finally brought the curtain down on the Wars of the Roses, or the Cousins' War, as it was called then:

'So here we are then', Lovell thought as he looked over his suit of armour once again. 'East Stoke, Nottinghamshire. Tomorrow is 16 June 1487 and anything can happen then. After coming all this way, from England to Burgundy, then to Ireland and then back again to England. Will we beat this Lancastrian upstart? At least we are in a good position here. We command the high ground, and we are also blocking the king from reaching Newark for fresh supplies. But I wonder if that wily Welshman will try and get out of a fight and buy peace again or try some other trick, like those offers of pardon he made last year? It hasn't been for nothing that this Tudor monarch has earned his

reputation for being devious. I mean, if fines and confiscations of property have brought more money into the royal coffers, then this Henry really knows how to play the devil's own game. I just know that if our Lambert Simnel ever becomes king in London, then I will certainly take a leaf out of Henry's book. But in the meanwhile, I had better go out and check our defences and preparations. My scouts tell me the king isn't far off.'

Lovell: Ah, there you are Lincoln. I was just coming out to see you about some last-minute details. Here, take a stool and tell me what you think. Do you think that we've reached the end of the road?

Lincoln: Well, if we have, John, then it's been a long road.

Lovell: I know. I was just thinking the same thing myself.

Lincoln: And now, to end up in this God-forsaken spot between Nottingham and Newark.

Lovell: Aye, you're right there. But what are our chances against the king? We've got about ten thousand men, including this German Schwartz and his troops.

Lincoln: True, and he is probably the backbone of our forces. I'm not too sure how these Irish will fight. I mean, they've got the will, but they don't have much armour and God knows what they'll do once the arrows begin to fly. A thin doublet doesn't offer much protection against an arrowhead.

Lovell: Aye, I was thinking the same. And our English fighters? Will they turn tail or will that devious Henry try and buy their peace? You know what, Francis? I think we should mix our English and the German troops together. That way they should give each other a certain backbone. What do you think?

Lincoln: I hope you're right there, John. After all, we've both been in a similar situation in the past and we've seen how men behave in battle, haven't we?

Lovell: Aye. That's what I was thinking of. So you know what we should do now? We should draw a plan of where we're going to place our men. I'm telling you, I went for a walk earlier this evening over the battlefield and I suggest the following: we'll group our men in a central block on the hill and make sure that our right flank extends over to that higher part, there.

Lincoln: What? To Burham Furlong?

Lovell: Aye. That's it.

Lincoln: Why?

Lovell: Because, my dear Francis, it means that we control the high ground and that Burham place has a steep side to it which means it'll protect our right flank.

Lincoln: And you're sure that the king will come from the south?

Lovell: Aye. He has no choice. If he wants to beat us here and prevent us from moving south, he'll have to attack us from the south. The south-west to be exact. This is a good spot we have chosen. He cannot surprise us from the north as the River Trent protects our backs. So you see, he has no choice.

Lincoln: Well, my friend, I hope you're right, but I don't share your confidence.

Lovell: Fear not, my dear Francis, we've been through all this before. Just think, this time tomorrow we'll be on the way south to London. But in the meanwhile, I suggest that we each make a quick round of the men and then get some sleep. Tomorrow we're going to need all the strength we have.

Lincoln: Don't take my words to heart, John. I always feel like this before a battle.

Lovell: That's all right, my friend. But tell me, what is our newly crowned King Edward doing at this moment? Sleeping, or talking of battle?

Lincoln: When I left him he was talking of battle and how he spent his time at the French court, but now I trow he'll have gone to his tent to sleep. Before leaving him I told him we'll all have a long day tomorrow. And now, before I go to bed myself, I'll go and look over in his direction. So good night, my friend, and may the Good Lord grant us courage and victory tomorrow.

Lovell: Amen to that, Francis. Amen."

"And Grandpa, I bet Henry was having a similar conversation on his side. I mean that his men wouldn't desert him and that of course, he'd win the day."

"I'm sure you're right, Sophie, especially if the rebel army consisted of between nine and ten thousand men."

"Yes, Professor Warkworth, but they can't have been a very united army. After all, there were German mercenaries, Irish peasants and anti-Lancastrian Englishmen. That must have made communication and the giving of orders somewhat of a problem."

"I don't think so, Harry. Remember, Henry VII himself had English, French and Welsh troops when he fought Richard III at Bosworth Field. And also, you have to take into account that battles weren't very sophisticated or technologically advanced in those days. I'm sure that if a commander shouted and pointed his sword in a certain direction, then his troops knew where to go and what to do.

"So the next day the rebels formed a line roughly half-way between East Stoke and the village of Elston, that is, a few miles south-west of Newark, and decided to wait there. They didn't have long. At the head of Henry's army was…"

"Henry."

"Oh no, Sophie. Henry was no military leader. He may have defeated Richard III two years earlier, but he was certainly a backroom general. No, his commander at the front was Sir John de Vere, the Earl of Oxford. He suddenly realised that he had come upon the enemy and now he had a problem. It was this. In his push northwards he now saw that he didn't have enough forces with him. He could send a messenger back to the king and tell him to catch up as soon as possible or…"

"He could beat a strategic retreat to Henry's position and then they could all advance together as a united army."

"Yes Harry, but there's a problem with that alternative. For if he retreated, even on purpose, it would probably have been understood as a sign of weakness which would then have encouraged the enemy to charge and for his own men to desert. No, he couldn't retreat, but he did have one more option. That was to stand and wait for Henry to catch up and then they all attack the rebels as a united army."

"But wasn't that dangerous, Professor Warkworth? Hanging about before a battle tends to make the men nervous, no? I mean that might be the chance for many of them to sneak away and desert."

"I don't think so in this case, Harry. No, I think the danger in hanging about, as you call it, was that he might be attacked by the rebels, and that the timing of the attack and the organisation of the rebel troops would be initiated by Lovell and his commanders instead."

"So Grandpa, what did the Earl of Oxford do?"

"He did the only thing he could do in such a situation. He charged the rebels. That is, he led his six thousand men against the rebel force of ten thousand and hoped that his more professional army would win the day."

"And I suppose that he hoped that Henry would catch up in the meanwhile."

"I suppose so."

"So what happened?"

"Well, Sophie, both armies let fly with clouds of arrows and the Irish men on the rebels' side really suffered from this as they weren't wearing any heavy clothes or armour. Then while Oxford was positioning his men for a charge, the rebels took the initiative and charged, forcing Oxford to retreat. This might have been a good short-term advantage for the rebels, but now it meant that they were a disorganised force, a bit like Harold's men at the closing stages at the Battle of Hastings. The result was that for an hour there was a massive scene of close hand-to-hand fighting, and…"

"But Professor Warkworth, couldn't Oxford send an urgent message to Henry to get moving and come and support him?"

"That's exactly what he did, Harry. And when the king's men joined the fray at last, the rebels began to retreat and so Henry saved the day by taking the pressure off Oxford and his men. Finally, the rebels broke ranks and retreated back up the hill they had happily charged down three hours earlier. They continued north towards the Trent and many were killed by the king's men on the way in a narrow gorge now known for obvious reasons as the Red Gutter. It must have been a really bloody battle. Over five thousand rebels were killed, that is about half of Simnel's army, while Henry lost about three thousand of his own men."

"Were the rebel leaders killed or were they executed later?"

"No, Sophie, there weren't many left after the battle. Lincoln, Captain Schwartz and Sir Thomas Broughton were killed, and…"

"And what happened to Lovell?"

"Ah, there's a bit of a mystery there. He was never seen alive again after that day."

"Do you mean that they found his body but they don't know exactly what happened to him?"

"No, not that either. They never found him on the battlefield afterwards, and some people think that he drowned in the Trent while trying to escape and that his body was washed away. However, other people think that years later they found his body in a sealed vault in the family home at Minster Lovell. When they broke this vault open, they found a skeleton inside, but it proved impossible to identify who it was and how it got there in the first place. But what you do have today is a large square memorial, the Burrand Bush stone, which shows where Henry VII placed his standard after the battle."

"And, Professor Warkworth, what happened to our hero, Lambert Simnel?"

"Well, Harry, at least we have a happy ending to this part of this anti-Henry plot. The young man was brought before Henry who had to decide what to do with him. The king was sharp enough to see that Simnel had been used and that *he* hadn't started any of this, so he decided to spare his life and…"

"Threw him into prison."

"Yes, Sophie, but only for a few days. At first he was imprisoned in Newark and then he was taken to London. There he was paraded around with the real Earl of Warwick so that people could see he was an impostor. Then after that Henry had the young man brought to court where he was put to work as a servant in the royal kitchens."

"You mean plucking pheasants and washing dishes?"

"Yes, I suppose so. But I think he must have been quite a bright young man as it was recorded later that he became one of the king's falconers. He eventually died aged about sixty."

"Which was a good age then, right?"

"Right. By the way, an interesting footnote to this plot is that Henry learned from experience and made sure that all parts of the country would be loyal to him. So when a tax-revolt broke out in the north, he sent the Earl of Northumberland to disperse the rebels."

"Do you mean the same earl who had failed to support Richard III at Bosworth Field?"

"Yes. And when Northumberland turned up with his men to put down this minor revolt, his men deserted and killed him for – as the records put it – 'disappointing' their Yorkist hero, Richard III in *his* hour of need."

"So Grandpa, after this Lambert Simnel plot was over, did Henry feel secure at last?"

"I don't think so, Sophie, because four years later, in 1491, the next Pretender, a young man called Perkin Warbeck, claimed that he too was the rightful heir to the throne. However, this time, this threat was much more serious and this time Henry was not so amused or generous."

"Do you mean that Perkin Warbeck paid with his neck?"

"Exactly, but that's another Pretender and another story."

Chapter Five
The Would-be King, Perkin Warbeck (1491-1495)

Perkin Warbeck   *King Henry VII*

"Grandpa, do you remember when you said that Lambert Simnel was the first Pretender to threaten Henry VII? What happened to the second one, Perkin Warbeck? You said he was a greater threat to the king, no?"

"Yes, Sophie. I think he was. You see, his claim to the throne was a much more serious affair as it didn't only involve the usual crowd of pro-Yorkist dissidents, Burgundians and Irish, it was also supported by King

James IV of Scotland."

"Do you mean this time that Henry VII felt himself threatened from the north as well as from the south and west?"

"Exactly."

"So who was this Perkin Warbeck? Was he an innocent dupe like Lambert Simnel, someone who was used by others?"

"Yes and no. He was certainly used by others, but I don't think that he was as innocent as Lambert Simnel. For a start he was much older. When he started out at the beginning of the 1490s he was seventeen years old, and I believe he really knew what he was doing."

"Was he also from Oxford?"

"No, he wasn't even English. He came from Tournai in Flanders, which is now in Belgium. He was the son of a boatman called Werbecque but somehow, despite his simple working-class background, he learned English. According to many people at that time he looked a lot like the younger one of the two princes who were supposed to have been murdered in the Tower of London."

"Richard, Duke of York?"

"Yes. And not only that, but this boatman's son was noted for the regal way he used to walk around."

"Why? Was he a snob?"

"I don't know about that, but when he met Lady Margaret of Burgundy, Edward IV and Richard III's sister, she felt that he had enough of the family look to be supported as another Yorkist claimant to the throne of Henry VII."

"You mean she was no longer interested in Lambert Simnel?"

"Yes."

"And how did he learn to behave like a prince and not like some smelly old boatman's son?"

"Well, the first report we have of this young man is when he was in the service of Lady Brampton. She was the widow of a Yorkist exile living in Portugal who was a known supporter of Richard III."

"So she was a genuine Yorkist?"

"Exactly. And it was through this lady that our hero met all sorts of other ex-pat Yorkists. In addition, he was also mentioned in a letter written by the Spanish king and queen, Ferdinand and Isabella. It also seems that he came into contact with Sir Bernard de la Force, an important Englishman, at the Spanish court."

"So in other words, he had somewhere to learn his courtly manners, etc?"

"Oh certainly. And while he was living in Portugal, he left the service of Lady Brampton and started working for a Breton merchant called Pregent Meno. According to a confession he made a few years later to Henry VII, and remember that you cannot believe everything that was written in such documents…"

"Because of torture?"

"Yes. Warbeck claimed that while he was walking around wearing clothes his master wanted to sell…"

"Like a medieval model?"

"Yes, he was addressed as the Earl of Warwick and then as Richard, Duke of York. He seemed to have liked his new role in life, especially when he was told he looked a lot like Edward IV. Soon after this, the young man, who acted like a prince, and who could now speak good English, set sail with Meno for Ireland on a business trip. There, the pro-Yorkist Irish, including the influential Earls of Desmond and Kildare, were prepared to support him as a figurehead in their ongoing fight against Henry VII. He stayed in Ireland for a few months and became known as the 'Merchant of the Ruby'."

"And so everything was going OK for this imposter?"

"Right, especially when in the summer of 1492 he received an invitation from the King of France, Charles VIII, to come to Paris. He proceeded to wine and dine Warbeck for a few months, while several important Yorkists, such as Sir George Neville and Sir John Taylor, came to pay him homage as their new leader."

"But tell me, why did Charles VIII want to get involved in this plot?"

"Power, Sophie. Power. That, and money, which is also power, is the usual answer for such questions. France was a growing power in Europe and Charles wished to take over the Duchy of Brittany, especially as Henry had invested so much money and men there in order to keep it pro-English or, at least, independent of

Charles VIII. Then, to top it all, the French king really annoyed our Henry by going and marrying the Duchess of Brittany. This really cemented the diplomatic relationship between Charles and Brittany."

"But what could Henry do about that? After all, wasn't this an internal French matter?"

"Yes, Sophie, it was, and Henry decided that war was now the most suitable way to solve this problem. He therefore declared war on France and crossed the Channel in October 1492. In the meanwhile, Charles wanted to invade Italy so, to keep his northern front quiet, he signed the Treaty of Étaples with Henry a few weeks later and that was the end of it. All in all, this war had included a nine-day siege of Boulogne and the death of one English knight. However, the best part as far as Henry was concerned was that he had made a profit out of it."

"How?"

"Parliament had voted him some money for his war-chest, and then as part of the peace treaty, Charles agreed to pay Henry fifty thousand francs a year."

"So everyone was happy?"

"No, not everyone. All of Henry's lords, knights and others who had hoped to make a quick buck out of the war were very disappointed. For them, this was not the way to do battle."

"And where does Perkin Warbeck fit in all this? We seem to have forgotten about him."

"Well, as part of the peace treaty, he had to leave

France. He returned to Burgundy, to the Duchess Margaret who welcomed him back as her long-lost nephew and named him the 'White Rose of England'. She supplied him with a guard of honour of thirty men who were dressed in the green and white livery of the House of York. Then, in addition, the Governor of Termonde, Hugh of Melum, was appointed to act as his special advisor."

"I'm sure Henry wasn't happy about that."

"Exactly. He tried putting pressure on Burgundy through the Netherland's Council of Regency, but they said that Margaret was a free agent and could do what she wanted. As a result, Henry imposed a trade boycott on the Netherlands. This actually backfired on him as there were riots in London, since this boycott hurt the English traders quite a lot.

"In the meanwhile, Perkin Warbeck's cause, that is, putting him on the English throne and getting rid of the Lancastrian Henry, was gathering momentum. He told everyone about how he had escaped death in the Tower although, unfortunately, his older brother, Prince Edward, had been killed. He also embellished this tale by adding that since then he had been wandering around Europe and…"

"And did everyone believe him?"

"Well, the funny thing is, it seems that they did. Various countries, such as Scotland, France and Denmark had vested interests in a weak and divided England, so they were prepared to recognise him as the rightful heir to the throne, as were several small states, such as the Netherlands and Saxony."

"So, Henry must have been furious by now."

"He was. But what could he do about it? He was in London, while Perkin the Pretender was safely living it up in Burgundy. The result was that Henry had Perkin officially declared as an imposter."

"Like he did with Lambert Simnel?"

"Yes. Then he broke off relations with Flanders. But perhaps a point more important for Henry was that he succeeded in planting a few spies in the Yorkist camp in Flanders. One of his spies, Sir Robert Clifford, was quite successful and managed to implicate all sorts of anti-Henry personalities who were later tried in England and then executed or heavily fined."

"That last bit sounds like our Henry."

"True. But the ironic part of this aspect of the plot was that one of the men who was incriminated was none other than Sir William Stanley."

"The man who had betrayed Richard III ten years earlier at the battle of Bosworth Field and who helped Henry's father, Henry VII?"

"That's right, Sophie. We'll make a historian out of you yet. The same Stanley who, according to Shakespeare, literally handed the fallen crown over to Henry on the battlefield, and declared him to be the new king, King Henry VII.

Then, in the summer of 1495, Perkin Warbeck, together with about five thousand mercenaries, crossed the Channel and sent an advance party to land on the Kentish coast near Dover. However, the local militia promptly overcame and imprisoned them. Henry hanged quite a few in various places along the south coast as a warning to what would happen to any other would-be invaders."

"I'm sure that taught Warbeck a lesson."

"Oh, it certainly did. He realised it would be stupid to attack Henry from the south, so he took the remainder of his men to Ireland, and from there he crossed the Irish Sea to Scotland, where he was very royally welcomed by King James IV. This welcome was so royal, in fact, that James gave Perkin his cousin, Catherine Gordon, in marriage and a goodly pension as well."

"Why? Didn't he know that he'd be making an enemy of Henry VII?"

"Of course. But that was nothing new. You must remember that Anglo-Scottish relations had been pretty bloody for years. So James called Perkin King Richard IV of England, named of course after the younger prince who had allegedly been killed in the Tower. Perkin must have enjoyed himself in Scotland because he remained there for two years before heading south to England. However, by now, James thought the time had come to improve his relations with England, so he later married Henry's eldest daughter, Margaret Tudor."

"But, Grandpa, if Perkin had moved south into England, surely Henry would have had his men there waiting for him, you know, like he did with Lambert

Simnel."

"Well, it wouldn't have done Henry any good to wait for Perkin up north because Perkin turned up in September 1497 near Land's End in Cornwall, where he'd arrived after a side-trip to Ireland. He became an immediate hero with the local Cornishmen who weren't feeling too happy with their king."

"Why?"

"First of all, there had always been a strong feeling of Cornish independence, and our Henry had been somewhat heavy-handed in trying to enforce his tax laws there. So, after leaving his new wife for safekeeping at St. Michael's Mount, Perkin set out for London with about four thousand men. He called himself King Richard IV and everything seemed to be going according to plan."

"But I can hear from the tone of your voice it wasn't going to stay that way."

"True. He reached Exeter in mid-September and demanded that the city surrender to him, immediately. It didn't. After waiting for two hours outside the city, Perkin attacked and succeeded in breaking through the north and east gates. There was some bitter fighting and our Pretender and his men were forced to retreat. They tried again the next day, but gave up pretty quickly, especially as the garrison now used their cannon on them. The rebels, however, were allowed to leave the battlefield without the usual scenes of pursuit and massacre, and so they continued on to Taunton."

"But, Grandpa, they were still getting nearer to London."

"I know that, Sophie, but be patient. On the day after he arrived at Taunton, Perkin heard that Henry's forces were moving west to catch him. So, with sixty men, he slipped away in the middle of the night and headed off in the direction of Southampton in order to find a boat and escape. Later, he claimed that he didn't want to see any more of his men being killed in his name. However, if this was true or not, or just some sort of excuse, it was at this point that his luck ran out. Henry's men controlled the coast, so he turned south instead of heading for London and managed to reach Beaulieu near the south coast where he sought sanctuary in the abbey."

"And was that the end of the very short reign of King Richard IV?"

"In effect, yes. He was caught by Henry's men and his wife was brought over from Cornwall. Henry went to great lengths to treat her as a lady, and there in front of his wife, Henry and his courtiers, Perkin publicly confessed that he was an imposter. Henry then sent Warbeck's wife to London in advance, where she joined his own wife's household. In the meanwhile, the king made a slower journey back to his capital, publicly displaying Perkin for the false prince that he was."

"So Henry really knew about the power of publicity."

"He certainly did. Later, probably as part of his public education plan, he executed a few of the ringleaders and then sent his commissioners to fine the rebellious Cornishmen, whom he referred to as a 'base crew.'"

"And, as usual, Henry made a profit out of the fighting?"

"Of course. And if you read what Sir Francis Bacon, the Elizabethan philosopher and statesman, wrote about him in his history of the time, you'll understand why Henry VII was not the most popular man in Cornwall. Look what it says here:

> *These commissioners proceeded with such strictness and severity as did much obscure the king's mercy in sparing of blood.*

"When Henry returned to London, he made Perkin publicly repeat his confession, and then imprisoned him."

"Where he chopped off his head."

"Whoa! Not so fast, Sophie. Remember, our Henry didn't execute the opposition unless he had no choice, or unless there was a profitable alternative to be had."

"So, what did he do?"

"Well, the funny thing was that, as our ex-Pretender was a foreigner, he couldn't be called a traitor, that is, within the eyes of the law. So he wasn't guarded too heavily, and he was even allowed to be with his wife during the daytime."

"That sounds fair enough, if a bit strange."

"True. Then after about six months, in June 1498, Perkin escaped from Westminster Palace, where Henry had imprisoned him. He fled to the monastery of Sheen, near Richmond Palace on the Thames. He was caught immediately and brought back to London where he was put in the stocks for a day and forced to make another public confession of his guilt. Then he was taken to the Tower and thrown into a dark and horrible cell. In fact, it was so horrible that the Spanish ambassador of the time wrote that the poor man 'sees neither sun nor moon'."

"And did Henry feel secure now? I mean now that Lambert Simnel was washing the royal dishes and Perkin Warbeck was 'being detained at His Majesty's pleasure'?"

"Yes, I suppose he must have breathed a sigh of relief. But then six months later, in February 1499, a friar and a man called Ralph Wilford, who was the son of a London cordwainer, that is, a shoemaker, tried a repeat version of Lambert Simnel. The young man said that he should be the real king as he was really Edward, the Earl of Warwick, and so was related to the past Yorkist kings."

"I'm sure Henry liked that one."

"I'm sure he didn't. By this time, Henry's patience had grown somewhat thin with all of these Pretenders, so he hanged Wilford and imprisoned the friar who, as a holy man, Henry didn't dare touch."

"And I suppose, by this time, Henry must have been

so nervous if anyone said 'boo!' to him."

"I agree. But by now we are coming to the last part of this plot, and here I suppose, I should paraphrase the Bard of Avon when I tell you about a 'plot within a plot'."

"What do you mean?"

"Well, Perkin was now in the Tower, and it seems as if his cell was quite close to that of the real Earl of Warwick who, as you remember, was the nearest claimant to the Yorkist throne. It also appears that several of the jailers were Yorkist sympathisers, and so Perkin and the earl were able to cook up a plot which involved escaping from the Tower. It also seems that Henry's spies knew all about this and even encouraged them, since they were looking for an excuse to get rid of these two plotters once and for all."

"And legally, of course, if they were plotting to escape."

"Exactly."

"But Grandpa, wasn't that a bit dangerous; a bit risky for the king? If the plot had got out of hand and the two of them had succeeded, then Henry might have been in real danger."

"No, Sophie. I don't think there was any real chance of that happening. Remember, Henry had his spies everywhere. As a result, in November 1499, Perkin and Warwick were brought to trial. This was held in Westminster Hall, and as such, the verdict would have been decided in advance."

"Guilty."

"Of course. The trial was just a publicity gimmick really, you know, like a Stalinist show-trial; a way of allowing the king to get rid of Perkin and Warwick in an apparently legal way."

"Which he did, of course."

"Of course. On 23 November, our hero, together with the Mayor of Cork, John Atwater, an Irish supporter and fellow plotter, were dragged feet first on straw hurdles to the scaffold at Tyburn, where Marble Arch is today. Perkin Warbeck was made to confess again that he was an imposter, after which he prayed to God for forgiveness and was then hanged. According to the records of the time, he 'took his death patiently' and didn't make a scene. Fortunately for them, and I'm not being cynical here, they were hanged until they were completely dead and not just strangled, before they were cut down, disembowelled, quartered and beheaded. Their heads were then set up on high on pikes overlooking London Bridge as a warning to other would-be imposters."

"And what happened to the Earl of Warwick? Was he hanged as well?"

"No. To conclude this sad and grim tale, the earl was beheaded five days later, and maybe because he was of royal blood, his head was not stuck up on a pike on London Bridge. He was buried at Bisham Abbey in Berkshire and Henry, despite his reputation for being mean, paid for the funeral expenses."

"So that, I assume, was the final act in Perkin Warbeck wanting to be king."

"Almost. As the contemporary records reported, over a dozen other people were brought to trial and six of them were found guilty. They were sentenced to be hung, drawn and quartered."

"Grandpa, I thought you said Henry didn't really like chopping people up."

"He didn't. In the end, only two of them were actually executed in public. A couple of them died quietly in the Tower, that is, without any publicity, and it is this last point, the quietness of it all, that has caused historians to ask whether the whole affair hadn't been cooked up all along by Henry himself as an excuse to get rid of the last Yorkist claimant to the throne, that is, the Earl of Warwick."

"Why, what questions have historians been asking?"

"Well, in Derek Wilson's book, *The Tower of London*, he asks questions such as: why were so many people pardoned?"

"You mean that they may have been planted by Henry as stool-pigeons?"

"Exactly. And then what would have happened to Henry's plans to marry off his older son, Arthur, to Catherine of Aragon, if the Earl of Warwick had still been alive? I mean, Henry was hoping to achieve respectability and acceptance by buying his way into the European royalty club. He was planning to marry off Arthur to the Spanish King Ferdinand and Queen

Isabella's daughter, Catherine of Aragon."

"I know, but didn't Arthur die when he was very young?"

"Yes, but he was married to her for about six months before he died. And meanwhile, Henry managed to get rid of the Yorkist de la Pole brothers, Edmund, Richard and William, either by exiling them, or sticking them in the Tower for life."

"So, Grandpa, that was really the end of the Yorkists and the Plantagenets."

"Yes. It certainly was. So now our Henry could sleep peacefully in his bed at night without worrying about any more Pretenders crawling out of the woodwork."

"But what about Catherine of Aragon? Didn't Henry, the eighth one, I mean, have a lot of problems with her?"

"Oh, certainly. But that was a different king and a completely different story. She never pretended or threatened to usurp the throne. And what with her pedigree and background, she never had to pretend that she was royal. She was a true blue-blood, through and through."

"I bet our Perkin wished he could have had some of that."

"Exactly."

Chapter Six
Lady Jane Grey, The Nine-Day Queen (1553)

The execution of Lady Jane Grey

"Grandpa, meet Jane. She's on the school hockey team with me. But now she's come over to help me with my maths homework."

"Hello Jane. By the way, are you the Jane Latimer that Sophie often talks about?"

"Oh no, Professor Warkworth. I'm the other Jane.

I'm Jane Grey."

"Oh dear. That's an unfortunate name."

"Why?"

"Don't you know what happened to the famous Jane Grey in history?"

"Do you mean Lady Jane Grey and the plot to make her the Queen of England?"

"Yes, I certainly do."

"Well, I know she was queen for a bit, but that's about all I know about her."

"If you don't mind, I'll fill you in about her."

"Oh, here we go Jane. When my grandpa gets a chance to talk about history, and especially about plots and conspiracies, there's no stopping him. I know, I'll bring in some coffee and some of his favourite chocolate digestive bickies and then he'll tell us all about Lady Jane Grey. Is that OK?"

Professor Warkworth smiled. "That's all right by me. So Sophie, you go and prepare the coffee and I'll start telling this Jane Grey all about her more famous, but definitely more unfortunate namesake. So, Jane, our story starts here, in the first half of the sixteenth century. Henry VIII was sitting on the throne and one of his courtiers was an ambitious but weak-willed man called Henry Grey."

"Hey! That's a coincidence. My father's also called Henry."

"I see, and is he also the Duke of Suffolk and the third Marquis of Dorset too, like his historical namesake?"

"Oh no, he's just plain Mr. Henry Grey, and so far his ambitions have got him to be the manager of a large computer store on the High Street. And... ah, here's Sophie with the coffee and bickies. Anyway, please continue, Professor Warkworth."

"So our historical Henry Grey decided to marry a lady called Frances Brandon, who was related to the royal family. She was the king's niece and therefore such a marriage could only do him good. This of course was especially true as she was also an ambitious young lady, and I think it would be true to say that it was she who ruled the roost in that particular household."

"Did they have any other kids, Grandpa?"

"Yes. They had three daughters altogether. Jane was the oldest, then Katherine, who was born three years later, and then Mary. Jane was the studious one, Katherine was the family beauty and poor Mary grew up to be very short with a bent back. So, in addition to being ambitious, the parents were very strict, especially the mother and so I don't think it would have been much fun to have been one of their daughters. And then, just to make Jane's life even tougher, the mother insisted that she, Jane, be treated as royalty, for she was determined that her daughter would be a valuable stepping-stone for the family's future."

"What a horrible way to be brought up."

"Exactly, Jane. Anyway, when our historical Jane was nine years old, she was sent away to the household of a Lady Katherine Parr in order to learn how to be a lady."

"Katherine Parr? She was Henry VIII's last wife, no?"

"Yes, Sophie. Now this of course was a very clever social and political move on the part of Jane's pushy parents. And in fact, it was also very good for young Jane as well. First of all, Katherine Parr was a very respected and educated lady, so Jane's academic education was not neglected and, secondly, Jane was treated with love and warmth for a change, something she was sorely lacking."

"So life must have improved for her, no? Now she had love and education and was far away from her horrible mum and dad."

"True Sophie, but in a way, it was a case of jumping from the frying pan into the fire."

"Why?"

"Katherine Parr's husband, her fourth that is, was called Thomas Seymour. He was also known as Baron Seymour of Sudeley, and like Jane's parents, he also saw the young girl as a way to further his own ambitions. He planned it like this. Jane, who was fourth in line to the succession, would be an ideal wife for the young King Edward VI. After all, they were of similar age, they were both intelligent and educated, and in terms of religion, they both tended towards the Protestant way of thinking."

"However, what Thomas Seymour didn't take into account was that his older brother Edward, Duke of

Somerset, who was then acting as the young Edward VI's Protector, had his own plans. These included marrying off Edward, the boy-king, to a Spanish princess, as well as marrying off his own son, Lord Hertford, to Jane Grey herself."

"I don't suppose young Edward had much of a say in these matters, right?"

"Right. But what neither of the Seymour brothers knew was that Edward, as he recorded in his diary, hadn't considered marrying Jane Grey at all. He had wanted to marry, as he phrased it, 'a well-stuffed and jewelled bride'. However, since Thomas Seymour didn't know anything about this, he informed Jane's father of his plans and naturally he agreed. But after some time had passed and he hadn't heard of any progress in this matter, Henry Grey decided to pay Thomas Seymour a visit at his Chelsea home. Seymour, grasping and ambitious as usual, said that if Jane's father really wanted to see some movement, he would have to sell Jane's wardship to him for two thousand pounds. Henry Grey agreed and Seymour immediately paid him five hundred pounds there and then on the spot."

"But Grandpa, didn't Edward VI know anything about these plots and plans?"

"Yes and no, Sophie. At first I think Seymour kept him in the dark, but later when he told the young king, who was about ten years old at the time, he said he wasn't interested at all."

"Serves Seymour right."

"Exactly, Jane. And later, when Seymour's older brother found out, he really lashed out at his younger brother for interfering in matters that were not his concern. Then they patched up their quarrel and Thomas Seymour continued flirting with the young Princess Elizabeth instead."

"That sounds dangerous."

"It was, my dear Sophie. For Seymour's big brother got to hear about it, since this – how shall I call it? – this flirtatious affair wasn't exactly carried out in secret. Then the two brothers had another row. This was because the Protector thought that Thomas was being very friendly with Princess Elizabeth and that he would rise to power hanging on to her petticoats, and so supersede him. These feelings were reinforced even further when Thomas tried to persuade his nephew, the king, to sign a document which would mean that the office of the Protector of the king's person would then be shared between them."

"And did Edward sign?"

"No, Jane. No way. His tutor, John Cheke, advised him not to and warned him not to become involved in his Uncle Thomas' activities. And then, to complicate matters even more, at the end of August 1548, Thomas Seymour's wife, Katherine Parr, gave birth to a little girl, but then she, Katherine, died a few days later of post-natal fever."

"Just like Edward VI's mother, Jane Seymour."

"Exactly. But now this new situation posed a problem for Seymour. Now that his wife was no longer there, he couldn't keep the young Jane Grey in his household any longer."

"Why not?"

"Why not? What a question my dear. To keep a young lady in your household who wasn't a very close relative in such a situation – perish the thought! Who would act as her chaperone? No, my dear Sophie, here you have to think in terms of mid-sixteenth century morality. As a result of this new situation, Jane's parents wrote to Thomas Seymour saying that they wanted their daughter back at home with them…"

"So that she could be brought up as a modest and virtuous young lady."

"Exactly."

"I bet that piece of news of news kept Jane happy."

"Well, Sophie, Seymour actually saved her from this. He brought in his mother, Lady Seymour, to run the household instead of Katherine and he also kept on his wife's maids-of-honour. He gave Jane's father another five hundred pounds and so the Seymour household was a respectable place for Jane to be. This then formed a crucial part in Thomas Seymour's long-term plans."

"How?"

"Because he was still thinking of marrying off Jane to the king. However, first he had to get the young man out of the clutches of his big brother, the Protector, to do so. This meant that he started looking around for supporters to organise a *coup* against his brother. Here Thomas Seymour exploited his position as Lord High Admiral to make sure that the navy would be loyal to him when he became the new Protector. In addition, he blackmailed the Vice-Treasurer of the mint at Bristol for ten thousand pounds."

"Apart from wanting the money, why did he do this?"

"He found out that the Vice-Treasurer had been clipping the coins and debasing the coinage."

"This Thomas Seymour sounds like a really lovely character!"

"Oh, he certainly was, Jane. He also encouraged piracy in the English Channel, on condition that he received a goodly chunk of the profits and he also demanded extra payment from ships sailing to Ireland. At the same time, he was still trying to influence the king to act against the Protector and to marry Jane, but here he began to sow the seeds of his own destruction. He was, as you would say, Sophie, so full of himself, that he bragged about his plans to everyone, and he didn't notice that he was beginning to get on the king's nerves. By the end of 1548, the Protector knew that his younger brother was busy plotting against him, even though several of Thomas' supporters, like Jane's father, had become very lukewarm in their support."

"But Grandpa, didn't big brother, Edward, do anything about this?"

"Of course he did. He couldn't afford not to. First of all, he was duty bound to protect the king and, at the same time, he had to look after his own neck, literally. Therefore, he started questioning all sorts of people who had been involved in his younger brother's plans – 'his disloyal practices' as he called them – and he even interrogated the king himself.

"Then in January 1549, Thomas Seymour really cooked his own goose. Accompanied by some armed men, he used a forged key and broke into the king's rooms at Hampton Court. But as Robbie Burns wrote, 'The best laid plans of mice and men all gang aft a-gley'."

"What happened?"

"Something very stupid really. The king's dog, which was in the bedchamber, obviously became very startled when a gang of armed men suddenly burst in. It started barking like mad and so Thomas Seymour shot the poor beast. The shooting must have made such a noise that a guard came over to investigate and…"

"That was the end of Seymour."

"No, not quite, Jane. He managed to talk his way out of this one by saying that he had broken into the king's chambers as a way of testing the efficiency of the king's guard."

"What a cheek!"

"And did he get away with it?"

"Yes and no. The guard let him go, but he also reported the matter to the Protector and the Privy Council. They decided that the best thing to do was to…"

"Chop off his head."

"Not yet, Sophie. No, they put him in the Tower and they interrogated everyone who was involved with his plots."

"And what was my namesake doing during all this time?"

"Oh, Jane, her ambitious parents saw which way the wind was blowing. They immediately hauled their precious daughter back to the family home at Bradgate in Leicestershire, since they naturally didn't want her, and of course themselves, to be tainted with the suspicion of treason. Here she cut herself off from the cruel world of plotting and pushy parents by immersing herself in her literature, philosophy and theology studies. Actually, she became quite a fanatic when it came to the new Protestant religion."

"And what happened to Thomas Seymour?"

"He was charged by the Council on thirty-three counts of treason which included plotting to marry Princess Elizabeth, as well as trying to seize control of the king and trying to take over the country."

"So he didn't really have a leg to stand on, did he?"

"No, Sophie, he didn't. The charges were read out to him while he was in the Tower and in fact his brother Edward, the Protector, tried to help him but another powerful noble, John Dudley, the Earl of Warwick, persuaded him otherwise."

"Why?"

"Oh, Dudley had other fish to fry, but we'll deal with

him later. And, if you haven't noticed, this whole sordid story about Lady Jane Grey is a series of one plot after another. As a result, the Council agreed that there needn't be a trial and soon after, in March 1549, Thomas Seymour was found guilty of treason. In addition to paying with his head, all his lands and property were to be forfeited. But now the Protector had a new problem."

"Signing his brother's death-warrant."

"Exactly. He put off doing so for a week, but then Dudley, whose own ambitions were being thwarted by this delay kept nudging the Protector to do his duty. In the end, the king gave his permission, and…"

"But Grandpa, he was only a ten-year-old boy."

"Yes, Sophie, but he was still the ultimate authority – the King of England. Therefore, on 20 March, the Lord High Admiral, Thomas Seymour, was executed on Tower Hill. By the way, the famous description of this says that when Princess Elizabeth heard about this, she is alleged to have said, 'This day died a man of much wit and very little judgement'. So now Edward Seymour could rule as Protector without feeling threatened by his younger brother's plots and machinations. But, as the saying goes, he was to know no peace."

"Why? Did the king fire him?"

"Oh no, Jane, much worse than that. At about the same time another powerful member of the Council, John Dudley, the Earl of Warwick, the man I mentioned earlier, started working against the Protector's policies. Remember, Edward Seymour was a Protestant and

Dudley at this point sided with the Catholics, though this was only for the time-being. Dudley also became the landowners' favourite as he was supporting them, as they had suffered because of the Protector. This Dudley was so successful that he managed to depose and even imprison his rival. Then his own coalition fell apart and Edward Seymour was released."

"But not as Protector?"

"Exactly. Now Dudley was number one in the Council and on the surface it looked as if he and Seymour had patched up their quarrel. On the one hand, Dudley was clever as he gave up the idea of England ruling Scotland but, on the other hand, he went and reversed the Protector's rather liberal land reforms by suppressing the peasants who had objected to the closure of the common lands."

"Why was that so important?"

"Well Jane, it was the common land, the land where the peasants were allowed to graze their animals and collect firewood for free. This meant that Dudley could easily influence his fellow lords to go along with him. All he had to do now was give them chunks of the common land which he had confiscated from the peasants."

"Oh I see. A Robin Hood in reverse. He stole from the poor and gave it to the rich."

"Exactly, Sophie. This meant that, at least with the common folk, the peasants, Dudley was not popular at all. However, in contrast, the ex-Protector became known as 'the good duke.' Then, and remember all this action was taking place against a backdrop of major religious change, Dudley, or Warwick, however you want to call him, now ignored his previous pro-Catholic tendencies and pushed ahead with the Protestant Reformation of England. And of course, he succeeded at the same time in grabbing much of the Church's remaining wealth for himself."

"Just like Henry VIII."

"That's right. Then, to consolidate his position, Warwick authorised a second *Book of Common Prayer* which he imposed on the Church through another Act of Uniformity. Then in October 1551, he promoted himself from John Dudley, Earl of Warwick, to John Dudley, Duke of Northumberland and Viscount Lisle."

"Was that such a big step up?"

"Oh Jane, it most definitely was. He was making a big point here. He was saying in effect that here I am, John Dudley, the first man of common, that is, not of royal, birth to become a duke. He also made sure that he was surrounded by a gang of yes-men as he handed out knighthoods to his family and friends. However, this was only stage one in his plan to gain the king's favour."

"I bet stage two was to send his rival off to the Tower."

"Exactly, Jane."

"And chop off his head."

"Not yet, Sophie. First of all, he had to have a reason otherwise a case of judicial murder wouldn't look very judicial, would it? Unluckily for the remaining Seymour, although he was quite popular with the man in the street, he didn't get on too well with the king. Dudley happily exploited this by informing the anti-Catholic king that that he would push ahead with more Protestant religious reforms while at the same time he brainwashed the young king by telling him that Edward Seymour was far too ambitious and a threat to the kingdom, etc."

"Just like Dudley himself."

"Exactly, except that it was Dudley who was now calling the shots. Anyway, he had Seymour, who was by now very much an ex-Lord Protector, brought to trial in Westminster Hall where of course he was found guilty of treason…"

"And sentenced to be executed."

"Exactly, but Dudley hadn't taken public opinion into account. Although he could officially, that is, with the Council's support, now do away with his rival forever, he decided to put this off and return Seymour to the Tower. He guessed that if he executed him there and then, he would have a major riot situation on his hands."

"So Seymour was saved, at least for the time being, right?"

"Right. Then Dudley organised a grandiose military parade so that he could show everyone who was now running the show. At the same time, he kept nagging the king to sign the death-warrant and in the end young Edward gave in and agreed to his uncle's execution.

This time there was no reprieve, and in January 1552, about six weeks after his trial, Edward Seymour, the one-time Lord Protector, made his final public appearance, but this time on Tower Hill in front of thousands of Londoners, who had in fact been ordered to stay at home."

"End of stage two. Now for stage three."

"Exactly, Jane."

"To grab the throne for himself."

"No, Sophie."

"Why not? He'd already grabbed a dukedom, why not a crown as well?"

"Well, not even Dudley thought he could get away with that one."

"So, Professor Warkworth, what was stage three?"

"Jane, stage three was to bring Jane Grey out of cold storage, as it were."

"Why?"

"Because the power-hungry Dudley now decided he was going to marry her off to his own son, Guildford."

"But Professor Warkworth, how would that help him grab the throne?"

"Elementary, my dear Jane. By this time, it was pretty clear that the young king was dying. However, before he did so, Dudley wanted to ensure that the newly established Protestant regime would continue after the king's death. Edward knew that according to his father's will, that is Henry VIII's will, the next in the line of succession would be his older sister, the very Catholic

Mary Tudor. Naturally both Edward and Dudley wanted to get around that one. Edward wanted to because of religion, and Dudley, maybe because of religion, but definitely because of his love of power."

"So you mean to say, Grandpa, Dudley had to persuade Edward to appoint Jane Grey, who was fourth in line of succession, to jump over Mary and Elizabeth Tudor?"

"Exactly, Sophie. But there was a problem with this."

"There always is. What was the problem this time?"

"The problem was that in the meanwhile Jane Grey had become betrothed to the late Protector's son, who was also called Edward Seymour, or Lord Hertford, to give him his correct title."

"This Lady Jane Grey plot is beginning to sound more and more like a TV soap opera."

"I know Jane, but believe me, it's all true."

"So anyway, how did Dudley solve this problem?"

"Oh, that was easy enough. He simply exploited Jane's over-ambitious parents and told them that if they broke the wedding contract, their fair young daughter would be next in line for the throne and that her new husband would be the son of the most powerful man in England. What could be better than that?"

"I bet Jane's parents really rubbed their hands with glee when they heard that one!"

"I'm sure they did, Sophie. They cancelled the wedding contract with Hertford and…"

"And sent out to their tailor for some new wedding

clothes."

"You're probably right there, Jane. So now everything was set for the wedding of the year. Now if you bring me that book over there, you'll see what our sixteen-year-old heroine looked like. Ah here we are, a description recorded by Battista Spinola, a Genoese merchant who was in London at the time:

> *… very short and thin, but prettily shaped and graceful. She has small features and a well-made nose, the mouth flexible, the lips red. The eyebrows are arched and darker than her hair, which is nearly red. Her eyes are sparkling, her colour good but freckled. In all, a charming person, very small and short."*

"She sounds quite attractive, Grandpa."

"She was, and she was also a very educated young lady. She spoke Latin and Greek and was also busy learning Hebrew as well."

"Why Hebrew?"

"So that she could read the Old Testament in the original. Remember the English version of the Bible then was the one written by Wycliffe and the country would have to wait for another sixty years before the King James version was published."

"And what was her new husband Guildford like?" Jane asked.

"And was he also good-looking and educated?" Jane added.

"Well, he was good-looking, but like his father he seemed to think a lot of himself and he was also very ambitious."

"So then he didn't object to this marriage, did he?"

"I doubt it, especially if it meant that he would become King Guildford I of England."

"And how did Jane react to all this?"

"Oh, at first she refused to have anything to do with it and said that she was already betrothed to Lord Hertford."

"I'm sure that didn't keep her parents happy."

"Exactly, but it didn't stop them either. Apparently, her mother gave her such a whipping that after that Jane gave in. As you'd expect, Jane never displayed any warm feelings towards her future husband before their wedding, and it was only towards the end of their short lives did they really show any signs of affection for each other.

"However, by now King Edward was seriously ill, probably with tuberculosis or some other lung disease. He kept coughing up a 'foul black liquid', but Dudley kept telling everyone that His Majesty was just 'temporarily indisposed' as they'd say today."

"And did people buy this story?"

"I don't think so, Jane, especially as he didn't show up at Jane and Guildford's wedding, and he was a close relative, after all. Anyway, after the wedding, the young people returned to live with their own families."

"That's a strange way of doing things, no?"

"Perhaps, especially to our twenty-first century ears. However, it seems that Dudley had made some sort of agreement with Jane's parents that if his forthcoming *coup* failed, then the marriage could easily be annulled as Jane wouldn't be pregnant or the proud mother of a future prince or princess."

"I see, a sort of insurance policy."

"That's right, Sophie, but more like a life insurance policy really. In the meanwhile, Dudley was busy trying to carry out stage three, that is, getting the progressively weak and dying king to appoint Jane as his successor. However, here Edward was a bit stubborn and asked that if Mary couldn't be the next queen, then why couldn't his half-sister, Elizabeth, who was pro-Protestant succeed him? After all, she was third, and not fourth in the line of succession like Jane."

"He had a good point there. So how did Dudley answer that one?"

"He said that was no good as Elizabeth was unmarried, and if a foreign prince married her then England might go Catholic again."

"This Dudley character really seems to have had an answer for everything."

"Yes, Sophie. He had to because Elizabeth wasn't fully convinced by all this. Then Edward suggested that Jane's mother succeed him, but Dudley made her promise that she would do no such thing. In the meanwhile, the king's health was going from bad to worse, so Dudley had to work fast. First, he started praising Jane's noble qualities and then he also told Edward that technically in any case both Mary and Elizabeth were bastards. This last point had been formally declared by an earlier Act of Parliament."

"So Grandpa, did he succeed in the end?"

"Yes he did. Under Dudley's guiding hand Edward wrote out a will – 'My Device for the Succession' as he called it – and ordered the crown to be left to 'Lady Jane and her heirs males'."

"And what about Mary and Elizabeth?"

"Oh, he wrote that they were to live in peace and harmony."

"And that was it?"

"No, not quite. First Dudley had to persuade the Council to countersign the new order changing Henry VIII's will. Few of them wanted to go so far as to tamper with a dead king's will, and besides, Dudley was not a very popular man and, according to law, Edward wasn't allowed to do what he had done."

"Why? He wasn't stupid or illiterate, was he?"

"Far from it, Jane. The reason was that although he was King of England, he was still a minor in the eyes of the law. In the meanwhile, Dudley had to make sure that the king stayed alive. He fired his doctor who didn't seem to be doing a good job and employed some female quack instead. None of this could be kept secret. And since they didn't have the ten o'clock news to broadcast health reports about His Majesty, Dudley told the king's attendants to prop him up by a window so that the people could see he was still alive and kicking, even though he wasn't kicking too much.

"In the meanwhile, Lady Jane Grey alias Mrs Guildford, was ordered to go to the king's apartments in the Tower, just in case he died. She refused to do so and her mother and Dudley's wife were very angry with her. As a result, Jane became ill and everyone concerned grew even more nervous about the whole situation."

"And did any of this help either Dudley or the king?"

"No, Sophie, it didn't. Edward died a few days later, leaving Dudley in charge."

"But Grandpa, didn't Mary and Elizabeth know anything about this? I mean, at least Mary must have known she was next in line for the throne."

"True, but Dudley managed to keep the king's death a secret for a couple of days. It was only after swearing them to secrecy did he tell the Lord Mayor of London and his aldermen that His Majesty King Edward had died and..."

"And that he'd appointed Jane to be his successor."

"Exactly. It was only later that day that he sent word to Elizabeth, not to Mary, mind you, that her brother had died. In the meanwhile, Mary must have learned or suspected something was up. She hurried south to London from Hertfordshire in disguise as she was scared she'd fall foul of some of Dudley's Protestant supporters."

"You mean that she already had a reputation for being a keen Catholic?"

"Yes, Jane, she had always been known for that. However, then she wrote a letter to Dudley and the Council, with copies being sent all around the country saying that it was strange that it was only now that she'd heard of her brother's death and that if Dudley behaved himself, she would forgive him. She also said that when she became queen, she wouldn't interfere with the religious situation in England."

"Professor Warkworth, what was Lady Jane Grey doing while all this was going on?"

"I was just coming to that, Jane. At about this time, after having received a few noblemen who bowed down in front of her and kissed her now royal hand, Dudley had her brought into the Chamber of State. Here he officially declared that Edward had died and that one of his last acts as king was to name her as his lawful successor."

"I bet that piece of news shook everyone up."

"I'm sure it did, Jane, especially as your illustrious namesake then went and turned the tables on the beaming Dudley by declaring…"

"Off with his head!"

"No, not quite, Sophie. She said, 'The crown is not my right. Lady Mary is the rightful heir'."

"That must have set a cat among the pigeons."

"I'm sure it did, Jane."

"And Grandpa, where was Dudley's son all this

time?"

"Oh, Dudley had made sure that his son was there. He wanted to make sure that he too was in on the act. Anyway, in the end, Jane gave in and very reluctantly sat on the throne…"

"To Dudley's great joy."

"Of course. Then he and the other lords swore allegiance to her. So as far as Dudley was concerned, Lady Jane Grey was now well and truly the first Queen Jane of England. Next day he had this declared all over London, while at the same time he had troops posted all over the city to make sure that there wouldn't be any rioting. Then later, dressed in the Tudor colours of green and white, she was taken to the Tower."

"The Tower! That wasn't a good omen, was it?"

"No Sophie, you've got it wrong. In those days the Tower of London was still serving as a royal palace as well. So where was I?"

"In the Tower."

"Right. So Jane, now beautifully dressed and wearing three-inch platform shoes to increase her height, was formally crowned Queen of England."

"And was Guildford crowned king?"

"No. Jane absolutely refused to have him crowned king saying that he could be a duke if he wanted instead. She also refused to sleep with him, which as Sophie would say, couldn't have made him very happy."

"And didn't the common people have anything to say about this?"

"No. They just kept quiet, firstly on account of the troops which were everywhere and, secondly, as Dudley wasn't very popular, Jane, who was seen as a puppet, didn't receive any popular support either. In fact, Dudley wasn't popular with anyone, including some of the most important lords, and ultimately this was to lead to the end of his plotting."

"And what were Mary and Elizabeth doing while all this was going on?"

"Elizabeth kept herself out of the way by saying she was staying in one of her country homes, or that she was ill or had a runny nose or something like that…"

"In other words, a 'diplomatic illness'."

"Exactly, and Mary was busy gathering an army and support in the area of Cambridge and East Anglia. In the meanwhile, Dudley, who from now on we'll call the Duke of Northumberland, also got his army of two thousand men together in London and prepared them to meet Mary's forces when they moved south."

"Professor Warkworth, wouldn't it have made more sense for Northumberland to move north and defeat Mary before she got too strong?"

"Yes, Jane, but he was too scared to leave London. He knew he wasn't popular and the thought of being caught between a possibly rebellious capital and Mary's forces to the north was obviously not a good idea. But now having said that, in the end he did march north and…"

"So he did decide to risk it in the end?"

"Yes, but I'm sure he wouldn't have done so had he known that half-a-dozen ships he had dispatched to patrol the East Anglian coast had rebelled against him and had gone over to Mary's side. That meant losing about two thousand men and a hundred great cannon. And if that wasn't bad enough, the Duke of Suffolk locked up all the councillors in the Tower to wait and see which way to jump. However, this idea was only partly successful as the Treasurer of the Mint had escaped and had taken a lot of the money with him over to Mary's camp.

"Then Northumberland suffered yet another setback. Some of the councillors somehow managed to get out of the Tower and declared that they were for Mary."

"They must have seen which way the wind was blowing and they didn't want to be caught on the wrong side."

"Exactly, Sophie. Remember, to be on the wrong side in those days could prove to be a fatal mistake."

"Yeah. Literally."

"Then these councillors declared that Mary was the true queen and everyone lit bonfires, drank wine and generally a good time was had by all."

"Except for the new Queen Jane, Northumberland and his men."

"Exactly."

"Grandpa, what was happening to them at this time?"

"Oh, what was to be expected. Northumberland surrendered and even ripped up the notices declaring

Lady Jane Grey as the new queen. At the same time, his chief supporters surrendered and the Earl of Arundel, who had been waiting for this opportunity, then arrested Northumberland."

"Why?"

"Because Northumberland had imprisoned him once in the past, so now he could have revenge. At the same time, Northumberland's servants ripped his badge off their clothes, so that they'd not be associated with him…"

"And get the chop."

"You really love that expression, don't you Sophie? But yes, you're right in a way, except in those days, the simple people were hanged, usually slowly, and not beheaded."

"So Northumberland's plot was over, then?"

"Yes. The bubble had burst. Northumberland was taken to the Tower, asked everyone for forgiveness and was put on trial for treason by his peers in Westminster Hall."

"And found guilty?"

"Of course he was, Jane. He pleaded for mercy and said he wanted to become a good Catholic once again. But none of this helped. He was executed on Tower Hill in front of thousands of people, but in a strange way, he was lucky."

"Lucky?"

"Yes. The executioner, who looked more like a butcher in a white apron, did a professional job and cut off his head with one blow. It wasn't always like that."

"And where were Queen Jane and Guildford?"

"They were the new Queen Mary's prisoners in the Tower."

"What? She didn't chop off their heads as well?"

"No, Sophie, she didn't. At this time she wasn't anything like the Bloody Mary she was to become. Jane and Guildford were given separate rooms in the Tower and were not allowed to meet. They were allowed to walk around the grounds and Mary was quite liberal with them, that is, despite her advisors' instructions. It is even possible that Mary had planned to release them later, but this never happened."

"Why not?"

"A few months after becoming queen, Mary decided to marry the Catholic King Philip II of Spain. This was, to put it mildly, not a very good idea. The average Englishman was suspicious of foreigners and even more so if one of them had the chance to become the ruler of England."

"So by doing so, Grandpa, was she going to lose all her popularity?"

"Oh, most certainly, my dear. And what is strange to learn today is that this queen, who was to have such a terrible reputation afterwards, succeeded the throne with almost everyone's support. That is, apart from the Protestant lords who opposed the execution of Jane and Guildford, the young couple's real danger came from Sir Thomas Wyatt."

"The famous poet?"

"No, Jane, his son who had the same name. At first he had been on Mary's side, but after he had heard about the queen's marriage proposal, he got together with several other important lords. These included the Duke of Suffolk, that is, Lady Jane Grey's father, who also wanted to overthrow Queen Mary."

"That doesn't sound too good for Jane."

"It wasn't. Wyatt's plan was to form four armies based in Herefordshire, Devon, Leicestershire and Kent which would then march on London. He started organising his four thousand men at Rochester and began to move off in the direction of the capital. At first it seemed as if the rebels would have the upper hand. But as more people joined him, officials loyal to the queen came along to promise a royal pardon to all of those who would abandon Wyatt. Also, at the same time, five hundred Londoners who'd been sent out to stop Wyatt then switched sides to join him."

"I see. Loyalty wasn't very fashionable in those days."

"Yes, you're right there, Jane. Therefore, during the last week of January 1554, a watch was kept on all the gates of London and all of the queen's men were issued with white coats. Despite everyone's advice, Mary stayed in the capital, and in fact she went to the Guildhall and gave a stirring speech. Here she said that Wyatt was only using her proposed marriage to King Philip as an excuse since what he really wanted was to attack her religion and take over the government."

"Were the people convinced?"

"Yes. They shouted 'God save the queen', and she was seen as a brave woman. However, two days later, Wyatt and his men got as far as Southwark, just south of the river. He set up some cannon to fire on London Bridge, but the larger cannon in the Tower were trained on him."

"Sounds like a stalemate to me."

"Yes, Sophie, it was in a way. And it was especially so as the queen refused to give permission to the captains of the guard in the Tower to fire on the rebels. Wyatt saw that he wasn't going to be able to cross London Bridge that way and enter the city, so under cover of darkness, he quietly marched his men westward and crossed the Thames at Kingston. From there he planned to attack the city from the west."

"Did he succeed?"

"Oh, he most certainly did, Jane. The rebels got right into the city and again the queen was advised to flee. She didn't and soon after Wyatt was captured, probably feeling very disappointed that more people hadn't flocked to his banner. And this brings us to the last part of the short but not sweet life of Lady Jane Grey."

"She was executed, no?"

"Yes, Jane."

"But, Professor Warkworth, that wasn't fair. After all, she'd been a prisoner in the Tower and had had nothing to do with Wyatt and his rebellion."

"I know that, Jane, but the queen's advisors kept putting pressure on her to get rid of Jane and Guildford."

"Why?"

"They said that these two were the potential cause of future troubles. They kept saying that Jane's father had said that he'd only support Wyatt if his daughter were restored as queen."

"So as before, Grandpa, it was Jane who had to pay the price for her parents' stupid plans."

"Exactly, Sophie. At first Mary was very hesitant to get rid of Jane and Guildford. Then she received a message from the Holy Roman Emperor, Charles V, saying that he wouldn't allow his son, Philip II, to come to England to marry her unless the unfortunate couple were removed, permanently."

"And so she gave in?"

"Yes, Sophie, she did. The sixteen-year-old Jane was given the chance of converting to Catholicism, but she refused. So, on 12 February 1554 Jane and Guildford were executed on Tower Hill. Guildford was executed first, that is, below her window in the Tower. She was forced to watch his headless body being carted away to the chapel. There her body would shortly join him together with those of the two Seymour brothers and Northumberland, the unloved father-in-law who had caused her to reign for nine days and then pay the price for his cruel ambitions."

"And, Professor Warkworth, what happened to Wyatt?"

"Oh, that's obvious, Jane. He was tried and found guilty a month later. He and dozens of his supporters were hanged and their bodies were left hanging on gibbets all over the capital and Kent as a warning."

"That sounds a bit grim."

"It was. But then Mary forgave quite a few other rebels and was even quite pleasant to Wyatt's wife, Jane."

"And did anything happen in the end to Jane Grey's pushy parents?"

"Yes, Sophie. Some sort of justice was served in the end, I suppose. Her father, who had tried to escape after supporting Wyatt, was captured, tried and executed about a week after the same was done to his daughter."

"And her mother?"

"She was spared, and then scandalised the country by marrying a very young horse master called Adrian Stokes within a month of her husband's execution. She then had three more children, two of whom were still born and the third one died after seven months. She then died in 1559, five years after her husband's execution."

"So in other words, Grandpa, anyone who came into contact with Lady Jane Grey and hoped to exploit the poor girl really paid the price."

"Exactly, Sophie. And what was really sad was that, from the very beginning, she didn't want anything to do with any of her parents plans at all. All the poor and unfortunate girl wanted was peace and quiet and to be able to sit and study her Latin, Greek and Hebrew."

"Exactly, Grandpa. She really was a poor and unfortunate girl."

Chapter Seven
Amy Robsart: Did she fall or was she pushed? (1560)

The death of Amy Robsart   *Amy Robsart's Tomb*

"Grandpa! Grandpa! Look at this article on the front page of the local rag. Look! It's about our MP, Robert Rosemount."

> *Amy Rosemount, forty-five, wife of Robert Rosemount MP, was found dead last night at the foot of the stairs in their home at Cummings Hall. The coroner, Edward Chadderton said, "It seemed that her death was caused by falling down the*

stairs which caused her to break her neck. However, we will only know what really happened after a thorough and exhaustive enquiry."

The police have not ruled out foul play, although at the time it is believed that Amy Rosemount was alone in the family home when the incident occurred.

"Well, my dear, that's certainly a dramatic piece of news for the local rag to print, isn't it? They usually print stuff about the local agricultural show or about drunk and disorderly behaviour at the 'Spotted Dog' or the 'Cricketers' Arms'.

"That's true, Grandpa. But I wonder why the police think that it may not have been an accident. People do fall down the stairs, you know. Maybe she just decided not to turn on the light or tripped on the hem of an evening dress or something like that. You know, death by misadventure and all that."

"Maybe…" The professor shook his head, showing that he didn't really believe in the 'accident' theory. "When someone of her status dies like that, the police are always on their guard, especially when a famous loudmouth of an MP is involved."

"Oh, do you mean her husband, Robert Rosemount?"

"Yes. Now he's a nasty piece of work."

"Why? When he came to give a talk in our school last term he seemed a very pleasant man."

"Pleasant or smooth?"

"Well, now you mention it, the word smooth would suit him better."

"Some people would say something even stronger. Like greasy."

"Why? What have you got against him? He's worked hard for the local people and the area, no?"

"Yes, yes. I know all that. But at the same time, he really knows how to look after number one."

"Like how?"

"Well, he was always a social-climber and a name-dropper for a start. Why, I remember when I went to that British Legion dinner last year, all he could do was drop names of all the ministers and royalty he had met. He made it sound as if he had tea and bickies with the queen and/or the prime minister every day, and that they just couldn't get on without him."

"So if he's not going to sing his own praises, who is?"

"No, Sophie. There's singing and singing. But if you didn't know, and this piece of news isn't published in that rag you're holding, it's a well-known fact that our local and noble MP, Robert Rosemount, was very friendly with the prime minister's wife, and that his own ever-loving spouse wasn't too pleased about that one, to say the least."

"Grandpa, what do you mean, 'it's a well-known fact'? It sounds more like gossip to me."

"That's true, my dear, but a couple of my friends at

the Legion are on the 'inside' about these sorts of things and so…"

"Are you saying, my dearest grandfather, that our local MP murdered his wife so that he could carry on with Lady…?"

"Whoa! I never said anything like that, but it's not the first time that things like that have happened, you know."

"Yes I know. Every other film has someone getting killed so that the husband or wife will be free to play around with…"

"No, no Sophie. I'm not talking about films. I'm talking about real life situations. In fact, the strange thing in this case is that it bears a fantastic similarity to another case in history that happened well over four hundred years ago."

"Why? Did another famous lady fall down the stairs?"

"Or was pushed. And not only that, but her name was Amy, and her husband was also called Robert."

"All right, Grandpa. I know you're itching to tell me this story, so let's hear it. But if I don't get my English homework finished tonight, it'll be your fault."

"Fair enough. So here goes. The name of our heroine was Amy Robsart."

"Never heard of her. Was she one of Henry VIII's or Charles II's mistresses?"

"No, not at all. She was the legally wedded wife of Sir Robert Dudley, the son of the Duke of

Northumberland, the duke who worked hard to make Lady Jane Grey queen. One day in September 1560, she was discovered lying at the bottom of a flight of stairs in her house, dead, with her neck broken."

"Wow! As you say, it really sounds a lot like the story we've just been reading about in the local rag. And did they find out who was responsible?"

"No. And that's the most interesting part of this Elizabethan mystery."

"Why? Didn't they hold an inquest or have some sort of enquiry? I mean, she was the wife of a duke."

"Yes, they did have some sort of inquest, but not like the ones we have today. I suppose that if they had used today's forensic knowledge and technology, we'd have had one less murder or accidental death to worry about, no?"

"So did they ever find out who actually killed this Amy Robsart if, as you are hinting, my dear grandpa, it wasn't a simple domestic accident?"

"You don't suppose I'm going to tell you the end of the story before you've heard the beginning, do you?"

"OK, Grandpa, let's hear it from the beginning."

"Right. Well, the enquiry probably went something like this:

'And you, my good man. Who are you?'

'I am, or rather was, sir, one of Lady Amy's servants, sir.'

'I see. And where were you on the day in question?'

'What question, sir?'

'The day in question, man. The 8 September.'

'Oh, sir. Yes, sir. I see what you mean.'

'Good. So where were you? Naturally as one of Her Ladyship's servants, you'd have been in the house on that day, no?'

'Yes and no, sir.'

'Please be exact. We haven't got all day. Now what do you mean – yes and no?'

'Well, I was in the house in the morning, sir. You know, cutting wood, laying fresh rushes on the floor and working in the vegetable garden and all that sort of thing, sir. You know, we grow all kinds of vegetables there and...'

'Yes, yes. That's very laudable, but where were you after that?'

'Oh, sir, now I know what you mean. Well, I wasn't in the house all day. Lady Dudley said that we servants could have half the day off, in the afternoon, that is, and go to the fair, sir. Only her housekeeper would remain behind.'

'What? Just like that. Just go to the fair?'

'Well, it wasn't an ordinary fair, sir. It was the special one. You know, 'Our Lady's Fair' and...'

'Which lady?'

'The Virgin Mary, sir. The fair is held every year on the Feast of the Nativity of the Blessed Mary, sir.'

'I see. And where was this fair?'

'At Abingdon, sir. A few miles south of Oxford, sir.

On the way to Didcot.'

'And how far is Abingdon from your lady's residence at Cumnor Hall?'

'A couple of miles, sir.'

'And did you go to this fair on your own?'

'Oh no, sir. I went with all the other servants. We were told, even instructed, to stay there until the evening as my lady wouldn't be needing our services until then.'

'And didn't you find these instructions, odd, er, out of the ordinary?'

'Yes, sir.'

'Had you ever been given instructions like that before?'

'No, sir. That's why I thought they were a bit strange. Usually, if any of the servants leaves the house, there are always a few of us left behind, sir. You know, to run messages for Lady Amy, or to…'

'Yes, yes. I know what the role of servants is.'

'And who gave you these instructions, as you call them?'

'I'm not sure, sir.'

'What do you mean, you're not sure? Surely you must know everyone who works at Cumnor, no?'

'Yes, sir. But what I mean to say is that I just heard them from one of the other servants. You know, one of the women who work in the kitchens, sir. But if I rightly recall it was Mrs Odingsell who told her.'

'And who is this Mrs Odingsell?'

'Oh, she is the housekeeper to Lady Amy, sir. Some

people know her as the widow who lives with Master Antony Forster.'

'And who is he, this Master Forster?'

'He is the owner of Cumnor Hall, sir.'

'What! Are you telling me that Cumnor Hall isn't owned by Sir Robert Dudley?'

'Well, not exactly sir.'

'All right. We'll leave that point for the time being. So, on the day in question, that is September 8, Lady Robsart was all alone in the house, except for Mrs Odingsell for company. Is that right?'

'No, sir. Mrs Owen was there as well.'

'And who is this Mrs Owen?'

'She was a good friend to my lady, sir. In fact, you could say her best friend, sir, and her closest companion. I know the two women used to share secrets between them and they completely trusted one another, sir.'

'Why? Wasn't your mistress friendly with Mrs Odingsell?'

'No, sir. Not really. I think my lady lived in fear of her. I'm not sure if this is malicious gossip, sir, and God strike me down if it is, but Mrs Odingsell was the aunt of Sir Richard Verney, and some people in the village think it was this man who murdered my mistress, sir.'

'And ignoring the village gossip, my man, what do you know about this Sir Richard Verney?'

'Well, sir, I know that he had once served as a page to Sir Robert Dudley's father and that he was devoted

to his master. I also know, but I shouldn't really be reporting this, sir, that there were rumours in the house you know, that is, among the servants, that my master was intending to rid himself of his wife, of my lady, sir, and so he sent for Sir Richard Verney.'

'And did this man come?'

'No, sir. Well, not at the time. But I know he sent a message that he would do his best to help his past master in the future in any way he could.'

'And how come you know all these presumably secret messages and confidences?'

'Well, sir, in a small household like Cumnor, there's not much that us servants don't eventually hear about, sir.'

'Hmm. Yes, I intend to agree with you there. So, on the day that Lady Amy Dudley died, or was murdered, that is, found dead at the foot of the staircase, she had been having a quiet meal with her two friends, Mrs Owen and Mrs Odingsell?'

'Not exactly, sir.'

'How so?'

'Because as I told you, sir, my mistress didn't care for Mrs Odingsell very much and in fact she asked her to go with the other servants to the fair at Abingdon. But Mrs Odingsell refused, saying that it was her God-given duty to attend on Her Ladyship at all times, sir.'

'So are you suggesting that your mistress ate her meal with Mrs Owen, and that Mrs Odingsell, whom she didn't like too much was also present at Cumnor, say in *another room?'*

'Yes, sir. Something like that.'

'And that this Mrs Odingsell was the link between Lady Dudley and Sir Richard Verney?'

'Yes, sir. And I also believe it was Mrs Odingsell who let Sir Richard into the house, sir.'

'What do you mean 'let him into the house'? Didn't Lady Dudley, as mistress of the house, have the right to say who would enter and who would not?'

'Well, yes, sir. I suppose so on normal occasions. But I believe that Sir Richard sneaked into the house without my mistress knowing anything about this, sir.'

'Sneaked in? How so? Speak up man.'

'Well, sir, Cumnor Hall is a fine old building, but it was not always used as a residential house, if you know what I mean, sir.'

'I don't. Please explain yourself.'

'Well, sir, at the beginning of the century, Cumnor Hall was a sanatorium for monks. Then it was rebuilt in parts and changed into the building which you see today, sir.'

'And what is the relevance of this?'

'Well, sir, when they were rebuilding the house, sir, certain secret passageways and doorways were added and... and...'

'Go on man. Stop mumbling.'

'Yes, sir. So, one of these passageways led to my lady's bedchamber, sir. It is my belief that it was through one of these secret doorways, that the murderer

entered the house and killed my lady, sir.'

'So, you are saying that the murderer, or the organiser of this terrible deed, was none other than Sir Richard Verney, and that he was aided by Mrs Odingsell, his aunt.'

'That's not for me to say, sir. I'm not a learned gentleman like you, sir. All I know is that my mistress' death was very beneficial to her husband, Sir Robert Dudley.'

'How so? He certainly didn't make any financial gain out of it. Surely he was secure in terms of money and property?'

'No, no, sir. I'm not referring to money or property, sir. I mean that he was now free to pursue his love affair with the queen, if I may say so, sir. At least, that's what some of the local people are saying.'

'Just take heed what you do say. You could end up in the stocks at the very least and maybe in the Tower if you walk around spreading tales like that, my man.'

'Please excuse me, sir, but I'm just repeating what certain people in the village were saying and also the gossip that I heard at the church, sir. I myself don't believe that...'

'No, no. Of course you don't. But just take heed not to repeat this seditious and malicious gossip again. Do you understand me? If not, it could be the worst for you.'

'Yes, sir. Absolutely, sir. Have you done with me now, sir? I would like to go home. My wife is waiting for me so that we may go to the market.'

'Yes. You may go. But just watch your chattering tongue, especially in the market and with your wife.'

'Yes, sir. God be with you, sir.'

"That night, the specially appointed coroner met with two of his peers and, over a meal of excellent capon and vegetables, all washed down with a good French wine, they began to discuss the mysterious death of Lady Dudley, the sweet and faithful wife of Sir Robert Dudley, the future Earl of Leicester."

'Now gentlemen, this murder, or at best, this sudden and unexplained death certainly smells like a barrelful of stale fish taken straight out of Billingsgate market. First, we have the dead and apparently unloved wife of Robert Dudley. Then, we have the curious knowledge about this Mrs Odingsell, who was supposed to be looking after the dead woman, but is in fact related to the alleged murderer, Sir Richard Verney.'

'Aye, and this knight is a more than devoted servant to Robert Dudley, who it seems would not cry too much if his wife suddenly died.'

'But how did she die?'

'She was found at the foot of a staircase in the house with a broken neck.'

'Well, my lord, that's a strange thing you are saying.'

'Why? People have been known to fall down the stairs before. And some have even been pushed. But I hope that isn't the case here.'

'I know that, but when I paid a social call on the Earl of Leicester a few weeks ago at Cumnor Hall, I distinctly remember thinking how short the flights of stairs are in that house.'

'What do you mean?'

'Well, the way the house has been rebuilt, the longest flight of stairs consists of about only eight or nine stairs. And between each flight there is a small landing.'

'So, what you are saying, my lord, is, that there is not one single, long flight of stairs in Cumnor. This means that if anyone were to take a fall, accidental or not, it does not seem likely that they would die from such an event.'

'That is indeed what I am saying. All I can suppose is that they would receive a severe headache, a few blows to the body and some unpleasant and possibly painful bruising.'

'And, by this my lord, are you implying any foul play?'

'Well, I cannot say exactly. What I have just said is merely speculation. But it does appear to me that if Sir Robert really wanted to make sure that his wife was indeed, how can I put this delicately...'

'Permanently removed from the scene?'

'Aye, that's it. Permanently removed from the scene, then she may have been murdered beforehand and then her poor dead body neatly placed at the foot of the stairs as though she had indeed fallen down them.'

'That seems to make sense, my lord. But tell me, how

could she have been murdered without her housekeeper, this Mrs Odingsell, discovering this deed?'

'Don't you see? She didn't have to discover anything. She already knew!'

'Do you mean to say that she was part of this terrible plot?'

'Well, it certainly seems like that to me, at least from what you have just told us, my lord.'

'You mean like that Macbeth *story in* Bellenden's Chronicle of Scotland?'

'Aye. Indeed I do.'

'Pray, my lord, which story are you alluding to?'

'Well sir, in his Chronicles, *Bellenden writes that the murderers of King Duncan were actually in the castle at the time and that Lady Macbeth, like our Mrs Odingsell, was not just an innocent personage present in the castle.'*

'Yes, my lord, it certainly does begin to sound like that. But why should Sir Robert wish so keenly to rid himself of his wife. By all accounts she seems to have been the model of gentility and faithfulness. Even if this son of Northumberland was known to have sown his wild oats elsewhere, as other men have done in the past, and doubtless will continue to do in the future, it was still not a reason to kill his wife, no?'

'But you forget, my good sir, the other lady involved here, in this 'oat sowing' as you phrase it so agriculturally, is none other than our gracious queen. We are not talking about some local harlot plying her

wares near the Clink Prison in Southwark.'

'Yes, I suppose you're right.'

'And I don't think that Her Majesty would approve of being referred to as the 'other woman'.'

'And what about Sir Robert himself?'

'Oh, my lord, it's common knowledge that he has been more than lovesick for Her Majesty for some time now.'

'Aye. You are right there. It is certainly no co-incidence that soon after she was crowned queen, one of her first acts was to promote him to become a Knight of the Garter as well as her Master of the Horse.'

'Well, that's definitely a good step up from being just an MP for Suffolk. I mean, being Master of the Horse means you are always in close connection with the reigning monarch, and that is just what I suppose Her Majesty had in mind in dishing out that particular plum.'

'You know gentlemen, I think you are being a little harsh, and may I say it, a little un-Christian with regards to Sir Robert. After all, he has served the Crown faithfully. He was Master of the Ordnance at the siege of St. Quentin some three years ago and he seems to have acquitted himself in a reasonable manner.'

'Implying that you haven't heard that he had not done so?'

'True.'

'But, my good sirs, let me interrupt you. Enough of this idle gossip. It is getting us nowhere. We are acting

in the manner that we belittle others for doing. Let us return to the matter which is the reason for this meeting, namely, who killed Lord Dudley's wife?'

'Or did she really fall down the stairs by accident?'

'You know, my lord, while I have been gnawing on this chicken bone, I've been thinking about this lady and Sir Robert. Do you realise that her background and lineage are far superior to his?'

'How so?'

'Well, when they first met, sometime in 1549, they were about seventeen years old. Her father was a knight from Norfolk, Sir John Robsart, and Sir Robert's father...'

'Lost his head. Quite literally.'

'Very true. Although he was the Earl of Warwick and later became the Duke of Northumberland, he became unstuck over that Lady Jane Grey affair. Poor lass, if ever I knew one, may I add.'

'You may. And it also cost the head of his other son. Now, what was his name?'

'Guilford.'

'That's right. He was the one married to the Lady Grey.'

'And our present Robert Dudley was probably saved from the same fate by the intervention of King Philip of Spain.'

'How so? What has the King of Spain got to do with all this?'

'Well, I don't know exactly. All I know is that Sir

Robert had served with the Spanish forces and, as it has been recorded, he succeeded fairly well there and so earned the king's gratitude.'

'But didn't Sir Robert first meet our queen in the Tower? That is before he was released.'

'Aye, and that's where people say their love affair started.'

'What! In the Tower? That's a grim place for a love affair.'

'Aye.'

'So this affair had been going on for some time, eh?'

'Yes. And you know what else smells about this 'unfortunate accident', as Sir Robert insists on referring to it? It is that some people were talking about it before it ever happened.'

'Please elaborate, my good sir. You have just made a very serious implication.'

'I will do so. Well, last year in April, the Spanish ambassador in England sent a report to his master, King Philip II, saying that Sir Robert Dudley had, er, how shall I phrase it...'

'Clearly.'

'Ah yes. Sir Robert has come so much into favour with the queen that Her Majesty visits him in his chamber night and day.'

'Aye, that's true enough. I've also heard that. And I'll tell you, my good sirs, what else I've heard, and this concerns his wife. According to various rumours circulating at court, she has a sickness, a malady in one

of her breasts, and that when she dies, Sir Robert will be free to marry the queen. And then that new Spanish ambassador fellow, Alvaro de...'

'Quadra.'

'Yes, him. Well, he also sent a report back to Spain saying that Sir Robert planned to poison his wife, and this was sent even before Lady Dudley was found dead in her home.'

'That's true. I've also heard that particular story. And I've also heard that the French ambassador also dispatched a report, not only saying that Her Majesty had slept with Sir Robert, but that he was even more specific and said that this had happened on New Year's Eve.'

'And didn't a German diplomat also talk about the poisoning of the same lady?'

'Aye. In fact, this story about poison was so widespread that a woman...'

'Anne Dowe, wasn't it? From Brentford?'

'Aye, she was sent to prison for telling such tales.'

'Well, not exactly for that. She was sent to prison for claiming that the queen had a son and that the father was none other than Sir Robert Dudley.'

'So, gentlemen, it would seem that if the sum of all of these diplomatic and other reports is true, our Sir Robert was certainly finding favour with Her Majesty, and that the air was thick with stories about Lady Amy's impending doom. These reports, together with what one of Lady Amy's more faithful servants told me this

morning, cause me to believe that the unlucky woman was murdered. Unfortunately, my belief in this is further reinforced when we learn about the size, or lack thereof, of the staircase where she was found. And, gentlemen, all of this is in addition to the fact that we know that there were secret passageways in the house which could have given a potential killer access to the poor woman.'

'And we should not forget, my lord, that this murder, or untimely death if you wish, happened when only Mrs Owen and Mrs Odingsell, a woman of whom we have not heard good report, were in the house, and all the other servants were at the fair."

"But, that's not fair, Grandpa. So they never found out who really murdered her, did they? Or if her death was a genuine accident?"

"No, my dear Sophie, they never did. But those who were responsible for her murder, if you do indeed believe that it was a murder, went to great lengths to cover their trails."

"Why? What did they do?"

"Well, for a start, the coroner's report was either lost or destroyed – either way, it was never seen again. In addition, the parish register, that great document for helping historians to ascertain the dates of all sorts of events, was also lost, or simply and conveniently disappeared. However, it is known that Lady Amy did have a classy funeral later in Oxford, and that Queen Elizabeth, probably for the record, told Sir Robert that he had misbehaved. This did not prevent the pair of them persisting with their love-affair which continued until his death in 1588."

"Wow! Another thirty years, or almost. But he never married her in the end, did he?"

"Oh no, Sophie. Sir William Cecil saw to that. Now there was a devious character, if ever I saw one."

"Cecil? Who's that, Grandpa?"

"Cecil, my dear, was William Cecil, later known as Lord Burghley. He was Queen Elizabeth's chief adviser, a sort of prime minister, and he and Dudley, our Earl of Leicester, were the greatest political enemies and rivals for the queen's attention at the time."

"So why didn't Cecil let Dudley marry the queen, and why were they such bitter enemies? After all, they were both Protestants, no?"

"Yes, my dear, they were. But they were both fighting for the ear of the queen, though in fact, I don't really think that Dudley had much of a chance against the wily old Cecil. You see, first of all, Cecil was twelve years older than Dudley, and whereas Dudley's family had suffered during the reign of Elizabeth's sister, Mary, Cecil had managed to carve himself out a temporary sort of career with the Catholics before jumping ship, as it were, and proving his loyalty to the new Protestant regime of Queen Elizabeth. So, when in January 1561, five months after Amy Robsart was killed, or merely fell down the stairs, the Spanish ambassador said that his master, Philip II, would support Dudley if he married the queen…"

"But weren't the Spanish sworn enemies of England?"

"Yes, they were later, but not at the beginning of her reign. Anyway, to cut a long and dirty story short, Cecil cooked up some anti-Catholic plots, which among other things, prevented a love-sick earl from marrying the queen. And of course, he did so because such a marriage had the support of Catholic Spain, and the Spanish king was a personal friend of Sir Robert Dudley."

"As you say, Grandpa, this Cecil guy really sounds pretty devious."

"Oh, he most definitely was. And by harping on about the 'ever-present danger of the Catholics', as he would phrase it, he prevented Elizabeth, as if she needed any prevention, from marrying various other potential suitors."

"Hence, the 'Virgin Queen'."

"Well, my dear. Maybe she was, maybe she wasn't. But that's another story. But all I can say is that young Amy Robsart seems to have been got rid of in vain, because Sir Robert Dudley never married the queen and the smell of her murder, or untimely demise as they say, clung to his name for a very long time afterwards. And that was even after he was promoted to become the Earl of Leicester as well as the Chancellor of Oxford University.

"Ironically perhaps, his own death was a bit of a mystery in a similar way to that of his wife's. In the same way that some historians explain Amy Robsart's death as a result of breast cancer and/or some sort of depression, they claim that Sir Robert did not die of a chronic intestinal complaint in September 1588 as claimed, but that he was poisoned by his second wife, Lady Lettice Knollys."

"Wow! Why?"

"Ah, so that she would then be free to marry her lover, Christopher Blount, that is, her husband's Gentleman of the Horse."

"And is it known or recorded what happened to any of the others who were involved in this rather mucky story?"

"Well, we know about the future careers of Queen Elizabeth and Sir Robert. The only other person of note whose subsequent activities are recorded is that of Antony Forster, the chap living with Mrs Odingsell. Soon after Amy's death, Sir Robert rewarded him for services rendered…"

"That's a delicate way of phrasing it."

"Exactly. And our Forster friend was also given large plots of land all over the country, including Cumnor Hall."

"Which he gave to his ever-loving widow, Mrs Odingsell?"

"No, not at all. He pulled most of the place down and then rebuilt it. That would have surely destroyed any evidence about secret passageways, etc. Then, just to make sure that no one would learn anything about the place, he gave Sir Robert the option to buy it in his will."

"Which he did."

"Exactly, my dear. And that was the way this Antony Forster fellow and Sir Robert Dudley decided to close up this murderous plot."

Chapter Eight
The Bank was mightier than the sword: The Ridolfi Plot. (1571)

Queen Elizabeth I

Roberto di Ridolfi

"Grandpa, did you know that the Bank of England isn't English at all, but Italian?"

"What do you mean, Italian?"

"Well, I'm exaggerating a bit, 'cos it's not really Italian, but it was the Italians who started banking. Our history teacher told us in class that the word 'bank' comes from the Italian word '*banca*', meaning the bench the Italian bankers used to sit on to carry out their business deals."

"Yes, Sophie, she's right there, except that they weren't banks for the man in the street, as it were. They were more like institutions for giving credit, etc. to merchants, lawyers, goldsmiths and the like in the latter part of the Middle Ages. It was only about three hundred years later that public banks, such as Barclay's, started."

"Yes, and she also told us about this Florentine banker called Ridolfi, who tried to bump off Queen Elizabeth I and put Mary, Queen of Scots, on the throne instead."

"Well, she was right in a way, but not, as you so delicately phrase it, about bumping off the queen, well, not him personally. Let's just say that he was part of an international Catholic network that wished to see Mary, Queen of Scots, replace Queen Elizabeth I."

"But he failed, right?"

"Right, but he was lucky because he didn't pay the price."

"But others did?"

"Certainly, Sophie. Several of them."

"So what happened? How come this Italian banker became involved in this affair – the Ridolfi Plot?"

"Well, my dear, it was like this. First of all, his name was Roberto di Ridolfi, and he was, as your teacher described him, a very successful Florentine banker. He had first come to England when Queen Elizabeth's older sister, Mary, had married the Spanish King Philip II. Naturally, the English Catholics were very pleased with this arrangement, especially as Mary's younger brother, Edward VI, had managed to establish the Protestant religion here. Now the Catholics wanted *their* religion – the 'true faith' as they called it – to be *the* religion of the land."

"And where does our Florentine banker fit in with all this?"

"Patience, my dear Sophie. Now Signor Ridolfi was what you kids would call a whizz-kid in the world of banking but, in fact, he must have been about forty when this plot blew up in everyone's face. Now since he was so good at the job of making money, he was much in demand, and although he was a staunch Catholic and Florentine, he held a key role in Queen Elizabeth's government. Even that hard-boiled and devious chief minister, Sir William Cecil, employed him. In fact, our Italian friend must have felt so much at home here, that he became involved in various unsuccessful risings in the north of the country where the Catholics had a stronger hold."

"I bet that didn't keep the queen very happy, her pet banker plotting behind her back."

"It didn't. He was arrested and Her Majesty's secret service, the MI5 of the day, led by Sir Francis Walsingham, ran a very thorough check on him."

"And what did they find?"

"Nothing. They searched his house and his bank and they found absolutely nothing, except the strict records of his business dealings. So they had to let him go.

Actually, they did more than that. They decided to use Signor Ridolfi as a double-agent and bring him over to their side, as the CIA would phrase it."

"That's a bit dangerous, isn't it? How would they know if he were to be trusted in the future, or if his information was any good?"

"That's exactly what the problem was. And as you so rightly guessed, my dear Sophie, our Florentine banker was not to be trusted. Not by anybody."

"Why?"

"Well, as soon as he, to continue with our CIA or FBI parlance, obtained security clearance from Walsingham and Cecil, he was off again."

"Meaning?"

"Meaning that in 1570, Signor Ridolfi got together with a Mr Leslie, the ambassador to Mary, Queen of Scots, or special messenger or whatever, and they hatched another plot."

"Which was?"

"Which was to use foreign Catholic armies to invade England, overthrow the wicked Protestant Queen Elizabeth and then crown Mary, Queen of Scots, as the new queen."

"Just like that!"

"No, not exactly. To employ foreign armies meant having to use a lot of cash. So Ridolfi, using his international and Catholic connections, got in touch with the most important Catholics of the day such as Pope Pius V, King Philip II of Spain and the Duke of

Alva."

"Who's he?"

"Alva? He was a Spanish aristocrat and his full title was Duque d'Alba, Ferdinand Alvarez de Toledo. He was a ruthless general and statesman who used his power to put down Protestant anti-Catholic riots in the Netherlands."

"In other words, a really tough guy."

"As you say, a really tough guy. And so you see, Sophie, as far as Ridolfi was concerned, he was the man for the job. And then, enter centre stage, as it were, yet another of Queen Elizabeth's tragic heroes, Thomas Howard."

"That doesn't sound a very heroic name."

"Well, his full name and title was Thomas Howard, Duke of Norfolk, fourth Earl of Surrey, Earl Marshal of England."

"Grandpa, with a handle like that, one would think that no harm could come to him."

"Wrong. Very wrong. Unfortunately, Norfolk, for that's what we'll call him, just happened to be on the wrong side at the wrong time. His father, the third Duke of Norfolk, alias the Earl of Surrey, was a courtier at the court of Henry VIII and was accused of treason after having risen high in the king's favour. However, to cut a long story short, he got on the wrong side of Henry VIII, who promptly imprisoned him in 1546, and there he stayed for six years until Mary Tudor released him. So you can see, his son, the fourth Duke of Norfolk, had a lot to live down."

"And did he?"

"Yes and no. As I said, he did do well at first and managed to curry favour with both the Catholic Mary Tudor and her Protestant sister, Elizabeth I. He commanded the English army which invaded Scotland and also ran the commission which investigated the problem between Mary, Queen of Scots, and the Protestant Scottish nobility. That was, as you would say, the climax of his career. The turning point came at the end of the 1560s when Mary, Queen of Scots, fled to England for sanctuary."

"Grandpa, this is a fascinating story, but how is it all connected with Ridolfi?"

"Patience, my dear. We are getting there, believe me. So where were we? Ah yes. Scottish Mary is now in England, and for the next twenty years or so, she will become the centre point, the magnet, for all sorts of Catholic plotters and conspirators who wanted to put her on the throne instead of Elizabeth."

"Including the Duke of Norfolk?"

"Yes and no. Yes, because he too wanted to see her as the Queen of England, but no, not in place of Elizabeth. He wanted Mary to succeed her instead. What happened was this: William Maitland, who was a prime minister of sorts to Mary, Queen of Scots, put forward a policy that Scotland should be allied with England instead of with France. To carry this out, he suggested to Norfolk that he marry Mary, Queen of Scots, and that after Elizabeth dies, Mary will become queen of both England and Scotland."

"But she was a Catholic."

"Yes, and that was a major part of the problem. So to carry out this plan, in March 1571, Norfolk foolishly signed a document stating that he was a Catholic and, as such, he would act as commander of Philip II's army whose job would be to put Mary, Queen of Scots, on the throne."

"That wasn't very smart."

"Sophie, I wholeheartedly agree with you. Anyone signing such documents then, knowing that Walsingham or Cecil was looking over his shoulder, should have had his head tested. But Norfolk was – how shall I put it? – rather full of himself, and so he signed.

"Then Ridolfi took these documents to Brussels and, after meeting up with the Duke of Alba, met a keen Scottish-Flemish supporter of Mary, Queen of Scots: a Mr Charles Baillie. It was Baillie's job to pass on secret messages to Norfolk and other important Catholics in England. In fact, Mary, Queen of Scots, used to write secret messages in invisible ink in order to keep in touch with her supporters."

"But how did Cecil find out about all these secret meetings and messages? He couldn't have had spies everywhere, could he?"

"Well, I'm not so sure about that. But both he and Walsingham do indeed seem to have had a very good network of spies and informers all over England and the

Continent. It is even said that the famous playwright, Christopher Marlowe, was one of them. And instead of him being killed in a pub brawl as is frequently claimed, Walsingham had him secretly spirited over to the Continent to act as a spy. But that's another story.

"Now, it was at about this time that Lord Cobham, the Warden of the Cinque Ports, sent a mysterious package that he had picked up to Cecil. Inside were all sorts of papers. Some were written in secret codes and referred to Mary, Queen of Scots, as well as to Norfolk, to the Bishop of Ross, and to various other important people. Naturally Cecil became very suspicious and had Baillie arrested and thrown into the Marshalsea prison. Baillie wouldn't 'sing' as they say on television, so Cecil planted a Mr William Herle in the prison in order to persuade him to spill the beans. Herle was only partly successful, so Cecil had Baillie transferred to the Beauchamp Tower in the Tower of London. There, he was tortured on the rack but, somehow, he didn't give everything away.

"Then to complicate the situation even further, the Bishop of Ross contacted Cecil complaining that a certain package of letters he'd been sent hadn't arrived. This spurred Cecil on to make greater efforts in wringing or racking the truth out of Baillie and in the end he succeeded. And this is how Baillie probably described his mission:

An opulently decorated room somewhere in the

Spanish Netherlands. In the centre is a massive wooden table topped by a candelabra. Lying on the table next to the candelabra is a sword and a pile of documents that need signing. The Duke of Alva is seated in a richly covered high-backed chair. Standing in front of him on the other side of the table, I am nervously wondering why the duke has had me brought here.

Alva: Señor *Baillie, I have a little task for you.*

Baillie: (Looking up at the stern and impressive face of the duke, dressed in a rich dark olive-green doublet and hose) Sí, Señor, *er… my lord, I…*

Alva: Sit down, Baillie. Bueno. *Even though I am a Spanish duke and you are a mere, how shall I phrase it? A mere commoner, we have a common purpose,* non? Sí, *to rid your country of its abominable Protestant Queen Elizabeth and then replace her with Her Gracious Majesty, Mary, Queen of Scots. Am I right?*

Baillie: Sí, *my lord. I do agree with you.*

Alva: Then this is what you are to do. Señor *Roberto di Ridolfi has informed me that you are to be sent to Antwerp. Do you know where that is?*

Baillie: (Nods his head) It's in the Spanish Netherlands.

Alva: Sí. *There you will be given some* documentos…

Baillie: Documents?

Alva: Sí, *documents. These you will take to England and then make contact with the* hermanos *Cavalcanti*
…

Baillie: The Cavalcanti brothers?

Alva: Sí, sí. *They are bankers and it is their task to help finance, how shall I say it in your English? Ah, sí, a revolution that will end the days of Elizabeth and her Protestant rule in England. Do I make myself clear?*

Baillie: Sí.

Alva: Bueno. *Then take yourself some of this wine. It is very good and, of course, it's Spanish. Now remember. These letters contain instructions and are… er…* comunicacion en clave.

Baillie: In code?

Alva: Sí, *in code. And don't forget. There are really two packets of letters. One that is real and one that is not real, er…* falso. Comprendo?

Baillie: Sí.

Alva: Bueno. *Now, if that monster, Cecil or that* araña, *what's his name? That spider, as the queen calls him, er, Walsingham, get their hands on the false packet, it is of no importance, as the real ones,* los genuinos, *must reach the Bishop of Ross. This you must remember all the time they are with you. The real message is that when the day comes, myself, with our Gracious Majesty, King Philip II, will send soldiers over to the east of England and your Elizabeth is (snaps his fingers imperiously) is no more.* Comprendo?

Baillie: Sí.

"Baillie was then dismissed and left to solve the problem of getting the genuine instructions into the hands of the Bishop of Ross. Unfortunately for Baillie, his message to the bishop was intercepted, and Cecil decided to use Herle to wheedle the information out of the bishop, but he failed. Cecil then decided to be more direct and dispatched three members of the Privy Council to interrogate the bishop. This time Cecil succeeded. His Excellency admitted that Mary, Queen of Scots, had been in communication with Ridolfi, the King of Spain, and the Pope, as well as the Duque of Alba, but he said that he no longer had the original letters. This half-answer frustrated the devious old minister no end, especially as he was forbidden from torturing this important member of the Church for more information."

"So for once, Grandpa, Cecil was beaten."

"Yes my dear, but salvation came from a completely unexpected source. John Hawkins."

"The Elizabethan sailor and slave-trader?"

"That's right. Someone informed Cecil that Hawkins was busy trying to rescue some English sailors from Spanish captivity. So, Cecil sought out Hawkins who admitted that he had already made contact with Guerau de Spes, the Spanish ambassador in London. This diplomat had, as a result, sent his friend George Fitzwilliam to Madrid to see about getting the English sailors released."

"That was very noble of Hawkins."

"Nobility be blowed, Sophie. Hawkins was in it for the money."

"You mean like the spy-swap deals that sometimes happened during the Cold War?"

"Exactly. So when Fitzwilliam returned from Spain, he sent a letter for Mary, Queen of Scots, from King Philip II. Cecil arranged for Fitzwilliam to visit the Scottish Queen and she gave him a reply which, of course, in a short time, was in Cecil's eager hands. Fitzwilliam then returned to Spain, collected his prisoners and Hawkins made a goodly profit. Philip II had obviously misjudged him and had thought he would change sides and help him with his forthcoming invasion of England."

"And where was Norfolk in all this? You haven't mentioned him for a bit."

"Ah, I was just coming to him. Now it was about this time that Fitzwilliam learned about Norfolk's plan to marry Mary and lend a hand with the Spanish invasion."

"So now, Grandpa, Norfolk was in deep trouble."

"Very deep. Right up to his ducal neck, in fact. But before Cecil could do anything about him, he had to have watertight evidence of his treason. Remember, our Thomas Howard was Earl Marshal, the Premier Duke of England. You didn't put such people on trial unless you were sure of the verdict. So Cecil went about collecting evidence as only he knew how. In his book, *The Elizabethan Secret Services*, Alan Haynes writes that Cecil managed to get his hands on some money and

coded letters which Norfolk had sent to Lawrence
Banister, one of his men in Shropshire. The money was
to be sent on to Scotland, to be used by supporters of
Mary, Queen of Scots. Cecil acted in his usual way.
Banister and two of Norfolk's secretaries were arrested
and racked in the Tower. They of course spilled the
beans, and Cecil, to be doubly sure, threatened the
Bishop of Ross with what the police call today, GBH..."

"Grievous bodily harm..."

"Exactly, if he didn't tell the truth. Cecil of course
couldn't, and wouldn't, have really racked the noble
Bishop however much he'd wanted to. However, Ross
decided not to call the Principal Secretary of State's
bluff and he spilled the beans, or a whole can of worms
as far as Ridolfi's plot was concerned. Naturally, the
names of the Duke of Alva, Norfolk and Mary, Queen
of Scots, came to light, and the Spanish ambassador de
Spes was declared *persona non grata* in England and
sent packing. In June 1572, Norfolk was executed for
treason to the general dismay of the English Catholic
community. And this was especially so because, while
he was on the scaffold, he publicly declared that he
wasn't a Catholic after all."

"Why did he do that, Grandpa? To save his neck?"

"Very possibly. That, or to prevent the rest of the
English Catholics from being besmirched with his
treachery. I don't know. Personally, I believe it was the
first reason."

"But surely, Grandpa, now Queen Elizabeth had

signed the death warrant for someone as important as England's premier duke, it wouldn't have been a problem for her to do the same for Mary, Queen of Scots, who was, after all, the focus of all the plots, no?"

"Well, as I said before, Sophie, yes and no. On the one hand, technically, to sign such a death warrant presented no problem. Both Cecil, Walsingham and even her court-favourite, Leicester, kept badgering her for ages to do so. But on the other hand, for one queen to execute another, especially when that other queen was her cousin, was not, in Elizabeth's eyes, a healthy precedent. In fact, she was so set against executing her potential rival that she tried to persuade Sir Amias Paulet, Mary's jailer, to murder his prisoner, but he refused outright."

"But Elizabeth did sign the death warrant in the end, no?"

"Yes. Eventually, in February 1587, some fifteen years after Norfolk had been beheaded for his part in the Ridolfi Plot, Mary, Queen of Scots, followed him to the block and was executed at Fotheringhay Castle."

"Where Richard III was born."

"Exactly."

"And what happened to Signor Ridolfi while all this was going on? I remember you said that he didn't pay the price for his plotting."

"That's right. When the whole plot blew up, and Baillie was being interrogated, Ridolfi was abroad. He eventually became a Florentine senator in 1600 and died peacefully, as far as I know, in Italy twelve years later, probably to the great disgust of Cecil's son, Robert, who had taken over from his father."

"So in other words, nothing ever came of Ridolfi's plotting and planning."

"Not really, except that it embittered some Catholics even more and it also caused Elizabeth and her ministers to become even more wary of the Spanish and of the English Catholic community. The guard on Mary, Queen of Scots, was tightened even more and the failure of Ridolfi's Plot sowed the seeds for future Catholic schemes and plots. The two most well-known ones being the Babington Plot and the Gunpowder Plot. But they're for another day."

"Or night. Somehow it seems more appropriate to talk about them at night."

"Exactly."

Chapter Nine
The Babington Plot: Kill one queen and crown another (1586)

Anthony Babington

"Grandpa, our new history teacher, Mr Wollaston, told us something today about a nineteenth century historian who was also a poet and a politician as well."

"Macaulay?"

"That's right. So you've heard of him?"

"Heard of Macaulay? Of course I have. And when I

was your age, my dear Sophie, I used to curse him regularly too."

"Why? Didn't you agree with his history?"

"No. Nothing of the sort. When I was in school, we had to learn reams and reams of his poetry off by heart, and I hated that. Even today, I can still remember whole verses of his poetry. Here for example, this piece, 'The Fight at the Bridge', from his epic poem 'Horatius':

> *Meanwhile in the Tuscan army,*
> *Right glorious to behold,*
> *Came flashing back the noonday light,*
> *Rank behind rank, like surges bright*
> *Of a broad sea of gold.*
> *Four hundred trumpets sounded*
> *A peel of warlike glee,*
> *As that great host, with measured tread,*
> *And spears advanced, and ensigns spread,*
> *Rolled slowly towards the bridge's head,*
> *Where stood the dauntless Three.*

How's that eh? Not bad for an old boy of over seventy, eh?"

"Wow Grandpa! I'm impressed."

"So am I, my dear. I haven't had to remember those lines for about sixty years I would say. That really shows how they hammered it into our heads in those days."

"Well, Grandpa, it's pretty stirring stuff."

"And you know what? Macaulay, or Lord Macaulay

that is, shares a name with another character in English history who was the complete opposite."

"Who do you mean?"

"Well, Macaulay was a highly respected historian who wrote a book, *The History of England from the Accession of James the Second*. He was also a successful politician and as I said, a poet. His full name was Thomas Babington Macaulay, and his opposite number, as it were, was also called Babington. Anthony Babington."

"And who was this Anthony Babington?"

"Anthony Babington was a Catholic plotter who unwittingly gave his name to the plot which in the end led to the execution of Mary, Queen of Scots."

"But Grandpa, surely as a Catholic, he wanted her to stay alive, no?"

"Yes, but his plot failed, with the result that he, she, and a good few others paid the price. Unfortunately for Babington he was up against perhaps the greatest spymaster of the Elizabethan age, an ardent, some would say fanatical, anti-Catholic Puritan called Sir Francis Walsingham. This man financed much of the queen's secret service out of his own pocket, and at one time he had about fifty spies and informers working for him, both here in England and on the Continent."

"So how did Babington's plot come unstuck? You would have thought that after the Catholics' failure with the Ridolfi Plot that they'd have been a bit more careful, no?"

"Well apparently they weren't, and this is what happened. Imagine the scene. We are at 'The Three Tuns' public house in Newgate market, London. A group of about a dozen men – Walsingham would probably have dismissed them as a terrorist gang – are sitting in one of the upstairs rooms facing the street. They have chosen this room as opposed to the larger room on the other side of the corridor on purpose, so that they can see if any of Walsingham's agents or soldiers are keeping an eye on them. In order to do so, they have left one of the heavy curtains slightly open and one of their number, Edward Jones, has been delegated to keep an eye out for any suspicious movement in the street below. A few tankards of cheap ale stand on the table, but the main centre of attention is the young man who has pushed his drink aside and is leaning forward on the large wooden table that seems to take up most of the badly lit room. His eyes are burning brightly as they reflect the external light of the two or three candles as well as the internal intensity of his own purpose:

Babington: Gentlemen, most of you who are gathered here tonight must know me, but some of you do not. For their benefit, I will tell you why we are here, but first of all, I will tell you a few words about myself. My name is Anthony Babington and I'm originally from Dethick in Derbyshire. I am twenty-five years old and I come from a good recusant Catholic family. My father's name was

Henry and my mother was called Mary.

Ballard: Just like the Blessed Virgin and Mary Tudor and Mary, Queen of Scots.

Babington: Exactly. Naturally I received a good but secret Catholic education and upbringing and as a result of that, I suppose, I was sent some twelve years ago to serve as a page to our gracious Queen Mary, Queen of Scots, when she was staying in Sheffield castle.

Savage: What do you mean staying there? She was and still is a prisoner, man.

Dunne: Aye, of Queen Elizabeth.

Tichborne: ... and her accursed lackeys, Cecil and Walsingham.

Gage: That's true, but let him continue. I want to know more about this man.

Babington: Thank you. After a while I left Sheffield castle and went to study law. But my friends, I didn't enjoy this pursuit and found it boring, so I left England for the Continent.

Gifford: Where did you go?

Babington: To the Spanish Netherlands and France. And while I was there, in Paris, I met an old soldier called Thomas Morgan.

Jones: Sounds Welsh to me.

Babington: He was. Now here was a man I felt I could really talk to. He hated Queen Elizabeth with a passion and so we had many a conversation about getting rid of her and replacing her with our beloved Mary, Queen of Scots. In fact, one idea we started working on was that we should kill that bastard daughter of Henry VIII and then seize all the ships in the Thames. After that we would start a general uprising and we would then kill all the queen's ministers especially Cecil...

Gifford: ... and Walsingham of course.

Babington: Of course. Now gentlemen, can you imagine what life would be like in England then, with our fair Scottish Queen Mary on the throne and that accursed Elizabeth buried deep underground? First of all we'd have a Catholic queen at our head and then all those terrible laws and fines for not attending their accursed Protestant services would be a thing of the past.

Salisbury: Aye, and our priests would be able to practise openly and they wouldn't have to look over their shoulders all the time and...

Barnwell: And go and hide in priest holes every time there was a knock on the door and...

Savage: ... and all the recusants would also be able to come out into the open and nobody would be forced to sell their property to pay these terrible fines.

Babington: What you say gentlemen is true. So what I propose is that we stop feeling sorry for ourselves and start fighting back.

Gage: How?

Babington: I propose that we start acting on a plan to see about rescuing our Queen Mary from her castle-prison and at the same time restore the true faith to this country.

Ballard: Easier said than done, young Babington. As you said yourself, first we have to rescue her. For that we are going to need guns, money and horses, and where are we going to get them? Remember, that damned spider, Walsingham, keeps his eyes screwed on us so very tightly that it's nearly impossible today for a good Catholic to breathe, let alone try and rescue a queen held in captivity.

Salisbury: Aye, he's right there.

Babington: Well my friends, things may not be as black as you paint them. While I was on the Continent, I was in contact with some of our fellow Catholics there who told me that once the spark of freedom had been struck here, then we would receive all manner of help from his Catholic Majesty King Philip II of Spain. Nothing of course would make him happier than knowing that he had such a dedicated band working here for the benefit of the Catholic religion.

Jones: So if that is true, Mr Babington, how are we first to bring about the release of our gracious queen from her prison and...

Tichborne: ... and even before that, Edward, how are we to inform her of our intentions, wherever she is?

Babington: Chartley. She's in Chartley Castle. She was moved there from the castles at Tutbury and Bolton.

Dunne: Hey! Wasn't it at Bolton Castle when she was going to escape by climbing down some knotted sheets one night?

Ballard: Yes. But one of her ladies accidentally gave the game away when she knocked over some furniture and that aroused the guards.

Babington: Gentlemen, this is all very interesting but we are not getting anywhere. Now, the first thing we must do is to make contact with our queen, but the question is how?

Tichborne: How about tying coded letters to an arrow and firing it into the castle. No one would know who fired it and it is a silent way of sending messages.

Barnwell: True, but it's not practical. First of all you would have to get close to the castle and...

Jones: ... and how do we know it would be her that picked them up? Just suppose that one of the guards or even one of Walsingham's men got hold of them and then decoded the letters, then the game would be up.

Gage: So how about disguising one or two of us and pretend to be servants or messengers and...

Habington: Wait! I have an idea. We could disguise ourselves up as delivery boys and take messages in that way.

Babington: That's a good idea but I doubt if it would work. I have heard that Walsingham's men are checking everyone who comes in and out of the castle. If they don't know you, at best they'll just send you on your way.

Ballard: And at worst?

Babington: They'll start asking you a lot of questions and...

Habington: Wait! I have had another idea and this is a much better one. If we cannot get into the castle as a carrier of boxes or barrels, how about using the boxes and barrels to carry us in?

Savage: What do you mean?

Habington: It's obvious, no? We should smuggle ourselves into the castle inside a box or barrel or something like that.

Babington: And how would you leave the castle? In the same barrel or box that is now supposed to be empty and light?

Habington: Hmmm. I hadn't thought of that one.

Babington: But my friend, you have just given me an idea. The important thing is to get the messages in, is it not?

Salusbury: Aye.

Babington: So we could smuggle the message in a barrel of ale or something like that. After all, they are always bringing barrels of ale into the castle and I'm sure they don't check all of them.

Gifford: But the message would get wet.

Babington: No it wouldn't. We could put it in a hollowed cork so they would remain dry and...

Gifford: ... and the queen could send us her replies in the same way.

Babington: Of course. And in this way she would not give up hope and she would be able to learn all about our plans.

"But Mary, Queen of Scots, was not the only one who would learn about their plans. For unknown to Anthony Babington and his fellow conspirators, one of their number, Gilbert Gifford, was on the payroll of Mary's greatest enemy, Sir Francis Walsingham. Gifford was a Catholic double-agent who at one time had trained for the priesthood and as such he was trusted in Catholic circles. He had worked for Walsingham for several years and so it was not surprising that all the information that he learned at Babington's regular clandestine meetings was soon passed over to his workaholic employer. The same was true for all the messages that were smuggled into Chartley, except that, for several of them, Walsingham himself had a hand in their content. It was not for nothing that Queen Elizabeth's spymaster's favourite axiom was 'Knowledge is never too dear'. The comparison of him and a spider was also very apt judging from the way he set out to trap his potential victims and then allow them to tie themselves up in knots within his fatal web.

"Babington insisted that all of the Scottish queen's messages be addressed to him personally, an action that perhaps in the short term was good for his ego, but in the long term would prove bad for his neck. Little did he know that the messages including such stirring phrases as 'we have vowed and we will perform or die' were not to be understood by Walsingham as mere rhetoric, but rather as bold and heartfelt expressions of intent. Walsingham of course had no intention of ever letting them carry out their plans."

"But Grandpa, didn't Babington and his men realise that they were playing a very dangerous game?"

"Possibly, my dear. In fact I would say that I'm sure that they were aware of the dangers involved, but I think that they suffered from the same disease that all plotters, conspirators and modern terrorists do. They think that they can outwit the authorities, whoever they are, the Walsinghams of Queen Elizabeth's day, or the CIA, FBI or the MI5 of today. Sometimes they succeed, but never completely. When they do, they bring the whole wrath of the system down on their heads, so in a way, their success causes their ultimate failure. But to get back to Babington, he was never anywhere near succeeding because Walsingham was keeping a very close watch on their activities all the time."

"You mean through Gilbert Gifford?"

"Exactly, but not only through him, but also through the use of his other men such as Thomas Phelipes and spies and double-agents such as Robert Poley and

Francis Mylles. For example, one evening at the beginning of August 1586, a couple of Babington's men met Poley, who they thought was on their side, and told him that they had heard of a plot to murder the Earl of Leicester, Queen Elizabeth's favourite courtier. They also told him that this plot included the killing and/or the kidnapping of Sir William Cecil, her elder statesman and chief advisor. These two men would then be replaced by Catholic advisors and England would return to the joyous days when Mary Tudor had sat on the throne."

"And Grandpa, did they really believe this?"

"Oh, I'm sure they did. Babington it seems had his head in the clouds and Walsingham, through his double agents, was happily leading him and his fellow conspirators by the nose. On Babington's side, it was certainly a case of believing what you want to believe and not really reading the writing on the wall. In fact, one evening Babington was so trusting that he left Poley alone in his room where he read the messages that he'd received from Mary, Queen of Scots, as well as some of his own notes about plots and plans."

"Well that wasn't very smart."

"As you say, my dear, that wasn't very smart, especially as Poley started copying down the relevant parts, and was only stopped when Babington returned unexpectedly early. Poley ripped up the notes, but Babington said that he himself would explain various matters when he met Walsingham and Queen Elizabeth in the future.

"However, in the meanwhile, Walsingham decided that the time had come to start arresting the plotters. One of the first to be reeled in was John Ballard who was charged with being a suspicious – that means Catholic – priest. Fortunately for Babington, he was staying in the same house at the time, and when he heard the noise and commotion downstairs, he managed to slip out…"

"Just in time to be caught shinning down the drainpipes."

"Not quite. He managed to get clear away and rushed over to the house of Chidiock Tichbourne, one of his fellow conspirators, who unfortunately wasn't at home. But even now, it seemed that Babington was still pretty naïve regarding Poley, for soon afterwards, he met him and another conspirator, John Savage. It seems that Savage had had enough of plotting and had decided that the time had come to act. Babington agreed and gave him some money to buy some clothes which would be more suitable to wear at court."

"So he could go there and bump off the queen."

"Probably, but it never came to that. Anyway, it seems that soon after this, the penny had dropped in Babington's mind."

"You mean that he realised that Walsingham was on to him?"

"Yes, so he decided to run away and lie low for a bit. However, he couldn't have been thinking very straight, for instead of running far away, to be clear of London, or staying with someone who wasn't known to Walsingham, Babington rushed off to the house of another member of his gang, Robert Gage. There he met John Savage who promptly fled like a frightened rabbit, while Babington and Gage changed clothes, in an effort to disguise themselves."

"You know, Grandpa, this is beginning to sound like a real Elizabethan cops 'n' robbers story."

"It is in a way, but in fact it was much more deadly than that. So, once Babington and Gage felt they were sufficiently well disguised, they took off for John Charnock's house."

"Another plotter?"

"Of course."

"It seems to me that this lot never learned from experience."

"They didn't, but that's par for the course. From Charnock's house they took off again and this time they set off for St. John's Wood, which in those days was really a woodland area north of London. Somehow two other plotters, Robert Barnwell and Henry Dunne, got to hear about this and they met Babington and Gage there."

"But Grandpa, if those two found out about Babington and Gage, couldn't Walsingham and his men do the same?"

"Exactly. And so within a week Walsingham started reeling in the other plotters. First of all, he sent his men to pick up Tichbourne, Tilney and Savage and then he arrested Poley."

"But wasn't Poley one of his own men?"

"Yes, but this arrest was either a cover-up or Walsingham never really trusted him, after all, he may have been acting as a double agent against him. By throwing him into some dirty old prison, it kept him out of the way so that if he was playing both ends off against the middle, as the Americans say, then he couldn't tip off the other plotters.

"In the meanwhile, Babington and some of the others remained on the run and they fled to the house of two staunch Catholic supporters, Bartholomew and Jerome Bellamy who lived near Harrow. There they cut off their long hair and stained their faces with walnut juice in an effort to disguise themselves even better, but it didn't help. A few days later, Walsingham's men turned up and arrested all of them, including the two members of the Bellamy family. In the investigation that followed, Bartholomew died on the rack, presumably after having divulged even more details about the conspiracy, and Jerome was executed. Some of the conspirators, that is, those who were not caught in Harrow, managed to evade capture for some time, but by the end of 1586, Walsingham had pretty well netted them all."

"So Grandpa, that was really the end of this conspiracy, no?"

"Yes. Actually I don't seriously think it had too much chance of success. First of all, the government, that is, Walsingham, was too good for them, and secondly, Babington was not the ideal man to be the leader of such a group. He was far too vain and impractical for the role he had chosen for himself and he never realised until the end that Walsingham had had him in his sights from the very beginning. If you want, Walsingham was a bit like a spider playing with a fly, or like a cat playing with a mouse."

"What do you mean? They never met up until he was caught?"

"Oh no, nothing like that. They met up all right, and each of them did so because each one thought that he could exploit the other. For example, one evening some time before this, Walsingham sent his men to pick up Babington and bring him over to his house. Babington had let it be known that he wanted to go over to the Spanish Netherlands to spy on his fellow Catholics, while in fact he really wanted to make contact with them and prepare the groundwork for a future uprising. In order to travel to the Continent, he needed a passport from Walsingham, and so it seemed that for once their purposes coincided."

"I bet that must have been a fun-filled meeting."

"Well, my dear Sophie, that depends on your definition of fun. Walsingham received him very well and started plying him with strong wine. Fortunately, Babington realised this and kept his wits about him and hardly drank any of it. And then, as luck would have it, while he was there, he noticed his name on an incriminating document and decided it was time to leave. This he did, and it was soon after this that he headed north out of London. But now we come to the last chapter of this grim story."

"The trial and executions."

"Exactly, Sophie, but how did you know?"

"Because, my dear grandfather, most of your stories end like that."

"Well, I can't change history now, can I? Of course, the trial itself was merely a formality and it was probably unnecessary to have tortured Babington and some or all of the others. Babington himself had written out two long reports confessing his role in the plot and no doubt Walsingham, aided by the rack, had obtained similar confessions from the others."

"So why did Walsingham torture them so much? I mean Poley, Gifford and some of the other people involved had already given him all the background information and details, no?"

"True, but first of all you have to remember Walsingham was somewhat of a fanatic in trying to rid the country of the Catholic 'fifth column', as he saw them. In addition, he wanted the Catholic community to see what would happen to anyone who plotted against the queen and the establishment. And so, the end of this particular conspiracy came in September 1586. The fourteen plotters were ordered to be executed on two successive days in two groups of seven. The first group, which included Babington, was dragged to the open area near St. Giles' on wicker hurdles. There Walsingham made sure that Babington, as the leader, would suffer even more because he was forced to witness the half-hanging, drawing and quartering of John Ballard before he himself underwent the same grisly end. According to a popular story, when Walsingham went over to the queen that night, rubbing his hands with glee and telling her all the gory details, she was so disgusted…"

"That she cancelled the remaining executions."

"No such luck. Instead, she ordered the drawing and quartering of the second batch of seven plotters not be carried out until they were dead, and this was a slightly more humane way of doing things. In a way Walsingham's plan backfired, at least in carrying out these grisly punishments in public."

"Why?"

"Because instead of being seen as religious conspirators who had wanted to kill their queen, they were seen by many as Catholic martyrs who had died bravely for their cause. It may possibly be argued that it was the execution of these men which inspired future Catholic conspiracies, such as Guy Fawkes and the Gunpowder Plot…"

"But that of course is another story."

"That's right my dear. But you know what? Perhaps the saddest part of Babington's conspiracy is that it convinced Walsingham that the quicker Mary, Queen of Scots, was out of the way, the better. It was true that he had been working to achieve this for ages, but Babington's plot was the straw that broke the camel's back. So a few days after the executions, she was taken out of Chartley castle and moved to Fotheringhay Castle in Northamptonshire. Walsingham was now in such a hurry to get rid of her that within three weeks she was put on trial for her life."

"On what charges?"

"Huh! That was no problem for Walsingham. With the evidence he had got from Gifford and the others, it was easy for him to have her charged with aiding and abetting various conspiracies aimed at destroying Queen Elizabeth and the Protestant establishment. Of course, she was found guilty, and despite the wishes of the queen, she was executed in February 1587."

"Why despite the queen's wishes? Surely it was safer for her to have Mary, Queen of Scots, out of the way. There'd be no more Babington type plots then, right?"

"Right, but Elizabeth didn't want to be held directly responsible for Mary's death. I mean that she had to sign the death warrant personally and this she did very reluctantly in the end. Remember, first of all, Elizabeth and Mary were related to each other through Henry VIII's sister, Margaret, and also Elizabeth, who was no fool, thought that if one queen could be executed, why not another, if there were a change in circumstances. So she ummed and ahhed for some time, and all the time Walsingham and Cecil were breathing down her neck to get on with it. Eventually she did, but then claimed that she had been tricked into signing the document by Cecil's secretary, William Davison."

"But couldn't Elizabeth or say Walsingham have had

it arranged that Mary was quietly poisoned or something like that?"

"Do you think they hadn't thought of that? Before this, Elizabeth had tried to persuade Mary's jailers to poison her, but this they had refused to do. Anyway, after Mary had been executed, Elizabeth then had Davison imprisoned in the Tower of London on the grounds that he had tricked her. He was also ordered to pay a fine of ten thousand marks, but this was never carried out. He was later released and quietly retired. Perhaps as a way of showing that she was sorry, Elizabeth ordered that the Scottish queen be buried in state at Peterborough Cathedral. There she lay for about twenty years until her son, King James I, had her body removed to a special tomb in Westminster Abbey. So it may be said that Mary, Queen of Scots, did have a royal end to her life."

"Yes, Grandpa, but not in the way that Babington and his fellow conspirators had planned it."

"Exactly."

Chapter Ten
Poison the Queen:
The Lopez Conspiracy (1594)

"Lopez compounding to poison the Queene"

"Grandpa, meet my friend Philip Mendoza. He's come over to help me find some geography material on the Internet."

"Pleased to meet you, young man. Mendoza, eh? Now that's an interesting name. Spanish isn't it, or is it Portuguese?"

"It's Spanish."

"But you're not Spanish, are you?"

"No, I'm English. But my ancestors were Spanish, that is, about three or four hundred years ago. Have you heard of the *marranos*?"

"Who or what were they Philip? Isn't that the name for a type of sheep?"

"Wrong animal, Sophie. No, *marrano* is the Spanish word for a pig or a filthy person. The Spanish used the name for the Jews who converted to Catholicism during the period of the Spanish Inquisition."

"When was that?"

"In the late Middle Ages. And there were lots of Jews then who were so scared of the Church authorities that they pretended to be good Catholics, but secretly they still practised their Jewish religion."

"But Philip, why were they so scared?"

"Well, if the Church caught you, or say a jealous or nasty neighbour told the authorities that they suspected you of being a secret Jew, a *marrano*, then you could be tortured or burnt at the stake in a big public ceremony called an *auto-da-fe*."

"But that sounds terrible!"

"It was. My grandfather told me that during that period there were about two thousand *auto-da-fe* burnings and at least thirty thousand executions. And then after that, in 1492, the Spanish government expelled all the remaining Jews from Spain."

"1492, but that's the year that Columbus discovered America, no?"

"Exactly, Sophie, and there are some people who

claim that he was also Jewish."

"So, Philip, was your family expelled from Spain as well?"

"I suppose so, Sophie, and then they probably went to Portugal, North Africa or Holland, you know, countries which would let them practice their religious beliefs without the fear of persecution."

"So why didn't they come here, to England? I mean you're living here now."

"Because Jews weren't allowed to live in England. Edward I had thrown them out in 1290, when they couldn't pay his special taxes anymore and they didn't return until Oliver Cromwell allowed them to do so over three hundred years later."

"Why did he do that?"

"Well, I suppose it was because of their international business connections. Don't you remember what we learned in our history class? While Oliver Cromwell was ruling Britain, the country was going through a major trade war with Holland. I suppose that Cromwell thought that if he allowed the Jews to return to England then this would help him."

"So do you mean, Philip, that between Edward I and Oliver Cromwell there were absolutely no Jews living in England?"

"No, not exactly. My grandfather told me that there were a few small *marrano* communities in London and Bristol, but they didn't have very good name."

"What do you mean?"

"Well, say if anyone wrote a play or poem or story that included Jews in it, they were always the baddies."

"Ah, you mean like the Jew in the Prioress' Tale in Chaucer's *The Canterbury Tales* that we read last term?"

"That's right. Or like that horrible guy, Barabbas, in *The Jew of Malta* by Christopher Marlowe."

"That's right Philip, but you're forgetting the most famous example of the wicked Jew in English literature."

"Who's that, Professor Warkworth?"

"Shylock, from Shakespeare's *The Merchant of Venice.*"

"Oh, of course. How could I forget?"

"And you know what, Philip, according to some literary critics, the anti-Semitic parts of the play may have been the result of an Elizabethan conspiracy which involved some of your *marrano* ancestors?"

"What, my *marrano*...?"

"Oh, don't you worry about my grandpa, Philip. He's always going on about plots and conspiracies in English history. You only have to say the name of a person or place and he'll tell you that someone there plotted to do away with the king or something like that. Isn't that true Grandpa?"

"Now don't you mock your aging grandfather, young lady. But it's true. There was a very famous plot which was discovered towards the end of Queen Elizabeth I's reign, and a *marrano* called Lopez was found to be slap-bang in the middle of it."

"OK Grandpa, tell us about this Lopez plot. I know you won't forgive us if Philip goes home without knowing that his ancestors were spies and plotters, and maybe even murderers."

"My dear Sophie, I'm pretty sure Philip's ancestors weren't involved in this as there were only a few dozen *marranos* altogether living in London then. Anyway, if you bring in another packet of chocolate digestives we can get on with the story of Roderigo Lopez and the plot against Queen Elizabeth I.

"So, cast your minds back to over four hundred years to the London of the 1590s. Queen Elizabeth had been reigning for over thirty years, the Spanish Armada had been beaten and destroyed, but the English were still scared of anything foreign. Especially anything Spanish. It was also during this period that the government was keeping a strict look-out for any signs of the Spanish trying another scheme to make England a Catholic country once again. And in the middle of this, we find the *marrano* family of Lopez living in London, in the parish of St. Peter-le-Poer."

"Was that safe for them to live there?"

"Yes, Sophie, I think it was, because our friend, Lopez, seems to have done pretty well for himself. He was a doctor by profession and he became the personal physician to several leading members of society, including the Earl of Leicester, Sir Francis Walsingham, and also Robert Devereux, the Earl of Essex. And then…"

"Not bad."

"Not bad, as you say. And then to cap it all, from 1586 he became the personal physician to the queen. In fact, the good doctor did so well that he was able to send his son, Anthony, to be educated at Winchester College. But that's the good part of this story."

"Why? Was he a crook as well? You know, a sort of Jekyll and Hyde character?"

"No, no, Philip. He was nothing like that at all. After all, in addition to being a well-placed doctor, he also made money from a monopoly he held for importing aniseed, and that was in addition to money he received from the estates belonging to the Bishop of Worcester. In fact, he had enough money to send some to support the poor Jewish *marrano* community in Antwerp, Belgium."

"So what crooked deals did he carry out then behind the queen's back?"

"Sophie, he wasn't a crook like you're thinking. He got into trouble because he was a spy. I mean, Walsingham and Cecil were more than delighted to use his knowledge of Spanish and Portuguese and other languages and get him to spy for them."

"Why? Wasn't it enough for him to be a big high-flying doctor? You know, 'by appointment of Her Majesty', etc?"

"No, Sophie, I don't think he had much choice in the matter. I mean, if Walsingham, Cecil or the Earl of

Essex asked you to do something, you did it. Remember, after all, Lopez was an immigrant belonging to a potentially persecuted minority and these top aristocrats were the equivalent of being important cabinet ministers today. That is as well as being very well in with the queen. However, for all that, I don't think our Signor Lopez played his cards right."

"Why do you say that?"

"Well, Philip, when Lopez thought he had picked up some interesting information, instead of taking it to the Earl of Essex, he contacted Essex's sworn political rival, Sir William Cecil directly, or even the queen herself, and only after that did he tell Essex."

"I bet Essex didn't like that one."

"Exactly. Especially since Essex was in the middle of a long-running battle with Cecil to gain the queen's political favour. For him, it was one thing to be her favourite courtier – her boyfriend, if you like – but what he, Essex, wanted was to have some political clout as well."

"I see, so when Essex went running off to the queen to say that he'd heard something interesting, she would tell him that she'd already heard it."

"Exactly, Sophie. And in this way, Essex would look a bit stupid in front of the queen, or at best, somewhat inefficient. If this wasn't rather tactless on the part of Lopez, then he rubbed even more salt into the earl's open wounds by admitting one day, to another dubious character, Dom Antonio, the Pretender to the

Portuguese throne, that he, Lopez, had cured His Lordship of a bout of venereal disease. I believe that this breach of professional conduct was carried out while the good doctor was drunk and he was to pay very heavily for it in the future."

"I bet that kept Essex happy, knowing that his doctor couldn't keep his mouth shut."

"Exactly, Philip. So the earl plotted revenge and he didn't have to wait too long for the golden opportunity to drop right into his lap. Not long after this, in October 1593, a Portuguese fellow named Estaban Ferrar da Gama was arrested on the suspicion that he had sold English national state secrets to Spain. Now, as Privy Councillor who was in charge of the Portuguese department of the Foreign Office as it were, Essex now used his authority to intercept all the mail and messages coming to England from Portugal. And then one day, lo and behold! A secret letter that da Gama had written to Lopez fell into Essex's ever-open hands. This letter was delivered to him by Dom Antonio and it said that a messenger was on his way from the Continent with some letters, which if they were discovered could prove fatal to both da Gama and to Lopez."

"I'm sure Essex was happy when Dom Antonio brought him that one."

"I'm sure that he was absolutely delighted, Philip. Therefore, as a result, da Gama was, as the newspapers say today, picked up for questioning…"

"That is, helping the police with their enquiries."

"Exactly, and he admitted that he and some others had been trying to negotiate some sort of peace deal with King Philip II of Spain. And then to make matters look even worse, da Gama himself tried to bribe a guard to take a secret message to Brussels and to pick up some incriminating letters there before they fell into the hands of the authorities."

"Wow! This plot is getting thicker and thicker."

"Very true, my dear. And then, to complicate matters even further, an ex-spy called Antonio de Vega reported to Essex that Lopez had agreed to poison Dom Antonio, the Portuguese Pretender, about six years earlier and that he would be well paid for doing so."

"But Lopez hadn't poisoned him."

"I know, but maybe now he wished he had, seeing the trouble Dom Antonio had got him into. And this was yet another piece of information for Essex who, after spending much time and effort in getting all sorts of Spanish and Portuguese documents and letters translated, had Lopez arrested in January 1594. He was then interrogated by Essex, Sir William Cecil and his son, Robert, who now spent much time filling in for his aging father. In addition, Lopez's house was searched for more evidence and given a very thorough going-over."

"And what did they find there?"

"Nothing my dear, Sophie. That is, nothing particularly useful. However, to make sure he could keep his eye on his prisoner, Essex had Lopez imprisoned at his own place, Essex House."

"Not in the Tower of London?"

"Wait a minute, Philip. That comes later. So, use your imagination. The Earl of Essex, now full of himself – he was really a rather shallow and conceited fellow – went racing over to the queen to tell her his good news, that he had uncovered a plot; a threat against the nation's security…"

"So she must have been very pleased with her boy-friend."

"Not at all. For when he told Her Majesty his joyful news, she replied that the Cecils, father and son, had already informed her, and to quote the cliché usually attributed to Queen Victoria, she was not amused."

"I bet Essex wasn't either."

"I agree with you there, Sophie. He took himself off in a huff and shut himself in his rooms for a couple of days. In the meanwhile, Cecil was not completely convinced that Lopez was really guilty of plotting against the state, so a week later he was interrogated again, but this time in the Tower where he was now being kept."

"See, Sophie. I knew he'd end up there."

"But of course, Philip. All the crooks ended up there. And usually ended up in pieces as well."

Professor Warkworth looked at Sophie and Philip and rolled his eyes.

"So when you two bloodthirsty characters have finished, we can continue. Now Essex, who was suffering from a severely bruised ego, then wrote a letter to one of his supporters, Anthony Bacon, the brother of Sir Francis Bacon, and probably hoped this would help him. Sophie, if you give me that book over there, the one about Walsingham and the Elizabethan spies, we will be able to see what Essex wrote. Ah, here we are:

> *I have discovered a most dangerous and desperate treason. The point of conspiring was Her Majesty's death. The executioner should have been Dr Lopez, the manner poison. This I have so followed that I will make it as clear as noonday.*

"And at about this time, Lopez confessed to everything, and as the records of the day state, he confessed 'more than enough'."

"So this time Essex must have thought that things were now going his way at last."

"Exactly, especially as luck would have it, another one of those shady semi-underworld Portuguese characters called Manuel de Andrade popped up and said that he too had heard that Lopez had indeed intended to poison the queen."

"But why would Lopez have wanted to do that? What was his motive?"

"Philip, I doubt very much if he did want to. After all, he was her personal physician and that must have carried some sort of respect and status, and I'm sure he knew what the price for treason was. In fact, the only answer I can give you is that Essex was looking for any excuse to get rid of him and all this so-called evidence was like a goldmine for him. Also, you must remember, Essex was an important aristocrat while Lopez was merely a foreigner and a Jew, or at least a converted one, and all that ran in Essex's favour."

"So in other words, Lopez didn't stand a cat in hell's chance, did he?"

"No, Sophie, he certainly didn't. He was put on trial very soon after, and even then it wasn't a real trial. He had to face a secret commission in the Guildhall, and all its fifteen members had been hand-picked by the queen herself. Naturally it included Essex, as well as his brother-in-law, Lord Rich, as well as Cecil Junior…"

"Sir Robert?"

"Yes, and the whole thing was conducted by the Solicitor-General, Sir Edward Coke. He was known to be a somewhat harsh and unpleasant person who throughout the trial kept referring to Lopez's Jewish background. Lopez was denied any defence counsel and admitted that he had confessed to these treasonous crimes."

"Why?"

"Because, Sophie, he said that he was afraid of being tortured on the rack."

"I suppose he was found guilty."

"Of course. That had been decided in advance. He

was found guilty on three counts. The first was for spying on behalf of Spain, the second was for planning to poison the queen, and the third was that he had intended to start a rebellion in England, although it was never made really clear when and how he would do so. Naturally he was sentenced to death by…"

"… by being hanged, drawn and quartered."

"Exactly. At Tyburn, where everyone could see. However, the queen wasn't very happy with this."

"So she quashed the verdict?"

"No such luck, Sophie. She didn't really want to execute her personal physician, so she delayed the hanging for about four months, which meant that the poor man 'shuffled off this mortal coil' at the beginning of June 1594."

"And was he the only one who was hanged?"

"Oh, Philip, you're as bloodthirsty as Sophie. As it is, another one of Essex's past employees, a man called Manuel Luis Tinoco who had played a minor role in all this, was also hanged. However, before this happened, he began to fight the hangman on the scaffold and this the crowd thought was great fun."

"What happened to da Gama, the one who was involved in this plot from the beginning?"

"Oh, he was hanged with Lopez and Tinoco as well. And like Lopez, he didn't make any fuss so the crowds were also somewhat disappointed."

"So poor old Lopez was the fall guy and Essex had his revenge."

"Yes, but in a way this story does have a happy ending. It seems that the queen wasn't really pleased with what had happened to her doctor. Maybe, and remember our Elizabeth was no fool, she saw through Essex's moves. She allowed Lopez's wife, Sara, to keep all her money and property, that is, not confiscate everything as she, the queen, was allowed to do, and she also allowed Sara to continue living peacefully at her home in London. And then to round off this sorry tale, young Anthony Lopez was allowed to continue with his studies at Winchester College, from where he'd been suspended, and not only that but the queen even had his fees paid as well. Finally, there is a legend that until her dying day, Queen Elizabeth wore the ring that Lopez had given her while he was serving her as her personal physician."

"Maybe, Grandpa. But that didn't help him in his hour of need, did it."

"Unfortunately, no. But since he had got himself involved with such shady characters as he had, as well as annoying the vengeful Earl of Essex, that was the price to be paid. Remember, history teaches us that plotting can be a very fatal experience."

"Very true, Grandpa. Especially if you are on the wrong side."

"Exactly."

Chapter Eleven
Stab the King:
The Gowrie Plot (1600)

The Gowrie Conspiracy   *King James I & VI*

"Grandpa, which English king or queen was the victim, or the intended victim, of the largest number of plots or conspiracies?"

"Well, I know that Queen Elizabeth was the intended victim of at least three Catholic plots, like the Babington one we talked about to replace her with Mary, Queen of Scots. However, if I stop and think for a moment, I think the winner of this dubious award would probably go to

Queen Victoria or Queen Elizabeth I's successor, King James I of England and the Sixth of Scotland."

"King James the Sixth of Scotland?"

"Yes, that was his first royal title."

"Grandpa, which plots are you thinking of?"

"Well, the most famous one you know."

"Guy Fawkes and the Gunpowder Plot."

"Exactly. But there were also two other lesser-known ones – the 'Main Plot' and the 'Bye Plot'. The first one aimed to replace him on the throne with Lady Arabella Stuart, the daughter of the Earl of Lennox, while the Bye Plot was an unsuccessful plot to kidnap him."

"That's three. What else?"

"There was the murder of Sir Thomas Overbury in 1613, which didn't affect the king directly, but it was aimed at him and directed by the highest levels of aristocracy in the land, and it should also be remembered that James' father, Lord Darnley, had also been killed, that is by being bombed and/or smothered to death one night while recovering from a bout of syphilis or smallpox."

"That's a pretty grim way to go."

"As you say. Then there is quite a strong theory that King James himself did not die peacefully or naturally in bed, 'full of years' as they say, but that he was poisoned. And then of course there was the violent attack on his life when he was still King James VI in Scotland, and this one was known as the Gowrie Plot."

"So that makes it seven. Yes, I suppose he wins the

Oscar for royal victims, or at least is a close runner-up."

"That's right, as there were even more attempts on the life of Queen Victoria, but no doubt, we'll talk about that good lady sometime in the future."

Sophie nodded. "So tell me, Grandpa, what was this Gowrie Plot? What happened and when was it?"

"It took place in Perth, in Scotland in 1600, three years before James became the King of England. This Gowrie Plot is not only a plot, but it's also a mystery as well, but we'll go into that later. So, Sophie, here is the story, or at least, the basic facts of it as we have them today.

"5 August 1600 was a good day for hunting. The sky was clear and there were no signs of rain, which wasn't a bad thing for Scotland, especially at Falkland Palace, Perth, where King James VI was preparing for a day's hunting. Hunting was his joy. Some said it was almost an obsession with him, and in that way he was very similar to many of the former Kings of England.

"As he stood by a tree in the courtyard of Falkland Palace, he looked around to see that the preparations for the day were proceeding as planned. The horses and the stablemen were there waiting, the food had been stowed away securely in large hampers and was now ready in a carriage that was to accompany them. Various courtiers, pages and squires were standing there lounging around in small groups discussing the forthcoming day's activities as well as talking about the latest gossip and politics:

"Did you na' hear about the French king, na' what's his name…"

"Henri the Fourth"

"Aye, that's him. Well, he plans to marry his niece, Marie de Medici, and a bonnie lass she is too, or so I've heard tell."

"That's not new. I heard about that a few days ago from one of Sir John Ramsey's men. But you know, he's only doing so in order to get his grasping hands on her estates in Tuscany."

"You're right enough there. But since she's a Medici lass, he'll no' be doing a bad thing there."

"Aye, and if you're talking about young lassies, what about that young Mary McGuire near Gowrie? You know, the lass who works in Sir Thomas Erskine's kitchen. She's with child again, and who can tell who's the father this time?"

"True enough. There's at least four lads I can think of, and I'm sure my wife can think of even more."

"Trust the lassies to know about the lassies!"

"Aye, you're right there. They really know how to gossip!"

"Anyhoo, there's Sir Hugh Harries o'er there. Let's get o'er and join him and the king. I see he's getting impatient to get started."

"Aye, 'tis a shame to waste a guid day like this."

"And they walked over to where His Majesty was

leaning heavily against a tree. It was common knowledge that he couldn't walk or stand up for long periods of time without leaning against a tree, wall or courtier. It seemed as if his thin legs just couldn't support the weight of his body for long. Some un-Christian souls said this was just so he could be close to pretty boys and courtiers, but this of course was never said out loud.

"Just as the king was mounting his horse, the sound of flying hooves was heard as a horseman, mounted on a fine but sweating light brown horse, galloped into the courtyard. The rider pulled up his horse expertly to a halt, jumped off and ran over to where the king was standing with his hand on the saddle. He made a cursory bow as he addressed His Majesty and roughly wiped the sweat off his face."

Ruthven: Your Majesty. You must come to Gowrie House at once! There's something ver' strange happening there.

King: What is it man? Wait a minute. You're young Alexander Ruthven, are you not?

Ruthven: Aye, Your Majesty. That I am.

King: And you're the one who opposed me over my proposals for taxation? One hundred thousand crowns, was it not? (The young man who had calmed down by now did not answer, but shuffled his feet noisily in the gravel, in embarrassment). And was it no' your guid father who manhandled my mother, Mary, Queen o' Scots, when her secretary, David Rizzio, was murdered? (The young man remained silent as the other courtiers and attendants were wondering what would be the outcome of all this). And, was it no' your father, William Ruthven, who kidnapped me when I was a mere lad of sixteen and held me in your Gowrie House place in Perth?

Ruthven: Aye, it was, Your Majesty.

King: And what happened then laddie? Tell me. What happened then?

Ruthven: You escaped Your Majesty, and then executed my father.

King: Just so. And now you wish me to return to your cursed Gowrie House? How do I know what for? Maybe you and your brother John want to kill me there.

Ruthven: But Your Majesty, believe me. That's not what I've come here about.

King: So what have ye come about?

Ruthven: Fear not, Your Majesty. It's not about the eighty thousand pounds you owe my family.

King: I should hope not indeed. Now tell me, and tell me quickly, what's all this about. We want to start the hunt and don't wish to waste time with such as you.

Ruthven: We have found a man near Gowrie House who claims he has found a pot of large gold pieces,

236

sire, and...

King: What manner of man is this?

Ruthven: I think he's a foreigner, Your Majesty, but I'm not sure. I canna understan' what he's saying so I don' know where he's from.

King:(Dubiously) And where are these gold pieces now?

Ruthven: I don't know, Your Majesty. My brother, John, ordered me to ride o'er here as fast as possible and inform you about it, sire. So you could come o'er and examine them.

King: Ruthven, how do I know I can trust you? Your family has done me a rare lot o' mischief in the past.

Ruthven: But the story of the gold is true, Your Majesty. And my brother did tell me to ride o'er here to bring you back wi' me to Gowrie House.

King: And you are now asking me to give up a guid day's hunting to ride over to Gowrie House with you to examine your foolish story about a farmer and his crock of gold?

Ruthven: Yes, Your Majesty.

King: Well, I'll think about it. In the meanwhile, I'm going hunting and I'm certainly not going to give up this glorious day. So guid day to you, young man. You may or may not hear from me later. Sir Thomas, let's be away.

"And giving the young Master of Ruthven a

dismissive wave, the king indicated that one of his attendants should help him mount his horse. As they set off, the king was heard to mutter to the horseman nearest to him:

King: I've never trusted those Ruthvens. Not the father and certainly not his sons. You canna trust them. Their family and the Stuarts have never got on together. I did not cry when I signed the death warrant for their father William, that I can tell you.

Attendant: But, sire, didn't you promise him a pardon if he confessed to the kidnapping?

King: What if I did? He was a villain, and kidnapping your king, your anointed king I may add, is a treasonable offence. But now let us forget that foul affair and proceed with the business in hand. I prefer to think about hunting and grouse rather than those Ruthvens and their story about a crock of gold coins.

"The hunt went well. A satisfactory number of pheasants and grouse were bagged, and a large stag was killed as well. The king and all his entourage had good reason to feel pleased with themselves as they cantered over to a quiet meadow to enjoy the contents of the well-stocked hampers. Then one of the attendants reminded the king about Gowrie House and the gold:

Attendant: Your Majesty, are you not interested in looking into this Gowrie House gold thing? It all seems a ver' strange story to me.

King: Aye, you're right there. 'Tis true, young Robbie, I am interested, but I'll only ride over to Gowrie House if I have an armed party of men with me. As I said, you canna trust those Ruthvens.

Attendant: But surely, Your Majesty, are you no' exaggerating a wee bit? They canna really be tha' bad.

King: Well, you hav' na been kidnapped by them, have you?

Attendant: Aye, Your Majesty, I suppose you're right. So I'll arrange an armed party for you. Will thirty men be enough?

King: I hope so. Tell the men we'll leave for Gowrie House after we've finished eating. I don't see why those Ruthvens and their stories should disturb our day's hunting.

"An hour later, King James VI, accompanied by a troop of thirty armed and mounted men set off for Gowrie House. After an hour's easy riding, the royal party was suddenly surprised to find that their way was blocked by an even larger group of armed horsemen who quickly surrounded them. The king had to raise his voice over the sounds of the assorted men, the shuffling horses and jingling harnesses to make himself heard:

King: Who are you and why have you stopped us? Do
you not know that we are on our way to Gowrie
House?

Horseman: Aye, we know that. We are the Earl of
Ruthven's men. We have been sent to escort you
there and to make sure you arrive there quite
safely, Your Majesty. If you did bu' know it, there
are some villainous people about on His
Majesty's roads and we wouldna' want you
coming to no harm now, would we?

Attendant: You need not have come in such large
numbers. His Majesty said he would come, and
come he has.

Horseman: Aye, we just wanted to make sure he did,
that's all. And now, Your Majesty, please tell
your men to sheath their swords and we will
proceed quietly on to Gowrie House where no
doubt my master is waiting to see you.

King:(Ironically) No doubt.

"James then noticed that three of Ruthven's men had
left, as if at a pre-arranged signal, and galloped off in the
direction of Gowrie House in order to warn the earl of
their planned arrival. Another hour was to pass before
the two parties of horsemen cantered into the spacious
forecourt of Gowrie House."

"Didn't the king suspect anything by now, not even
a little bit?"

Professor Warkworth shrugged. "I don't know,

Sophie, but let me continue telling you this weird and wonderful story. So here we are, a curious king and a vengeful Scottish aristocrat. So picture the scene: Standing at the top of the steps by the main doorway, John Ruthven, the current Earl of Gowrie, is resting his large hands on his hips, the fingers of his left hand gently stroking the hilt of his sword. As the king at the head of the large group of horsemen drew up to the foot of the steps, Ruthven approached him and made a quick bow. The earl then ordered his men to dismount and see to their horses and when the king's men prepared to dismount, Ruthven told them to remain as they were, for the time being:

Ruthven: Your Majesty. Right glad am I to host you here in my humble home. 'tis no' often we are so honoured here at Gowrie House. However, I fear that the evening meal is not quite ready, but I pray you to take some ale to refresh yourself in the meantime.

King: Is that all the refreshment that you have for your king? Ale? I'll go without. I do not need your refreshment. And what about this man with his crock o' gold coins? Was no' that the reason I was bought here?

Ruthven: Aye, Your Majesty. But we'll see about him later. But in the meantime, would you do me the kindness of waiting in the house till the evening meal is ready?

King: And what about my men?
Ruthven: I'll see to their welfare, Your Majesty. Do not
concern yourself about them.

"Before the king could say anything else or express himself about the apparent meanness of his host's reception, he found himself surrounded by a dozen of the earl's men who escorted him up the steps into the house. At the top of the steps, Alexander Ruthven took over from his older brother and indicated that the king should follow him. James saw that he didn't have any choice, and with his usual rolling gait followed the younger Ruthven, being aware that he was being closely followed by the earl's men at every step."

"And wasn't the king allowed to take any of his guards with him? Not a single one?"

"No, Sophie, at least that's what we've been told. But let me continue. So, once they were in the house they walked through several rooms, all panelled with dark wood and complete with portraits of Ruthven ancestors or scenes of Scottish highlands, lakes and forests. Approaching the long gallery at the back of the house, the king noticed that each time they passed a room, Alexander made sure that one of his men closed the doors firmly shut.

"After what seemed a long walk, they arrived at a small door at the end of the dimly-lit corridor. Producing a large black key, Alexander Ruthven ushered his royal visitor into the chamber and followed him in. As he noisily finished locking the door, he whirled round to face His Majesty who was startled to find the young man now holding a dagger. I was right after all, James thought. He does indeed intend to kill me. James looked around desperately. Shouting wouldn't help. The room had been well chosen. It was too far away for anyone in the house to hear him. And in any case, even if they did, by the time they would have reached him, Alexander and his dagger would have completed their grisly task.

"The king saw that he had no choice. He would have to try and persuade young Ruthven not to carry out his mission. Now he had decided on a course of action, the king felt remarkably calm. Speaking as clearly as he could, he told his would-be assailant that no good would come from all this:

King: Even if you do succeed in killing me, what good will it do you? Do you really think that you will get away with it? My men, who outnumber yours, will hunt you down and you'll be hanged like a common criminal. That is, if they don't cut you up first.

Ruthven: But you executed my father.

King: (Not reacting) Do you really want to look like that deer we killed in the forest this afternoon? All bloody and swords sticking out of it looking like a squashed hedgehog? Of course not. You're young, laddie. Think o' that. You have all your life in front of you. Fear not. I'll pardon you for

your youth. No doubt your brother set you up to
this. Now just you think on what I've said.

"The heir to the Ruthven fortunes did so and after a few minutes, stuck his dagger back into his belt. Walking over to the door he muttered something about seeing his brother and left the room, but not before locking the door securely. Ten minutes passed and he returned, his hand clutching his dagger again, and he told the king: 'My brother says you are to die, so be prepared'.

"He had hardly finished saying these words when the king pushed him against the wall near the turret window. Before Ruthven could recover from this surprise attack, the king had somehow wound his arm around his neck and shouted, 'Treason! Treason!' out of the open window. It was a desperate move but it paid off. for just then, the king just happened to see Sir John Ramsey walking in the grounds below with Sir Thomas Erskine.

"'Treason! I'm betrayed. Up here!' he shouted and increased his hold on the half-strangled Ruthven's neck. Suddenly the king's attacker shook himself free from the royal stranglehold and stepped back to face his king. As the young man was trying to recover his senses, Sir John Ramsey, accompanied by a few of the king's men burst into the unlocked room. They lunged at Ruthven, stabbed him and drew the young man's blood.

"Instinctively, Ruthven dropped his dagger and put

his hands to where Ramsey had made his bloody mark. As the red stain began to spread out over his doublet, the king cried out, 'Strike him low! Strike him low!' Stabbing him again, Ramsey and the king watched the bleeding Ruthven collapse and stagger out of the doorway and then tumble down the stairs like a punctured red balloon, spurting blood as he did so. At the foot of the stairs, Sir Thomas Erskine almost tripped over the falling body of his king's would-be murderer. Without waiting, he took out his sword and ran the prostrate body of Alexander Ruthven through with his heavy sword. Alexander looked up at his attacker, his eyes concentrating for a second. 'Alas, I was not to blame for this' he murmured, and his head flopped to one side, his eyes sightless.

"Yanking his sword out of the dead youth, Erskine, now accompanied by Sir Hugh Harries, charged up the stairs to find the king, looking for a servant. As the three knights were bending over their seated sovereign, a noise was heard outside the room. John Ruthven, the third Earl of Gowrie, stood in the doorway. This time his hand was not stroking the hilt of his sword, for his weapon was now out and ready for action. But he was not ready enough. Suddenly, their swords withdrawn, Ramsey, Erskine and Harries all leapt at him. Ruthven did not stand a chance. Leaping backwards he found that his escape was cut off as several of the king's men had blocked his retreat down the staircase. As he raised his sword to attack Erskine, Ramsey made a low thrust under the earl's uplifted arm and stabbed the instigator of the Gowrie House plot through the chest. As Ruthven crashed to the floor in a pool of blood, his final expression was one of shock and surprise. With his death, the Gowrie House plot was over."

"Grandpa, that's a great story, but is it true? I mean all that stuff about finding a crock of gold coins and then luring the king to Gowrie House in order to bump him off. It does really sound a bit steep to me."

"Not only to you my dear, but it has, as you say, sounded a bit steep to generations of historians ever since."

"But Grandpa, isn't there any proof about this story? Didn't anyone hold an inquest of some sort? I mean, two aristocrats were killed and the king's life was threatened, no?"

"That's true. It's known that several accounts of this plot were recorded at the time, but the king had them all destroyed, all but his own version, that is. And as you can guess, historians have been sceptical about that one seeing what the king had done with the others."

"Well, what about the story of the crock of gold? Was that proved at least? I mean a crock full of gold coins can actually be seen and felt, no?"

"That's true, Sophie. But that part of the story has seemed to have faded away in light of the Ruthven attack on the king himself. But there are some things about this that we do know for certain. One, there was no love lost between the Ruthven and the Stuart families. Two, the king certainly set out for a hunting trip and then travelled over to Gowrie House. And three, if he did want to bring about any harm to the Ruthvens, he wouldn't have entered 'enemy territory' as it were with only a small band of his men.

"Yes, I suppose you're right, but it still sounds really weird to me."

"And not only to you, my dear, but in addition, I'm also pretty sure, that knowing his past record with the Ruthvens, the king certainly wouldn't have allowed himself to become separated from his escort to be led off to an isolated room at the back of the house. This is especially true as in his book, *Historical Enigmas*, the historian Hugh Ross Williamson writes that Ruthven had changed the family crest to include an armed man pointing at the crown, with the words 'For Thee Alone' inscribed on it.

"It is also known that King James, despite his being able to overpower Alexander Ruthven in the upstairs room, was more of an academic than a man of action. Physically, he was always very unsteady on his legs, and he was quoted as saying that if he hadn't been a king he'd have probably been a university man instead. And apart from anything else, we know that it was King James who was the initiator and organiser of the Bible that bears his name. So that when later he said to a minister in Edinburgh that it was well-known that he wasn't a bloodthirsty man who was out to revenge the

Ruthvens for their past behaviour, I think we can believe him."

"So what was behind this plot then?"

"Well, I think the situation was like this. Queen Elizabeth had been on the throne since 1558, that is, for forty-two years which, it must be admitted, was an extremely long time and especially so then. It was obvious that her time was drawing to a close and that, as she didn't have any children, the important question of the day was who was going to succeed her? There were two main candidates. The first was our King James whom we have just been talking about and who was supported by the Protestants, despite the fact that his mother was the Catholic Mary, Queen of Scots..."

"And the other was...?"

"The Infanta Elizabeth of Spain, the daughter of Philip II..."

"... who was supported by the Catholics."

"Exactly."

"But wait a minute, Grandpa. If she was Spanish, then I'm sure your average Englishman didn't want a foreigner, let alone a Spaniard on the throne."

"True, but you must remember that Philip II had married Elizabeth's sister, Mary, so the Infanta, the Spanish princess, did have some claim after all. In addition, I don't think that aristocratic Spaniards took the feelings of your average Englishman much into consideration. Now, if we mix all this up with English party politics of the time, we'll see where the Gowrie

House plot fits in."

"But Grandpa, there weren't any party politics then, were there?"

"No, not in the sense of the New Labour and Conservative parties, but rather parties grouped around central figures, in this case, Sir Robert Cecil, Queen Elizabeth's chief adviser, her sort of prime minister, and Robert Devereux, the Earl of Essex, the queen's favourite courtier and reputed lover. Now Essex, as pro-Protestant, had been engaged in some secret correspondence with King James about becoming the next King of England after Queen Elizabeth. Essex's plan was that, at the appropriate time, James would march south to the Anglo-Scottish border and demand that the English government recognise him as the new king. He would send the Earl of Mar as his ambassador to London, and for his part, Essex would try and take over the government in London. His efforts of course would be backed up by the new and grateful King James of England and Scotland. In theory, it was a good plan, but…"

"… it failed."

"Exactly. But I'll tell you why and about Essex's plot later. But for now, just remember that Sir Robert Cecil, he who had inherited his father William's natural deviousness, reverted to his true colours. He fully supported the succession of James over that of the Spanish Infanta, who now disappears from the scene."

"But how does the Earl of Gowrie fit into all this?"

"Well, he, in fact, like some other members of the aristocracy, had some sort of tenuous claim to the throne."

"How? He was Scottish, no?"

"Yes, but Henry VIII's sister Margaret had married the Scottish King James IV almost a hundred years earlier, which meant that the Earl of Gowrie and James VI both had claims to the English throne, although in fact James' claim was stronger."

"So in other words, you are saying that either of these two wouldn't have been too sad to see the other one get pushed out of the way?"

"Exactly, my dear Sophie. And that brings us to the ever-open question of this mysterious plot, which might also have involved an Anglo-Scottish conspiracy, to boot. The question is, did King James somehow have the situation worked out so that his men had an excuse to kill his rival, or was it Gowrie's plan to do the same, but in reverse? As we've seen, it went wrong for Gowrie and he paid the price for its failure. As Robbie Burns, Scotland's national poet wrote, 'The best laid plans o' mice and men gang aft a-gley'."

"So we don't really know who was trying to kill who."

"Exactly. And then of course there's another theory."

"With you, my dear grandpa, there always is. What is this other theory then?"

"It is possible that the Earl of Gowrie was supported by Cecil and…"

"But wait a minute, Grandpa. You've just told me that Cecil was supporting this Spanish Infanta lady."

"Yes, but unwillingly. He knew as much as anybody else how the English would have hated to have a foreigner, especially a Spaniard on the throne, and as we have noted, Mr. Cecil's other name was Mr. Devious. What I'm saying is that he may have been playing both ends against the middle."

"Meaning?"

"Meaning not only exploiting the Catholic Infanta, but also using Gowrie as a rival to King James. As I said before, only when Essex and the Gowries were safely and permanently out of the way did Cecil arrange for King James to succeed Elizabeth.

"Unfortunately, however, we shall never know the whole truth. As I said earlier, the king destroyed all the records except his own. We know that two and a half years later James did succeed the queen and proceeded to work hand in glove with Sir Robert Cecil until the latter retired in 1612. King James became known as 'the wisest fool in Christendom' and the Gowrie plot was largely forgotten. In its stead, he left historians with other plots such as the Main and Bye plots to get on with…"

"To say nothing of the Gunpowder Plot, and this is where we came in."

"Exactly. And speaking of plots, I think it's time I moved myself out of this armchair and got on with weeding my vegetable plot before your grandmother takes a dagger, or more likely a garden hoe, to me."

Chapter Twelve
Usurp the Queen: The Essex Rebellion (1601)

Robert Devereux, Earl of Essex

"Grandpa, do you remember talking about the Earl of Essex when you were telling me about the Lopez Conspiracy?"

"Yes."

"So was he really such a disgusting character as to

get someone executed, especially by being hung, drawn and quartered, just because he annoyed him?"

"Well, Sophie, Lopez did more than that. If you remember, he also spread the word that Essex, who after all was his employer, had venereal disease and I'm sure his lordship wasn't too pleased about that."

"OK. There I agree with you, but to make Lopez pay with his life still sounds a bit steep to me."

"You may be right there, but you have to remember who Essex was."

"You mean his position? Where he stood in the aristocratic pecking order?"

"No, not just that, but his character as well. I mean that he was a hot-tempered, flamboyant show-off type of fellow who had little self-control and who didn't think or plan ahead too much."

"Sounds like a really spoilt little rich boy to me."

"He was, and then in addition to all that, he spent much of his life being up against our old friend, Cecil."

"Which one, father or son?"

"Both. At first he was in opposition to the older Cecil, Sir William, who later became Lord Burghley but, later on, towards the end of the sixteenth century, his son Robert took over. The father died at the ripe old age of seventy-eight in 1598 and, by then, young Robert was well-entrenched in the saddle. I suppose if we continue with this horsey comparison, you could say that Essex was a light flashy racehorse in comparison to the solid plodding carthorse, Cecil."

"So, Grandpa, what happened to this flamboyant Earl of Essex? Did he get his just deserts, I mean, for causing Lopez to be executed?"

"Oh, he certainly got his come-uppance, but I'm not sure if, like your Signor Lopez, he didn't pay too high a price in the end for his incompetence and rashness."

"Why, what happened to him?"

"Well, Sophie, if you have time and I have enough chocolate digestives, I'll tell you all about him. The Earl of Essex, or Robert Devereux, the second earl that is, was born in 1566 with a silver spoon in his mouth. His father was the first earl and young Robert was ten years old when he succeeded his father. At the time, everything was going very well for the handsome and dashing young man. He was educated at Trinity College, Cambridge, and he also had all the right connections at court which of course then was the centre of power."

"Because of his dad?"

"No. They were probably due more to his stepfather, the Earl of Leicester, who was Queen Elizabeth's favourite courtier. In addition, it was also probably due to this gentleman that young Essex first tasted the more exciting aspects of Elizabethan life."

"Such as?"

"Well, in 1586, when our hero was a brash young man of twenty, he joined his stepfather at the Battle of Zutphen in Holland. The queen had sent troops there to fight the Spanish, you know, the usual battle of the English Protestants supporting other Protestants against the Spanish Catholics. However Leicester hadn't done so well and had lost a lot of men including his own nephew, the famous poet and courtier, Sir Philip Sidney. Essex however, had better luck. He fought bravely and was knighted for his efforts.

"Then the following year, he succeeded his stepfather and became the queen's Master of the Horse, a very important job as it meant that he always had to be in close proximity to Her Majesty. This of course kept him very happy. But then the following year he went and annoyed the queen somewhat by going and marrying Sir Philip Sidney's widow, Lady Frances Walsingham, the daughter of the queen's spymaster."

"Why did that annoy the queen?"

"Well, my dear, Sophie, if we take Essex's stepfather as an example, it seemed that the queen preferred her favourites to be eligible young bachelors without pretty wives hanging around their necks – that is, wives who were much prettier than the ageing queen herself."

"So was that the end of Essex's climb to the top?"

"Oh, no. This young man was to experience many ups and downs. In the meanwhile, he tried to keep the queen happy by running and financing a secret spy service, but of course, in doing so, he often got in the way of Sir William Cecil who was not so impressed, since both he and Walsingham were also running their own variations of MI5 and MI6."

"Whose was better?"

"Cecil's and Walsingham's of course. They were

both thirty years older and had more experience and contacts than Essex. But then Walsingham considerately died in 1590, so Essex now faced less opposition. In addition, by then, the younger Cecil, Sir Robert, had got more deeply involved in the murkier side of Elizabethan politics.

"And so, a couple of years later, Essex took part in one of Sir Francis Drake's expeditions to Portugal, and then in 1591 he himself commanded an expedition to Normandy. The aim of this was to help the French King Henri IV fight the Catholics who were giving him some trouble."

"So, so far it seemed to be going OK for our hero."

"Yes, I suppose so. Then after this French adventure was over he spent the next few years at home where he became involved in the Lopez Plot."

"And got STI, a bout of venereal disease, as well."

"Yes, that is, if he hadn't picked it up earlier. So as a result of all what I have just described, Essex had got himself some good publicity, as the media people would say today."

"Why what else did he do? Spread his cloak out over a puddle for the queen just like Sir Walter Raleigh was supposed to have done?"

"No, something even more heroic than that. He was one of the commanders of a successful attack on the Spanish port city of Cadiz. At the time, this seemed like a good thing, but in the long run, it accomplished very little except to annoy the Spanish even more.

"By now we have probably reached the high point in his career. Soon after this he was created Earl Marshal, Master of the Ordnance, Chancellor of Cambridge University as well as serving as an unofficial sort of Foreign Minister."

"So, Grandpa, you can't deny it, our hero had arrived with a vengeance."

"Well, Sophie, yes and no."

"Ooh, I hate it when you give that answer. Why yes and no this time?"

"Well yes, it was true that he was very happily basking in all those honours and titles…"

"And no?"

"And no, because as the saying goes, pride comes before a fall."

"And he fell."

"Yes, my dear, very badly. Apparently he seemed to have become so conceited over his success at Cadiz that he set off in 1597 to try and capture some Spanish treasure ships off the Azores in the Atlantic Ocean. His expedition failed. In addition to that, there was now a new political wind blowing. Feelers were being put out about starting peace negotiations with Spain especially as the queen had had enough of this long drawn-out and expensive war. The Cecils were advising the queen that this would be a good idea and she probably agreed, since she really hated financing military adventures which she thought were a waste of money. It was one thing for her to support and sponsor state piracy, like having Drake,

Hawkins and Frobisher go and capture Spanish galleons all bursting with gold doubloons, but to pay for an army and a Navy on a regular basis didn't seem to make much financial sense to her."

"So now you're saying that Essex and the Cecils were really at each other's throats?"

"Exactly. This also meant that Essex, who was a very impulsive fellow, was also becoming very careless in how he treated the queen. She might have regarded him as her favourite courtier, but she never ever let anyone forget that she was Number One, and that she wasn't going to share that title with anyone."

"Why? What terrible thing did he do?"

"He literally turned his back on her one day in front of everyone at court!"

"Oh Grandpa. How shocking!"

"My dear, Sophie. You obviously don't know anything about the rules of Elizabethan courtly etiquette. You do not turn your back on the monarch, especially if her name is Queen Elizabeth Tudor."

"So she sent him to the Tower and chopped off his head."

"Not quite. But she was so annoyed and insulted by this public insult and gross display of bad manners that, depending on which history book you read, she slapped his face or boxed his ears."

"Or both."

"Possibly. But as a result, he stormed out of the court and stayed away for five months and only came back in

September 1598. Then he and the queen made it all up between them again and…"

"And everything was hunky-dory, as my American friend, Ashley, would say."

"No, not quite. Because during this period, the Irish were beginning to get out of hand again and one of their leaders, O'Neil, the Earl of Tyrone, had started a rebellion. Essex's name was being bandied about as a possible leader of an expedition to be sent out to put down these noisy Irish rebels. However, there were a few personal and political questions to be sorted out first. It was only in March 1599 that Essex finally set out for Ireland, having persuaded the queen to agree to two of his conditions."

"I can guess what they were. One, she chops off William Cecil's head, and two, she chops off his son's."

"Not quite. One, she cancels all the debts that Essex had inherited from his father, and two, she appoints the Earl of Southampton, who was then out of favour, but who must have been one of Essex's buddies, to be the General of the Horse. The queen agreed and so Essex set off for Ireland in March, with the good people of London shouting, 'God bless Your Lordship' and 'God preserve Your Honour' etc. while in the background, Sir Robert Cecil was smiling from ear to ear."

"And his dad?"

"He was dead. He had died the year before, so young Robert, who was about thirty years old, was now minding the store."

"So why was Cecil smiling so much? Essex now had the chance to come back from Ireland as a winner, you know, the queen's man who knows how to impose law and order, no?"

"Not really. You see, first of all, Essex was now out of the way, away from court and where all the action took place, and also Ireland had a reputation of being the graveyard of reputations."

"And was it like that for Essex?"

"Oh yes, my dear. It certainly was. As soon as he arrived, he ran into stiff opposition from the Irish rebels, and within three to four months his army of sixteen thousand men had melted away to a mere quarter of that number."

"Why? Were the Irish such great fighters?"

"That's part of the answer, while the other part is that many of his men deserted him and many others died of disease, etc. Then, to make matters worse, the queen fired Southampton and sent Essex a letter not allowing him to return to England as he had planned to do. The next stage was for Essex to go and put down a rebellion in Ulster."

"Sounds familiar. The British fighting in Ulster."

"That's true. This Essex story is just one chapter in the very long centuries-old Anglo-Irish saga. The result was that Essex went off to Ulster, failed and considered returning to England. Fortunately, he was talked out of doing such a rash deed and instead he arranged to meet O'Neil, the rebel chief, and come to some sort of agreement or cease-fire with him. This he did, and the fighting stopped, at least for a while."

"So that was good, no? I mean the fighting came to an end and the queen wouldn't have to spend any more money on her army."

"Perhaps so, but in fact she was furious since she considered that the truce that Essex had signed was more favourable to the rebels than to the English."

"And, Grandpa, I suppose that while this was going on, Cecil was having a good laugh."

"I suppose so. And then after Essex had finished with O'Neil, he jumped on his horse and galloped off to London."

"Without permission from the queen?"

"Without her permission. According to the popular story, he arrived at the queen's palace at Nonsuch in Surrey in his muddy riding clothes and burst into the queen's private chamber while she was wearing her royal nightie and with her hair in rollers."

"I'm sure that would have hit the headlines if they had existed back then."

"It did, well, at least the Elizabethan equivalent. But somehow, love overcomes all, because she didn't box his ears this time and according to the contemporary records, Elizabeth was seen to be very pleased and thanked God that even though he had suffered so many storms abroad, he had returned home safe and sound."

"I'm sure Cecil wasn't pleased about that."

"Exactly, but soon Essex was in hot water again, and

this time all the way up to the Elizabethan ruff around his Elizabethan neck."

"Why? What now?"

"He was accused by the opposition, that is, those aristocrats who couldn't stand him, of having left his post in Ireland without having obtained royal permission to do so beforehand. As a result, it was decided to look into Essex's behaviour and conduct during the war at a special meeting of the Star Chamber. However, unfortunately for Essex, he wasn't allowed to attend it in order to defend himself or justify his behaviour at all."

"Grandpa, that doesn't sound very fair to me."

"It wasn't. And I wouldn't be surprised if Sir Robert Cecil didn't have a hand in this. So, six months were to pass, that is, with Essex being held under house arrest until June 1600 when he was brought before a hearing at York House. After a lengthy session, his punishment for desertion, that is, rushing back to London without permission, was read out."

"The chop!"

"Don't be so bloodthirsty, my dear. No, he was fired from all his public offices and duties, except his Mastership of the Horse. In addition, his monopoly for the importing of sweet wine was cancelled and this one really hit home because this was Essex's major source of income."

"So by now he'd really hit rock bottom, no?"

"Very much so, my dear. And this is the scene where

Essex the rebuffed lover and favourite of the queen turns into Essex the bitter and angry plotter. He was determined to have revenge on Sir Robert Cecil and his pals whom he saw as responsible for his grim situation, that is, no money and no political clout."

"So, Grandpa, what did he do? Did he try and sneak into the palace at night? Or did he pay someone to kill Cecil in some lonely dark London alleyway?"

"Oh, no, my dear Sophie. Nothing like that. Such actions were not Essex's style. If he were to act at all, it would be big and bold, and for everyone to see."

"And was his action big and bold?"

"Yes and no. It was certainly no sneaky affair, but it turned out to be much less grandiose than what he had planned. So, between the time of his downfall over Ireland in the summer of 1600 and February 1601, Essex began plotting to have his revenge. You know, contacting people who had a grudge against Cecil or the establishment and having secret meetings and all that sort of thing. His basic plan however was pretty simple. He would gather around him all those malcontents and others who had a chip on their shoulder, and they would all go in a body to the court and force the queen to fire Cecil, Raleigh and the others and then bring about a new state of affairs. But, he said, the queen wasn't to be harmed."

"Sounds a bit like a *coup d'état* in a banana republic to me."

"Exactly."

"And did it work?"

"Hear me out and you'll see. So Essex being Essex, he couldn't organise something like a *coup d'état* quietly like all good plotters should. No, there were all sorts of people who kept coming and going to Essex House, his London home. Now, the authorities of course, who were always jumpy and on the lookout, became very suspicious. I mean all sorts of people like unemployed soldiers, Puritan priests as well as aristocrats such as Sir Charles Danvers were forever attending meetings there and so the queen's Privy Council decided to send one of the Lord Treasurer's sons to find out what was going on.

"This man then reported back about what he had seen and heard, and on February 7, Essex was summoned to court to account for his behaviour as well as to be personally reprimanded for holding unlawful gatherings. He was ordered to leave London and go and stay in one of his country homes where he would be out of the way."

"Did he do all this?"

"No, not at all. In reply, he sent a message to the queen, who incidentally he hadn't seen for months, telling her that he was sick and couldn't come. And yes, they decided to have some pre-*coup* entertainment as well"

"What, Grandpa, did they bring in some dancing girls or the Elizabethan equivalent?"

"No, no. They commanded Shakespeare's band of

players to put on for them a special performance of his play, *Richard the Second*."

"What was so special about that?"

"Because, my dear, this play, *Richard the Second,* deals with overthrowing the monarchy and that at the end of the play, the king is murdered."

"I see, and I bet that didn't go down well when the news leaked out."

"You're right, and then the same evening Essex called all his chief conspirators together and they decided to put out a story that there had been a plot to murder him by a gang of four Jesuits."

"Why did he say that?"

"Well, first of all, Essex knew that he was very popular with the ordinary 'man-in-the-street', so he would appear to be the poor underdog and so gain their sympathy. Secondly, it was always good policy to blame the Jesuits and Catholics for anything that smelled bad. That was a sure way of gaining public sympathy."

"And did his plan work?"

"No, not really. The next day, Essex decided to carry out his *coup*. According to the records, 'three hundred of prime note' gathered at Essex House and while he was giving them their last-minute instructions, the Lord Keeper with three other lords were dispatched by the queen to find out what all the fuss and commotion was about."

"How did she hear about this so quickly?"

"Well, don't forget, Sophie, London wasn't the big

sprawled out city that it is today, and also, all these places, like Essex House and the palace, weren't really too far away from each other. Besides, knowing Cecil, who was really a cunning old fox, the authorities had their spies and tell-tales all over the place."

"I see. So what happened next?"

"When this deputation of four lords turned up at Essex House and ordered Essex to disperse this unlawful gathering, Essex promptly took hold of them and locked them up in his library. Then he and his men set off in the direction of the city, but this in fact showed bad timing on his part."

"Why?"

"Simply because his plans hadn't been completely worked out. Remember, my dear Sophie, if you wish to carry out a *coup d'état*, make sure that all your people are in position and know what they are supposed to do. This wasn't the case with Essex. The arrival of the four lords had caused him to rush his plans, and so Essex and Co. set off for the city, not fully prepared for what would happen. By this I mean that they had no contingency plans and no Plan B to fall back on if Plan A failed. The original plan had been to ride over to St. Paul's Cross, make a public announcement about their cause and then wait for hundreds of people to join them."

"But this didn't happen."

"Far from it. Since he'd been rushed, Essex in his usual impulsive way set off with most of his men behind him on foot as they hadn't had time to get their horses.

That was one thing. Another thing was that Essex hadn't taken a prepared speech with him, so all he could do was to shout out that there were plans afoot to murder him. So instead of arriving at St. Paul's Cross to make his announcement, he went to the sheriff's house, the commander of the city's militia and told him what was up."

"And then the sheriff arrested him?"

"Not quite. The sheriff went to consult with the Lord Mayor of London, but in the meanwhile, Essex had been officially declared a traitor. The queen and her court assembled their troops and made ready to put down this *coup*, or as it has been called since then, the Essex Revolt or Rebellion. By this time, I suppose Essex saw that things weren't going too well so he sent one of his chief plotters, Sir Ferdinando Gorges, back to Essex House to release the four lords from the library. Gorges then accompanied the lords back to court to see what could be done, I suppose to try and come up with some sort of compromise or honourable retreat."

"I bet the queen wasn't in much of a listening mood."

"You're right. And especially as her former lover had been declared a traitor. The result was that Essex decided to take himself and his followers back to Essex House, but on the way they found that the queen's troops had cut them off at Ludgate Hill. Essex then tried to give them the slip by going home another way and in the meanwhile he had someone burn some incriminating documents. However, he was unsuccessful again and discovered that the authorities had blocked off the other way he had chosen. This meant that by the time it was evening, the whole affair had fizzled out. Essex, Southampton and some other important lords were arrested and taken to the Tower and their houses were searched as well. The government declared a state of emergency and a watch was kept on the ports."

"That was over-reacting a bit, wasn't it?"

"Probably, but remember, until the authorities had completed their investigations, they couldn't know how widespread or not this whole affair was. Unfortunately for Essex, the Council didn't waste any time, for within two weeks, on February 19 to be precise, Essex and Southampton were put on trial at Westminster Hall, to be tried by the Lord High Steward, the Lord Treasurer and twenty-five other members of the aristocracy."

"Nothing too big for the Earl of Essex, eh?"

"Exactly. I'm also sure that several of the lords wanted to be seen to be there as a way of proving their loyalty to the Crown."

"What was he charged with exactly?"

"Oh, the usual things. Surprising the queen's court, entering the City of London with the purpose of inciting a rebellion, as well as being armed. He was also charged with defending, that is, preventing Her Majesty's troops from entering his house and stuff like that."

"So in other words, Grandpa, they really threw the whole book at him."

"Oh yes, Sophie, they certainly did. Essex had really

played himself right into their hands this time. But this time, as opposed to the post-Ireland investigation, he was allowed to defend himself. However, one of his past friends, Sir Francis Bacon, who Essex had been counting on, now turned his back on him and acted as one of Her Majesty's judges.

"In addition to that, having to defend himself against the bullying of Sir Edward Coke and the wily old Sir Robert Cecil also meant that the results of this trial or investigation were pretty well a foregone conclusion."

"Hmm, so in a way it sounds as if Essex got some of what he had dished out to poor ol' Lopez in the past."

"Exactly. And yes, just to make sure there would be no judicial slip-ups, various officials were sent to speak to Essex in the Tower and, after he confessed to the above charges, he decided to implicate various other people who had taken part in the plot, including the Earl of Southampton who …"

"Wasn't he one of Shakespeare's patrons?"

"Yes, Sophie, but none of these big names cut much ice with the judges. The result was that the punishment for treason, the death penalty, was to be carried out a few days later, on 25 February 1601."

"The government certainly didn't waste any time, did they?"

"No, Sophie. Justice was to be carried out swiftly, as a warning to any other would-be plotters. However, unlike other cases, justice was not going to be seen to be done, at least not by too many people. That was because the court agreed to grant Essex one of his last wishes, that is, to be executed privately and not on Tower Hill in front of a huge mob."

"Hmm, I'm sure that was good to know, especially when they were going to cut your head off."

Professor Warkworth shrugged. "Perhaps, but now we come to the last chapter in Essex's action-packed life. On 25 February, he was taken out to the inner courtyard in the Tower of London and only about a hundred people were allowed to witness this bloody event. In keeping with tradition, he forgave the executioner and then started praying. When he'd finished, he removed his black hat and cloak and stood there, flashy as ever in a bright red jacket. His last words were, 'O Lord, into Thy hands I commend my spirit', and then he laid his fair head on the block."

"Grandpa, I'm not sure I want to hear the rest of this."

"You're right my dear. It wasn't very nice at all. The executioner didn't do a good job and it took him three blows to remove the head. After that, things of course had to be done in style, for this was Essex's body after all, so he was buried by the Duke of Norfolk and the Earl of Arundel."

"And that was the end of the Essex Rebellion."

"Yes, but there was of course some clearing up to do. Various lords and others who had sided with him were tried. Two were beheaded on Tower Hill, and two others, of a lesser rank, were hanged at Tyburn. Other more minor players had to pay very stiff fines. One of these was a Robert Catesby who had to sell one of his country houses in order to pay a fine of four thousand marks, which was a small fortune. This embittered him so much that it is not surprising to find out that he became one of the leading lights in the next major plot against the government, the Gunpowder Plot."

"Which of course we'll talk about later."

"Of course. But you know Sophie, one of the interesting things that I've found out about Essex's life is that there was quite a connection between his and his father's life too. In addition, Essex's own son, the third earl's life also continued in his father's footsteps in much the same way. So, it seems that there was a strong thread that wound its way through the three generations of Essex, or to give our unhappy earl his full title, Robert Devereux, second Earl of Essex, Viscount Hereford, Lord Ferrers and Lord Bourchier."

"Wow! He certainly collected titles and honours while he was around."

"Oh, he did that all right. Now in connection with his father, there were three things they had in common. First, his father was promoted to be a High Marshal. Second, he was sent to Ulster to put down a rebellion, which he did with great cruelty, and finally, he too died at the age of thirty-five, although this time it was from natural causes."

"And Essex's son?"

"The third earl, the son of our impetuous hero was like his father in that he inherited the title at the age of ten and he also fought the Spanish at Cadiz. Also, like his father, he started off as a staunch supporter of his ruler, in this case King Charles I, but then turned against him, though in a much more organised way than his father had done."

"How?"

"The third Earl of Essex, who was also called Robert Devereux, fought on Cromwell's side during the Civil War and even led the Parliamentary army at the Battle of Edgehill in 1642. Here he did quite well, but when he turned south, it was like a repeat performance of his father's military career in Ireland…"

"He was defeated by the locals?"

"That's right, my dear. After he had led his troops into a defeat at Lostwithiel in Cornwall, he passed the command over to Major-General Skippon and abandoned the Army just like his father had done in Ireland over forty years before. As with the second earl and the queen, he was severely reprimanded by his ruler, Oliver Cromwell in this case, and then he resigned from the Army. Perhaps it was no coincidence that he died within a year…"

"Just like his father had done after his failure in Ireland and the trial that followed."

"Exactly, except that this time, this Earl of Essex died in bed."

Chapter Thirteen
The Gunpowder Plot, 5 November, 1605

The Gunpowder Plotters. Guy Fawkes is third on the right.

"Grandpa, do you remember when you said that the best-known mystery in English history is about Richard III and the princes in the Tower?"

"Yes."

"Well, what do you think is the best-known plot in English history?"

"Oh, that's an easy one, Sophie. The Gunpowder Plot, of course."

"You mean Guy Fawkes and all that, and blowing up

the Houses of Parliament and killing the king?"

"Yes, but that was only half the story."

"There was more?"

"Oh, certainly. Blowing up Parliament was only the first part of what Guy Fawkes and Co. had planned to do. Their plot was much more grandiose than that."

"So why isn't that part as famous as the rest of the plot?"

"Probably because the first part, that is, trying to blow up the king and Parliament is the most dramatic part of the story, while the second part, that is, kidnapping the king's daughter, Princess Elizabeth, and setting her up on the throne as a new Catholic queen, never happened."

"Yes, I suppose you're right, Grandpa. I mean the image of Guy Fawkes hiding in the dark cellars under the parliament building just about to light the blue touch-paper does have a certain dramatic element to it. And then getting caught just as he was about to do so really adds to the drama. By the way, was it just some rotten coincidence that he was caught, or did someone squeal on him?"

"Well, my dear, that's a difficult question to answer, because no one knows what really happened before Guy Fawkes was caught. There are all sorts of theories of course, and there's also the famous document, the 'Monteagle Letter,' which was supposed to be a warning letter. However, the question is, who wrote this letter and why? But you know, instead of jumping into the middle of this story, let's go back to the very beginning.

"Guy Fawkes was born in 1570 in York. His family, especially his mother, were recusants, Catholics who practised their religion in secret. Life in those days can't have been too much fun for the Catholics. Remember Mary Tudor, Bloody Mary, as the Protestant historians call her, had died only twelve years earlier, and her younger sister, Elizabeth, now queen, as well as her advisers..."

"... Cecil and Walsingham..."

"Exactly, were scared stiff that the Catholics, of whom there were still many in England, would stage a comeback as it were. Therefore, any time there were signs of the Catholics making any sort of protest, the authorities would come down on them like a ton of bricks."

"How?"

"The usual methods. Huge fines, confiscating land and property, as well as prison sentences if necessary."

"They didn't burn them at the stake or chop off their heads?"

"No, not usually, that is unless they really went too far, like carrying out acts of treason or things like that. I think Queen Elizabeth was too shrewd to execute too many people. After all, she wasn't interested in creating new Catholic martyrs. There were more than enough as it were for her. No, it seems that if the Catholics practised their religion secretly, or at least, didn't make a lot of noise about it, then she was prepared to turn a blind eye to them. In the end, what Elizabeth was interested in was peace and quiet at home and not an ongoing state of fear and repression. Besides, fining people brought in money to the state's coffers. Chopping off heads or burning people at the stake only created more martyrs."

"Like her father and her sister, Mary, had done?"

"Exactly. Now, in the meanwhile there were several Catholic plots which aimed at removing her and replacing her with the Catholic Mary, Queen of Scots."

"Like the Babington and the Ridolfi Plots?"

"Yes, but thanks to the inefficiency of Babington and others and the efficiency of Cecil and Walsingham's spy networks, these plots came to nothing. However, these plots still managed to keep the Catholic kettle bubbling as it were and give them a bad name. I suspect that as usual it was the small number of Catholic extremists who gave the rest of their co-religionists a bad reputation."

"Like the various ISIS terrorists and Al-Qaeda gang giving ordinary peace-loving Muslims a bad name today."

"Exactly. So, imagine the joy of the English Catholics when at the beginning of 1603 Queen Elizabeth I died after reigning for forty-five years. The new king was the son of the Catholic Mary, Queen of Scots, that is, King James VI of Scotland who became King James I of England as well. The transfer of power and of dynasties went pretty smoothly, thanks to various people including Cecil junior, that is, Sir Robert Cecil. He had inherited the task of being the unofficial prime minister from his father, who had died five years beforehand. The English Catholics now saw that this was the opportunity to press their case and remind the king of his Catholic background and how the wicked Protestant Queen Elizabeth had chopped off his mother's head.

"However, unfortunately for them, King James wasn't interested in any of this. All he wanted was a quiet life. He wasn't interested in turning England upside down again as Mary Tudor had done half a century earlier. So instead, he said a few nice words to the leading Catholics and sent them on their way. They felt that life for them would be better, while in fact King James carried on more or less with the same policies that Elizabeth had pursued. I say more or less, because in actual fact he went one stage further than Elizabeth. He signed a peace-treaty with King Philip II's son, King Philip III, of Spain."

"Wow! That was revolutionary. I mean after the Spanish Armada and all those years of fighting. So what made him do that?"

"Well, first of all it was good for trade, and secondly, neither England nor Spain really wanted to go to war at that time. King James I and King Philip III may not have liked each other very much, if at all, but they both realised that peace was better than war."

"I bet your English Catholic extremists were pleased with that one. I mean their king was now making peace with the chief Catholic ruler, that is, apart from the Pope."

"Exactly. But in everyday terms it didn't make life in England any easier for them and the system of fines and other punishments continued as before. In fact, it was so bad, that one of them, a Robert Catesby, known by his friends as Robin, decided to do something about the whole situation. He gathered a few other discontented Catholics together in a London inn called The Duck & Drake in order to discuss what to do."

"Was Guy Fawkes there?"

"He most certainly was. But our red-headed hero was the only one present who was not related to the others in terms of family connections."

"So why did they rope him in? How did they know they could trust him? After all, he may have been one of Cecil's spies for all they knew, no?"

"Yes, Sophie, that's true, but they roped him in because they had first checked him out and found out that he was an expert on gunpowder."

"How so?"

"They discovered that he had served for several years in the Spanish Netherlands as some sort of sapper, a kind of military engineer, and that he was also known as a good God-fearing Catholic. But to continue with our story. One day Catesby and four of his Catholic associates were sitting around in The Duck & Drake. He had asked them all to meet him there because he wished to disclose his plan to them on how to bring about a radical change for the benefit for the Catholic population in England.

So, my dear Sophie, use your imagination and cast your mind back to The Duck & Drake inn to over four hundred years back in 1604. To Sunday 20 May 1604 to be precise:

Catesby: And so gentlemen, I think that before we start we should all introduce ourselves, especially as while I know my cousin – my second cousin, that is, Thomas Wintour who knows me as Robin – not all of us know each other well, especially our new friend here, Guy Fawkes.

Fawkes: Excuse me, Robert, but if you are going to use my name, please call me Guido and not Guy.

Catesby: Why? Jack Wright here told me that your name was Guy. That's the name he said he knew you by when you were both growing up together in York.

Fawkes: He was right then. But when I was soldiering in the Spanish Netherlands my Catholic friends there called me Guido and since then that has become my real name.

Catesby: So be it. Anyway, Guido here doesn't know any of us except Tom Wintour who brought him over from Flanders, and I think we should all take turns in introducing ourselves. Is that agreed?

All: Agreed.

Catesby: So I shall begin as I was the one who invited you all over to this somewhat rundown drinking establishment.

Wintour: You're right there. Even the ale tastes somewhat rundown.

Catesby: True, but let me start. First of all, let me tell you that Tom here and I are second cousins and that both of us are part of the huge Vaux-Tresham-Throckmorton-Monteagle-Habington clan.

Wright: Habington? Weren't some of them involved in the Babington Plot nearly twenty years ago?

Catesby: That's right. That was Thomas Habington. He managed to stay out of Walsingham's clutches for a few weeks after Babington was caught, but in the end he was hanged, drawn and quartered together with Babington, Ballard and the others.

Wright: And wasn't Monteagle the Catholic lord who tried to defend the Catholic cause in Parliament?

Catesby: Right again. But mark you, he had to spend four days in the Fleet prison for his pains.

Percy: He was lucky to be released after only four days. Others have been kept in there for much longer.

Catesby: That's true enough, Thomas. But now let me tell you something about myself. I'm just over thirty years old and I can count among my ancestors William Catesby, one of Richard III's most important advisors. My father was also called William and one of my first memories of him is when I was eight years old and the queen's soldiers came to our house and arrested him, together with Sir Thomas Tresham.

Fawkes: Why? Because he was a Catholic?

Catesby: Yes, but not just because of that. They arrested him because he was a Catholic whom the authorities thought had helped Father Edmund Campion stay out of Walsingham's clutches. It's true that they released my father later, but after that it seemed to me that whenever Walsingham wanted a scapegoat, he'd arrest my father and other prominent Catholic recusants. He'd either put them in prison for a while or fine them heavily.

Percy: Or both.

Catesby: That's right. In fact, in the end my father ended up paying about a fifth of the value of his estates in fines.

Wright: And what were you doing all this time?

Catesby: Me? I had started studying at Oxford but I left before taking the final exams for my degree.

Fawkes: Why?

Catesby: Because that would have meant taking the Oath of Supremacy – you know, the oath stating that Queen Elizabeth was the Head of the Church.

Fawkes: So what did you do?

Catesby: I went abroad to take a course in Catholic religious studies. I was there on the Continent for a few years and then I returned and married Catherine Leigh, my beautiful wife from Warwickshire. We had two sons, William and Robert. Unfortunately, William died when he was very young, but my canny young Robert is still alive.

Percy: Well Robin, that's the way of the world. Some survive and some don't.

Catesby: I know that, Thomas, but unfortunately my beautiful and beloved Catherine died soon after, and so for the past ten years or so I've been on my own – that is, with my mother of course at her country home in Ashby St. Ledgers in Northamptonshire – but I've never remarried. I'd never find anyone like my Catherine so I haven't even looked.

Wright: So what are you saying? Has the life of a bachelor been good for you or not?

Catesby: I don't really know. I miss my Cathy a lot and I always will. But on the other hand, I have a lot of true friends and so I've never been lonely or felt that I'm on my own. And of course, I really got to know the value of friendship when you, Jack and I were imprisoned together several years ago.

Fawkes: Why were you three in prison? What had you done?

Catesby: Oh, that was part of Cecil's anti-Catholic campaign when Queen Elizabeth was ill. The authorities were so scared that we Catholics would exploit the occasion to start a rebellion, or something like that, that they arrested many leading Catholics like myself. So that's when I met Jack Wright here and his brother, Kit, as well as my kinsman, Francis Tresham, and a few other good people. Luckily we were all released after the queen recovered, but then I got into trouble again, but this time it was my fault and not just because I was a Catholic.

Wintour: Are you talking about the Essex Rebellion?

Catesby: Aye. That's right. I thought that as he was supported by the Catholics and the Puritans, and all the others who were against Cecil, we would succeed in getting rid of that odious man and all his party, but it didn't work.

Fawkes: Why? What happened?

Catesby: Oh, we marched with Essex all right, right into the city. But there we found that we were up against the queen's men. There was some sort of scuffle and I was slightly wounded, but it was nothing serious. A mere scratch made by a sword. Anyway, in the end, I and several others found ourselves under arrest.

Fawkes: For treason, no doubt.

Catesby: Not quite, but it could very easily have been. However, fortunately for me, the authorities thought I was really only a very small fish in this particular pond and so I was fined instead. But I must add, it was a mighty large fine.

Fawkes: How large is mighty large?

Catesby: Four thousand marks. I had to sell one of our family homes, the one at Castleton, to a local wool merchant to pay it off.

Wright: But that didn't break you, did it, Robin?

Catesby: Fortunately, no. And then I became involved in the Spanish Treason Plot, that is, together with Jack Wright's brother, Francis Tresham, Lord Monteagle and Father Henry Garnett.

Fawkes: And what was that about?

Wright: Robin, I'll tell him. The idea was to send Thomas Wintour here and me to Spain to see if we could obtain help, either financial or military...

Wintour: Or both.

Wright: Yes, to re-establish Catholic rule in this country, you know, from King Philip and the Spanish authorities and the Church.

Fawkes: And what happened?

Wintour: Nothing. We got some promises of help, but nothing else.

Wright: That's right. The Spanish said they'd support us after we had succeeded in establishing Catholic rule in this country, but until then we would be on our own.

Fawkes: So that's exactly where we stand at the

moment. Unless we can bring down this King James and his parliament, we are not going to get any help.

Catesby: Exactly. Except in a way, it's worse than that. If you gentlemen remember, a few months ago, that is, at the beginning of the year, the king read out a new proclamation. He ordered all Catholic priests to leave the country and stated that all past fines for recusancy which hadn't been paid would have to be paid, and in full.

Percy: Aye Robin, but that's not all. Don't forget, he introduced another bill into Parliament last month that stated that all Catholics should be ex-communicated.

Wright: That's right Thomas. We, as Catholics will be completely ruined if that bill is passed. We will have no status at all. We'll be just like the Jews were in England three hundred years ago. Well, I for one have had enough of this persecution. I've already suffered enough during the past queen's reign, and like Robin, I was also arrested and thrown into prison when that accursed queen fell ill.

Wintour: Aye, but fortunately for you she recovered soon after, otherwise you'd still be rotting in the Tower.

Percy: That's right. That is, if they hadn't executed you in the meanwhile.

Wright: True. And then to rot in solitary confinement in

the Tower after Essex's fiasco was another grim experience.

Fawkes: So I see you gentlemen are very familiar with the Tower of London.

Wright: Oh, we certainly are. But after Essex's Rebellion I decided to lie low for a while and so I moved to Lincolnshire.

Catesby: Aye, but then you moved to one of my houses at Lapworth in Warwickshire.

Wright: That's correct, and that's where I've been living until recently.

Fawkes: And where were you, Thomas? Have you also stayed away from London?

Percy: Aye, man. I have that. I was even further away than Lincolnshire. I was living at Alnwick.

Fawkes: In Northumberland? Near the Scottish border?

Percy: Aye. I was serving my kinsman, the Earl of Northumberland. I was his agent, his collector of rents. I was so good at it that he made me the Constable of Alnwick Castle. But then I got involved in a swordfight with one of the Border Scots, so I had to lie low for a while.

Fawkes: But how did you become involved with Robin?

Percy: Oh, through our mutual Catholic connections. In fact, recently I said to Robin when we were discussing our present state in England with friends, and I'll say it again, 'Shall we always talk and never do anything about this situation?'.

Catesby: Aye, that's true enough, Thomas. And that's why we are here now, Guido. To do something!

Fawkes: Well, I'm glad we're not here just to talk. But before you say more, tell me, Thomas, are you also from the North?

Wintour: Oh, no. Not me. I'm from Worcestershire. From a good Catholic family, just like the rest of us. In fact, my uncle Francis Ingelby was a priest, and he was hanged, drawn and quartered over fifteen years ago.

Fawkes: I see. And what have you been doing in the meanwhile?

Wintour: Well, like you, Guido, I went over to Flanders, and I also spent some time in France. At first my Catholicism didn't really mean much to me, but when I saw how much we were being persecuted, I began to believe more in our cause and in the end I even travelled to Spain to get support from King Philip. In fact, it was while I was travelling about on the Continent that I first met you in Flanders.

Fawkes: That's right. But now we have to see what can be done to relieve the situation for us Catholics in England.

Percy: Very true, Guido. We must stop this endless crying and talking and do something instead. Something that will change the situation. And for ever. We must do something that will be remembered forever."

"That's right, Grandpa. They tried to blow up the Houses of Parliament."

"Yes, Sophie, but it wasn't as simple or as quick as that."

"Why not?"

"Well, first of all, they had to get their hands on enough gunpowder. Then they had to store it far away from inquisitive eyes. And then after that, they had to move it into position under the Palace of Westminster, the building where Parliament used to sit. In other words, the plotters had to contend with many logistical problems, including the finding of a suitable date for their action, and this itself was a problem."

"Why?"

"Because while they were planning to carry out their plot, Parliament decided to change the date when the king, his family and all the MPs would be present for the opening ceremony. At first they planned on some date in February 1605, but then there was a scare about the plague breaking out in London. Therefore, they decided to postpone the opening of Parliament until after the summer, that is, to reopen Parliament in October 1605."

"But surely that should have given the plotters more time to get organised, no?"

"True, but it also meant that there was a greater possibility of more people learning about what they were up to."

"Yes, I suppose you're right. But wait a minute, Grandpa. You just said October, but Bonfire Night is in November."

"Yes, I know that, Sophie, but during the summer of 1605, it was decided to postpone the opening yet again because of the plague. This time the authorities decided the official opening would be on November 5, and since then, that has become the most famous date in English history, that and 1066."

"That's right, Grandpa. Everyone knows those two dates even if they don't know anything else about history. But what did Guy Fawkes and the others do in the meanwhile, that is apart from biting their nails while waiting?"

"Oh, my dear Sophie. They had lots to do to keep themselves occupied. First of all, they had to find lodgings that were as near as possible to the Palace of Westminster. Then they had to plan and actually dig a tunnel from below this house which would end up under the Parliament building itself."

"That must have been a problem, I mean getting hold of a place that was convenient for them, and especially one with a cellar."

"Well, if it was easy or not, they did manage to get hold of such a place which was near enough for their purpose. And after that, according to tradition, they began to dig a tunnel. However, they didn't have too much luck as they found it hard going. You must remember that, apart from Guy Fawkes, these plotters were not used to heavy manual work. And in addition to all this, water from the Thames started to seep into their tunnel."

"So did they abandon it?"

"Yes, but then they had a stroke of luck. Thomas Percy, the one who was related to the Earl of Northumberland, was appointed as a Gentleman Pensioner and with this title he then had the right to mix with all the high society of his day. This meant of course that no one questioned his presence when he appeared in the Palace of Westminster and…"

"So he could get away with murder, as it were."

"Exactly, Sophie. This also meant that he was able to rent a house from a man called Whynniard and this house had a cellar which was situated so that it extended to just below the House of Lords."

"That was lucky for them."

"Exactly. So Percy, in his new role as Gentleman Pensioner, then took on a servant, a Master John Johnson, who was in fact none other than our hero, Guy Fawkes. So now all they had to do was to clear out all the loose rubbish from Whynniard's cellar and store their gunpowder there instead."

"But wait a minute, Grandpa. Wouldn't the other people who had cellars down there start asking questions and be suspicious if they saw barrels of gunpowder lying around?"

"Oh, the gunpowder plotters weren't as naïve as all that. As with all respectable citizens of the time, they let it be known that they were storing wood for winter fuel in the cellar. However, underneath their piles of wood, they were busily accumulating barrels and barrels of gunpowder. And in addition to all this, my dear Sophie, you must remember that we are talking about underground cellars, and the darkness down there certainly worked in the plotters' favour."

"So, Grandpa, how much gunpowder did they actually succeed in storing down there?"

"Well according to the records, they had about thirty-six barrels of gunpowder, that is, well over a tonne of the stuff."

"Wow! If that lot had gone up, there surely would have been a real fireworks display!"

"Oh it certainly would have been that all right. But as we know, it never happened."

"And did this band of plotters remain so small? I mean, if they had plans to bring about major changes in the country, then five plotters wouldn't have been enough, right?"

"Right. From this time on, that is from the autumn of 1604, other men were recruited to join them. The first one was Robert Keyes. He was about forty years old and his background was similar to that of Guy Fawkes. His father was a Protestant, but his mother was a practising Catholic. Keyes' job was to look after Catesby's London house at Lambeth, which it just so happened was on the other side of the river facing the Palace of Westminster. This of course facilitated moving the gunpowder that Catesby had bought from over the river straight into Thomas Percy's cellar. Then it was through Keyes that another man, Ambrose Rookwood, joined the conspirators."

"Grandpa, how did Catesby and the others know they could trust the new men? I mean, Cecil had his spies all over the place, no?"

"True, but it so happened that virtually all the central group of the plotters belonged to one of three large well-known Catholic families – the Catesbys, the Wrights and the Percys. This was probably their best way of preserving the necessary secrecy."

"I see, and as you said, Guy Fawkes was known to them through his army service, but that leaves one more, no?"

"Yes, the most aristocratic one of them all. The suave, rich and debonair Sir Everard Digby, but I'll tell you more about him later. Just let's say, that like Fawkes he wasn't related to them, but like Rookwood, he was recruited as a keen Catholic supporter and because he could supply the necessary logistical support in the form of money and horses. In fact, he joined this gang only in about October 1605 and there are theories that he was never told everything and that he didn't really know what he was letting himself into."

"By the way, Grandpa, what did they want horses for?"

"For getting away from the scene of the crime – the seventeenth century equivalent of getaway cars. The plotters realised that as soon as they had blown up the Palace of Westminster they would have to get away from London and the authorities as fast as possible and it was plotters such as Rookwood and Digby who were particularly useful here.

"So in the end there were thirteen conspirators who made up the inner circle. The first five included the instigator of the plot, Robert Catesby, as well as Guy Fawkes, Thomas Wintour, Thomas Percy and Fawkes' schoolboy pal from York, Jack Wright. Later, Wintour's brother, Robert, joined them as did Jack Wright's brother, Christopher, who was usually known as Kit. Then the Wintour's brother-in-law, John Grant, was brought in as was Catesby's cousin, Francis Tresham. Then we have Robert Keyes and his kinsman, Ambrose Rookwood, and finally Sir Everard Digby and Catesby's servant, Thomas Bates. There we are, thirteen in all."

"But wasn't thirteen an unlucky number?"

"Yes, as it turned out."

"But, Grandpa, tell me more about this Sir Everard Digby. He sounds quite fascinating. I mean, how often do you hear of rich aristocrats who mix with plotters who spend their time plotting in badly-lit inns and places like that?"

"Oh, Sir Everard was certainly an aristocratic sort of chap. He was a tall and athletic-looking courtier who was very wealthy, very popular and was a keen sportsman and horseman. He was madly in love with his wife, Mary, who loved him just as much in return."

"In other words, he had it all."

"Exactly."

"So what made him join Guy Fawkes and Co.?"

"Well, he and his wife were converts to Catholicism, but at first neither of them knew that the other one had done so. When they found out, they were both pretty shocked and then very pleased. As a result, they built a secret chapel in their country home for their own use and for the use of their new-found Catholic friends. And as I said before, as with Ambrose Rookwood, Sir Everard Digby was very useful for the plotters as he was able to help them financially and he also had a stable of fine horses which would be used for their future escape plans. In the end, his job was to remain in the Midlands and be ready to help the plotters after they had fled London. He was also able to round up a group of Catholic supporters who would then back up the plotters when they took over England and changed the clock back to a Catholic regime."

"But it still sounds to me, Grandpa, like they still didn't have enough people to carry out their plan. I mean, a central core of plotters and a few others doesn't sound like really enough men to me to turn the whole country around."

"You're right. And that was one of the main weaknesses of the whole conspiracy. They were too few and they wanted too much. Obviously, just to blow up the king and his parliament wasn't enough to get the Catholics back into power again. And to bring back the 'good old days' of Mary Tudor, the plotters would have needed hundreds, if not thousands of supporters spread out all over the country, something they never had. Naturally, as they were scared of letting too many people into their secret, they remained a very small band of ardent conspirators to the very end."

"And their end was pretty grim, right?"

"Right. And the irony is, that according to tradition, despite all their safety and security precautions, it was a member of the Catesby-Wintour-Tresham extended family who caused their final and untimely demise."

"Wow! You make that sound very dramatic. Who was this rotten apple in the barrel, the traitor to the cause? Was he a jealous cousin or jilted lover or something like that?"

"No, no, my dear Sophie, he was anything but that. He was an established lord and a respectable and respected aristocrat. His name was Lord Monteagle and he was related to the chief plotter, to Robert Catesby himself."

"How?"

"Catesby's cousin Francis Tresham…"

"One of the plotters?"

"Yes… had a sister, and she was married to Lord Monteagle."

"So how and why did he betray them? Was he a Catholic too?"

"Yes, Sophie, he most certainly was. He came from a very strong Catholic family and in 1599 he went to fight for Queen Elizabeth I in Ireland under the command of the Earl of Essex. The following year he joined Essex's abortive rebellion against the queen and then had the misfortune to fall into the Thames while trying to make his escape afterwards. He then surrendered to Sir Robert Cecil and was fined eight thousand pounds, which must have been a huge fortune in those days. Then two years later he financed a trip for Thomas Wintour..."

"The plotter?"

"Yes, as well as helping the well-known Catholic priest, Father Tesimond, obtain Spanish help for the English Catholics, but they failed. Then the Scottish King James VI became the King of England as well, but although he somewhat disappointed the English Catholic community, he rewarded all of those who had been involved in the Essex Rebellion. Monteagle's lands were restored, and he was allowed to take his place again in the House of Lords. The new king also personally asked the French King Henri IV to release Monteagle's brother from his Calais prison.

It was also at about this time that Monteagle wrote a letter to the king saying that although he had been brought up as a Catholic, he hinted that he was now a Protestant and that he had been blind and ignorant in the past with regard to his religious beliefs."

"In other words, he was a bit of a turncoat. I mean because King James didn't prove to be especially pro-Catholic, Monteagle did the same."

"Yes and no. While he did make out that he was no longer pro-Catholic, he did in fact continue with his Catholic lifestyle, and in fact his daughter became a nun. It was said that, in the end, when he died in 1622 he received the last rites as a Catholic."

"So, Grandpa, how did this Lord Monteagle betray the Gunpowder Plot?"

"Well, Sophie, it was like this. One evening at the end of October 1605, that is about two weeks before *the* night, Monteagle was sitting down at his London home, just about to get on with his supper, when a servant came in carrying a letter, which had just been delivered. It was this letter that has since become one of the most mysterious and puzzling aspects of the whole Gunpowder Plot."

"Why?"

"Well, first of all, it was unsigned and secondly, as you will see in a moment, it was badly written, that is, without any capital letters and punctuation."

"Trust you to notice that, Grandpa, you being a university professor."

"No, my dear Sophie. That's not the point. The point is, why was it written like that? Was the writer genuinely illiterate, or was he literate but doing his best to disguise his writing? Here, let's have a look at a picture of it in this *Illustrated History of England.* Here we are. Page 207:

my lord, out of the love i bear to some of

your friends i have a care of your preservation therefore i would advise you as you tender your life to devise some excuse to shift of your attendance at this parliament for god and man have concurred to punish the wickedness of this time and think not slightly of this advertisement but retire yourself into your country where you may expect the event in safety for though there be no appearance of stir yet i say they shall receive a terrible blow this parliament and yet they shall not see who hurts them this counsel is not to be condemned because it may do you good and can do no harm for the danger is passed as soon as you have burnt the letter and i hope god will give you the grace to make good use of it to whose holy protection commend you to the right honourable the lord monteagle

"Yes, Grandpa, I see what you mean about it being badly written. But tell me, who would have tried to disguise their writing like that, assuming of course, that that was the writer's intention?"

"Well, one theory I've heard is that the writer of this mysterious letter was none other than the Earl of Salisbury, Sir Robert Cecil, himself."

"What? You mean King James' chief advisor?"

"Exactly."

"But why would he write such a letter, and why would he send it to Lord Monteagle?"

"Well, according to some historians, Cecil was very interested in blackening the name of the Catholic community in England, and they claim that in fact it was Cecil who set Guy Fawkes and the other plotters up."

"Do you mean to say that Guy Fawkes and Co. had been duped all along? That they were the fall guys, the patsies?"

"Yes, Sophie. As you say, Guy Fawkes and Co. were indeed made out to be the patsies, the scapegoats. So that being the situation, Cecil would be able to arrest them before they could blow up the king and his parliament. And of course, by doing so, he would have had the perfect excuse to arrest any Catholic he wanted. In addition, he would also have been able to pass some more very tough anti-Catholic legislation."

"And of course, nothing would have happened to the king and his parliament."

"Exactly. And in this way, Cecil could have his cake and eat it, too."

"But, Grandpa, has this theory ever been proved?"

"No, Sophie, it hasn't. But it certainly makes sense, especially as the Cecils, both father and son, to say nothing of the equally devious Sir Francis Walsingham, often used people as *agents provocateurs* or as stoolpigeons in prisons. One of their favourite tricks was to let someone who they'd caught off the hook, sometimes almost literally, but on condition that they switch sides and become a double-agent instead."

"So, Grandpa, after Cecil got his hands on this letter, what did he do then?"

"Well, on the surface he didn't appear to do very much at all."

"What? Didn't he rush over to the palace and tell the king?"

"Oh no. Cecil had received instructions from His Majesty that he was going off for a few days' hunting in Cambridge and didn't want to be disturbed. And this by the way is why the Catholic historian, Antonia Fraser, thinks that the Monteagle letter was a fake. She claims that if it had been genuine, then Cecil and the king wouldn't have been so complacent knowing that a gang of Catholic plotters were planning to blow them all to kingdom come. However, whatever the truth is, Cecil did in fact discuss the whole affair with several other lords and I'm sure he felt that, with or without the king's personal knowledge of this warning letter, he had everything under control. Also, there's another well-known theory behind this Monteagle Letter."

"What's that? That Guy Fawkes was a double-agent?"

"No, but one of the other plotters was, or at least the one who sent this letter anonymously to Monteagle. This one was Monteagle's brother-in-law and he was scared that His Lordship would die in the planned explosion."

"Which plotter are you talking about?"

"Francis Tresham. He was one of the last ones to be recruited. It also seems that Monteagle's servant knew the two Yorkshire plotters, Jack and Kit Wright, and that he may have warned the plotters that they had a traitor in their midst. When he heard about this, Catesby's first reaction was to discuss it with Thomas Wintour. Then the pair of them set out to confront Tresham with what they had heard."

"I bet that wasn't a very pleasant conversation."

"I'm sure it wasn't. But apparently Tresham managed to convince them that he was completely innocent and so they decided to drop the whole thing. Now they had only about ten days left until 'D-Day', as it were, and…"

"Not 'D-Day' Grandpa, but 'G-Day', Gunpowder Day."

"Fair enough, G-Day. But we'll let that pass. So sometime during that period Cecil *did* inform the king and the trap was set to catch the plotters."

"And what were they doing during this period?"

"They were busy with the last-minute logistics, you know, like checking the gunpowder was in place and that it hadn't gone damp. They had also planned that only the plotters who had to be in London were actually there, as the others had ridden away to the Catholic areas of the Midlands. Later, under questioning, Tom Wintour said that he had tried to persuade Catesby to call the whole thing off, but Catesby had belittled the importance of the Monteagle Letter and now all they had to do was to wait for Guy Fawkes to light the blue touchpaper, as it were."

"Which of course he never did."

"Exactly. So on 4 November, while several of the plotters were in or on their way to the Midlands, others such as Catesby, Thomas Percy, Jack Wright, Robert Keyes and Tom Wintour and Guy Fawkes of course were still in London. They must have been feeling pretty confident and later that evening Catesby left London and headed north to put plan B into action; the Catholic Rebellion that would bring down the Protestant regime."

"You mean setting up the king's daughter as the new pro-Catholic queen?"

"Exactly. So later that night Keyes gave a timepiece of some sort to Guy Fawkes so that he'd be able to time the fuses. Then Guy Fawkes went down to the cellar to set off the gunpowder, all thirty-six barrels of it, and it is here we come to the classic and most dramatic scene of this plot."

"You mean Guy Fawkes being surprised and caught red-handed by the king's men?"

"That's right. They were led by the Earl of Suffolk, Sir Thomas Knyvett and John Whynniard, the man who had rented out the cellar to Thomas Percy. And yes, I suppose this famous scene in that dark but lantern-lit cellar must have gone something like this:

Soldier: Sir! Sir! We've just found a man there skulking

around behind some barrels over there in the far corner.

Suffolk: Was he on his own, man?

Soldier: Yes, sir. But Sergeant Fletcher and two other men are standing guard over him now.

Knyvett: Good. What was he doing when you caught him?

Soldier: Nothing, sir. He was just sitting there. As if he was waiting for something or someone. Y'know, sir. All hatted and booted. But anyway, sir, I took this timepiece off him. It looked somewhat suspicious.

Knyvett: A timepiece eh? So let's go over and see what's this all about. Soldier, lead the way, and for Jesus' sake be careful with that lantern. Whynniard, you too come with us. We might need you.

Soldier: Yes, sir. Please follow me and make sure you keep your head bowed low, sir. There are some low beams about a bit further on. I've already knocked my...

Suffolk: Yes, yes man. Go ahead and stop talking! We don't want this fellow whoever he is to escape in the dark.

(A few minutes later, Suffolk, Knyvett, Whynniard et al. stood facing the three soldiers who were guarding Guy Fawkes. The plotter was wearing a wide-brimmed conical hat and a

dark coloured heavy riding-cloak. He kept looking around and at the guards as if he were looking for a way to escape.)

Suffolk: All right. You three men. Leave him be. He's not going to run away from here. But just keep your eyes open. Now man, what's your name and who are you?

Fawkes: Johnson, sir. Master John Johnson. Servant to Thomas Percy, Gentleman Pensioner, sir.

Suffolk: Johnson eh? That's a common enough name. And pray, what are you doing, skulking around here in the dark at this time of night all dressed up as if you are going for a long ride?

Fawkes: I'm checking that my master's firewood is ready and dry for the winter, sir – that the damp hasn't got to it, sir.

Knyvett: What? In the dark?

Fawkes: No, sir. I mean yes sir. I mean I had a lantern with me, but I must have dropped it when I heard your men. I wasn't really expecting anyone else to come down here at this time of night, sir.

Suffolk: No, I'm sure you weren't.

Knyvett: Now let me look at you closely. Guard, bring another lantern over here. There, lift it high up. Yes, next to his face, man. Hmm. So you say you're a servant to this Thomas Percy?

Fawkes: Yes, sir.

Suffolk: Now answer me this, Master John Johnson, if

*that's who you are. How long have you been a
servant to this Gentleman Pensioner?*

*Fawkes: For a few months, sir. I cannot remember
exactly when I began in his employ, sir, but it
must have been before the summer season.*

Suffolk: And are you a valuable and devoted servant?

Fawkes: Yes, sir. Most certainly, sir.

*Suffolk: So valuable and devoted in fact that when you
come down here in the middle of the night, you
have to wear a heavy cloak, to say nothing of the
wearing of a large hat, boots and spurs, eh?*

Fawkes: I don't know what you mean, sir.

*Suffolk: Oh, I'm sure you do, Johnson. It means Master
John Johnson, that you are not who you
say you are and that you are not doing what you
say you are doing. I say that it means that you
are here after a long journey, or you are about
to embark on one.*

Fawkes: Oh no, sir. I...

*Knyvett: Soldier, check his boots and spurs. Are they
wet or covered with mud?*

Soldier: No sir.

*Suffolk: Master Whynniard, tell me. Aren't we standing
in a cellar that is rightly yours?*

*Whynniard: Yes, sir. That is, according to the property
deeds it is mine. And yes sir, I did indeed rent it
out to a Master Percy, and...*

*Suffolk: And tell me if I am wrong, but isn't this cellar
situated immediately underneath the Palace of*

Westminster?

Whynniard: Yes, sir. It is situated exactly under the Palace of...

Suffolk: That's enough, man. You, sergeant, take a couple of men and a lantern each and check out the area where you caught this Johnson fellow. Now! And you Master Johnson, you will remain here until they return. You two guards, bind his arms in the meanwhile.

(A few minutes passed and the sergeant returned with his two men. They were running and somewhat out of breath.)

Sergeant: Sir! Sir! All of you! We must get away from here! The whole cellar over there is full of gunpowder! Barrels and barrels of it, sir!

Knyvett: Full you say? Of gunpowder?

Sergeant: Yes, sir. Barrels of it! All hidden under faggots of wood and kindling, sir.

Soldier: There are thirty-six barrels, sir. I counted 'em myself.

Knyvett: Are you sure they're gunpowder and not wine, man?

Sergeant: Yes, sir. They're gunpowder all right, sir. I remember its smell, sir from when I was fighting in...

Suffolk: Yes, yes. We'll hear your stories later. Now let's move out of here. You men, take this Johnson *man upstairs and we'll meet you above ground in a few minutes.*

Soldier: Sir, before you go, sir, what shall I do with these?

Suffolk: With what, man? It's hard to see clearly down here.

Soldier: With these matches and touchwood, sir. I found them on the prisoner, on Master Johnson I mean, sir.

Suffolk: Give them to your sergeant. Now let's get moving. We've got a long night ahead of us. Sweet Jesus only knows what this Johnson man wanted to do with that gunpowder! Let's get moving. It may even blow up while we are standing here. Ho there! Bring a light over here and let's go."

"And then, Grandfather, did they lock Guy Fawkes up in the Tower?"

"Oh, no, Sophie. Not immediately. First of all, he was taken to the palace and interrogated in front of the king."

"Did they torture him?"

"No, at least not at this stage. They asked him who he was and he admitted to being a Catholic from Yorkshire and that he had been a soldier in the past. When they asked him to explain what he had been doing with a letter addressed to a Master Guy Fawkes in his pocket he said that that name was just an alias."

"And did he tell them about the plot?"

"Yes and no. He admitted that he had planned to blow up the king and Parliament and the whole palace, but he wouldn't tell them if anyone else was involved."

"And then he was tortured?"

"Yes, but not before telling the king that he had intended to blow him back to Scotland."

"I bet that can't have pleased His Majesty."

"I agree with you. It's funny, you know, but even when he was confronted by the king and Cecil and Co., Guy Fawkes couldn't forget his own anti-Scottish prejudice."

"And what happened to the other plotters? I mean Guy Fawkes was then sent to the Tower, no? So where were the others?"

"Well, Sophie, they were all over the place, that is, between London and the Midlands. But by 7 November, after various incidents in and around the Midlands, they had all managed to meet up at Holbeach House in Staffordshire. This was, and still is, a large, red-bricked country house which then belonged to Stephen Littleton, one of their later supporters."

"How did they end up there? Surely that's a long way from anywhere to start an uprising, especially in those days. After all, it's not as if they could have given orders on their mobile phones or anything like that."

"That's very true. The thing is, the plotters had planned beforehand to aim for the Midlands, which was pro-Catholic country. But what happened was that the king's forces, who had begun chasing them, pushed them further west than they had intended. So by 7 November, most of the plotters found themselves in this country house, probably feeling very sorry for themselves."

"Why?"

"Because, by then, they must have realised that their plot had failed. And not only that, but they were now surrounded by the king's men who were determined to flush them out of their bolthole. The plotters must have known that they would be seen as traitors and would probably receive very little mercy if captured. And then, on top of that, a terrible accident occurred which certainly can't have helped their already jagged nerves."

"What happened?"

"On their way over to Holbeach, they had got hold of a large supply of gunpowder. This they had loaded onto an open wagon, but it had got wet in the rain."

"Wait a minute, Grandpa. Don't tell me they tried to dry it out in front of a fire."

"Yes, Sophie, that's *exactly* what they did do. They spread it out all over the floor in front of the fire, and of course a spark landed on it and some of it, which had now dried off, exploded."

"But surely that would have killed them, no?"

"Yes, but in this case it didn't. I think that perhaps because the gunpowder wasn't compressed in a compact container and also because some of it was probably still damp meant that the explosion was somewhat limited.

However, it was bad enough to burn and blind two of the men and that must have unnerved the others who were now watching out for the king's men."

"How long were they there before the king's men arrived?"

"Not long – about one day. The king's men arrived that night and they immediately surrounded the house. Very soon after that, they shot and killed Kit Wright and they also seriously wounded Tom Wintour in the shoulder. Then Ambrose Rookwood was badly wounded and it was also at about this time that Catesby took Thomas Percy downstairs with him to the courtyard, so they could face the king's men from down below."

"That doesn't sound a very clever move, going outside, I mean."

"It wasn't. But maybe because the house was full of smoke, as well as the smell of burnt flesh and the screams of the wounded men, they thought they'd have a better chance outside. But whatever the reason was, they went outside and stood next to each other by the heavy wooden entrance door. According to tradition or the records, Catesby then said to Percy, 'Stand by me Mister Tom and we'll die together'."

"And did they?"

"Yes. Just as they were standing there, a soldier called John Streete loosed off a lucky shot and the same bullet killed both Catesby and Percy. And by the way, if you go to Holbeach House today, you'll still find bullets embedded in the door as well as the old hiding holes for priests inside. However, these have been covered up with glass as the place is now a nursing-home and it wouldn't be good publicity if the old dears kept falling down secret holes in the floor or suddenly disappearing behind the walls, now would it?"

"And Grandpa, how long did the rest of them hold out for?"

"Not for too long. Some of them tried to sneak out in the dark but they were captured within a day or so. Within a short time, eight of them were under lock and key in the Tower of London, while Thomas Bates, who was a servant and therefore deemed a lesser mortal, was held in a separate prison in Westminster."

"Eight of them? You said there were thirteen altogether."

"True, but four of them were killed at Holbeach, and soon after they arrived at the Tower, Francis Tresham, Monteagle's brother-in-law, died of some internal inflammation. Of course, it has since been claimed that he was got rid of after he had implicated the others in the plot. Then soon after this, the eight remaining plotters were interrogated and brought to trial at Westminster at the end of January 1606. And that, my dearest granddaughter, was more or less the end of the Gunpowder Plot."

"And did they receive a fair trial at least?"

"Oh no, certainly not. It was more like a show-trial, like they used to have in Stalin's Russia or in Nazi

Germany. As far as the authorities were concerned, all they were interested in was that their kind of justice was seen to be done and you can be sure that Sir Robert Cecil wasn't going to leave anything to chance."

"Did the king attend the trial?"

"Hmm, it's possible that he was present, but if so, he was hidden behind a curtain and heard everything that way. Remember, he'd already been the target of several attempts on his life so he obviously wasn't feeling very forgiving with regards to the plotters who were now standing there on trial. In fact, soon after Guy Fawkes had been captured, the king had stated specifically that torture was to be used and, as an academic, he'd instructed that Guy Fawkes should be racked *'et sic per gradus ad ima tenditur'* or, in everyday English, 'from the gentler tortures to the worst.'"

"Ugh! Nasty."

"Yes, Sophie, very nasty. And so that's exactly what happened. Guy Fawkes was tortured, that is, on the rack in the Tower of London. At first he wouldn't say anything, but after three days he was broken, mentally and physically and he confessed and divulged all the details he knew about the plot. By the way, if you look at the records and compare how he signed his name before he was tortured and how afterwards, you can see he was really and truly given the full treatment as King James had instructed, *'ad ima tenditur'*, to the very worst."

"And were the others tortured?"

"No, not as far as I know. I think that as soon as they saw the physical and mental state of their fellow plotter, there was no need. Besides, I don't think that the authorities wanted to parade a group of broken-down men at their trial. After all, it wouldn't be good publicity as it were and, besides that, Cecil wasn't really interested in creating another group of Catholic martyrs."

"So how long after all this was their trial?"

"Well, the majority of them were brought to London very soon after their capture at Holbeach, but a couple of them, Robert Wintour and Stephen Littleton, the owner of Holbeach, were captured at the beginning of 1606, that is about three weeks before their trial."

"But, Grandpa, you said it wasn't a real trial. Didn't they have lawyers to defend them or anything like that?"

"No, they…"

"And what about Magna Carta? Weren't they supposed to have been defended by lawyers?"

"Sophie, remember, Magna Carta was written by the nobles for the nobles, and not for the commoners who wanted to kill off their king."

"Yes, I suppose so."

"So, Sophie, the eight of them were paraded on a platform in the centre of Westminster Hall and from there they faced the Lord Commissioners, who included a couple of ex-Catholics who wished to show what *they* thought of these plotters. The Attorney-General, Sir Edward Coke, was a particularly nasty man and he fully played out his role in demonstrating how terrible and murderous Guy Fawkes and Co. really were."

"So, in other words, it was pretty obvious what the verdict was going to be."

"Exactly. They were all found guilty of high treason and for that there was only one penalty."

"The chop!"

"No, no, nothing as quick or as clean as that. The chop, as you insist on calling it, was for aristocrats only. Guy Fawkes and his men were all commoners so they were all to be hung, drawn and quartered. That is, hanged until they were half-choked but not dead, then cut down and then they were to have their guts drawn out of them and then be beheaded. Then the rest of the bodies were to be cut into four quarters and distributed around the country."

"Ugh! But why such a terrible punishment?"

"Well, Sophie, firstly to act as a deterrent to other would-be plotters, and secondly, the body parts were sent to different towns and cities in the country to be placed over the city gates or other central places to act as a very real and bloody warning, a deterrent as it were. Remember, the government couldn't show any of this on the ten o'clock news."

"The same way the authorities stuck heads up on poles on London Bridge?"

"Exactly."

"And was this horrible sentence really carried out on all eight of them?"

"Yes, in fact on even more than these eight plotters. You see, for several months afterwards the authorities continued to round up other Catholic supporters all over the country. Some were executed in three months later in April, while Henry Garnet, one of their spiritual supporters, was executed a month after that. But as I said, the main bunch was executed in two groups of four at the end of January 1606 on two consecutive days."

"So I suppose that their executions were a very public spectacle."

"Oh, they definitely were. The plotters were dragged to the place of execution – St. Paul's churchyard – on the first day, and then to Westminster Old Palace Yard on the second day. They were taken there on wicker hurdles and then they had to climb up onto the scaffold. There they were allowed to say a few words or prayers and then they were dispatched."

"Didn't any of them try and run away or try and commit suicide as a way of escaping their terrible fate?"

"No, no, they couldn't. They were too closely guarded for that, but apart from that, these plotters saw themselves as martyrs for the cause, and escaping or suicide would have been understood as a sign of weakness or cheating. But I must say that while they were waiting by the scaffold, Thomas Bates' wife did manage to break though the crowds and embrace her husband, who then whispered to her where he had hidden a large sum of money for her. Ambrose Rookwood's wife was also there among the crowds, and when he saw her, he shouted out, 'Pray for me, pray for me!' but otherwise, apart from their final words and prayers, the plotters were silent.

"Perhaps the most dramatic aspect was that the man the plot is named after, Guy Fawkes, did succeed in cheating the executioner in a way at the end."

"How? Did he swallow some poison or something like that?"

"No Sophie. He was the last of the eight to be executed, and I think it was done like that so he'd be forced to witness the suffering of his fellow plotters. Somehow he managed to get his broken body to the top of the scaffold, and after the noose had been put around his neck, he jumped and broke his neck. This of course killed him and so he didn't suffer the agonies of drawing and quartering as the others had done."

"So, Grandpa, that I suppose was the end of the Gunpowder Plot."

"Yes, but it didn't mean the end of the various Catholic plots which followed over the next two hundred years. It wasn't until 1829 when the Catholic Emancipation Act was passed, that the Catholics were granted full equality under the law."

"But that was too late for Guy Fawkes and Company," Sophie added.

"So anyway, if you're a Catholic in England today, you shouldn't celebrate Bonfire Night, should you? I suppose you should celebrate the deaths of King James and Sir Robert Cecil instead."

"Exactly, but that's not a very Christian sentiment, Grandpa, if I may say so."

"Yes, my dear. You are right."

Chapter Fourteen
Colonel Blood and the (almost) theft of the Crown Jewels (1671)

Colonel Blood's gang stealing the Crown Jewels

"Grandpa," Sophie said. "You know that my friend, Harry, went on a school trip to the Tower last week and…"

"And?" Professor Warkworth answered, looking at his granddaughter and her friend while wondering where this was leading.

"And afterwards we talked about some of the stories you've told us about."

"And?"

"And, yes, Professor Warkworth," Harry continued. "I said to Sophie that nearly all the conspiracies and plots we've talked about ended up with people having their heads chopped off at the Tower of London, or at least being tortured there."

"That's right, Harry, but such were the ways of justice in those enlightened days."

"But, Grandpa, were there any plots that actually happened in the Tower itself, I mean apart from prisoners trying to escape or things like that?"

"Sophie, I'm sure there must have been. I'm sure that if those thick grey walls could speak, they would divulge the bloody details about all sorts of plots and mysteries. Maybe we would finally find out who really murdered the princes in the Tower, or who Perkin Warbeck, the would-be usurper of Henry VII, really was, or…"

"Or if Richard III's brother, Clarence, was really drowned in a barrel of Malmsey wine," Harry added.

"Exactly."

"But seriously, do you know if any plot was hatched there which actually involved the Tower itself, like one of the guards planning to kill the king or queen, or something like that?"

"No, Sophie, I can't think of anything as dramatic or

as far-reaching as that, but there certainly was a plot to steal the Crown Jewels that were stored there for safekeeping."

"When was that?"

"In 1671."

"And who planned that?"

"Colonel Blood. Colonel Thomas Blood."

"That was his real name? You're kidding!"

"No, Sophie. I kid you not. That was his real name."

"And did he succeed in stealing the Crown Jewels?"

"And end up in the Tower? And was he executed?" Harry added.

"Wait a minute, Harry! I see you're as bloodthirsty as my granddaughter. But I'm not going to answer all your questions now. There's no point in ruining a good story if I tell you the end now, is there?"

"I suppose not, Grandpa. We've got some time so let's hear about Colonel Blood and the Crown Jewels."

"Fair enough. So, let's start at the very beginning, in 1618 in Ireland. This is where our infamous hero, Thomas Blood, the self-styled Colonel Blood, was born. His father was a man of means and had made his money from property in a couple of counties near Dublin and in County Wicklow. However, despite his Irish background, Thomas came over to England when he was quite young and, when the Civil War broke out in 1642, he became an officer in King Charles' army. Then later, he changed sides and fought most of the rest of the war on Cromwell's side."

"And did he succeed in England?"

"Yes, Harry, he did very well here. He even married quite a wealthy lass from the north, a Miss Holcroft from Lancashire. Then after the war, as an officer, he was paid for his services by being given plots of land in Ireland instead of hard cash. As for his war record, it's not known what part he actually played, but some historians claim that he may have worked as a spy for the Parliamentary army, that is, the Roundheads."

"And what happened to him after Charles II was restored to the monarchy?"

"Then, unfortunately, his luck ran out, for now he was on the wrong side. However, luckily for him, Charles II was not a vengeful sort of king and only a few people paid for their pro-parliamentary loyalty with their heads. It is true that the body of Oliver Cromwell was dug up and hanged in chains at Tyburn, but in general, people were only too pleased to start afresh and go about rebuilding their lives. Our hero, Colonel Blood, had to forfeit all his lands and, of course, this annoyed him somewhat."

"I'm sure it did," Harry said.

"So, for revenge, he decided to capture the Duke of Ormonde."

"Who was that?"

"The Duke of Ormonde, or to give him his full title, James Butler, twelfth Earl and first Duke of Ormonde, was an Anglo-Irish Protestant aristocrat who was one of the chief representatives of the English Crown in

Ireland. He was the king's man who confiscated Blood's newly acquired estates. Ormonde held this position for several long periods, beginning with the English Civil War and continued until his death in 1688.

"At first he was a successful military commander who easily defeated the Catholic rebels. Later however, the Catholic Confederates, the Irish Catholics' noble-led government, over-ran most of Ireland and Ormonde left the country. As a result, Cromwell dealt pretty swiftly and bloodily with the Catholic rebels, a fact that is still well remembered in Ireland today.

"After Charles II was restored, he promoted Ormonde to be the Lord Lieutenant of Ireland, and he worked hard to improve the general economic situation there. It was during this period of his life that the paths of Ormonde and Colonel Blood crossed for the first time."

"Why? What did Blood do to Ormonde?"

"Nothing much. He just tried to capture the duke, although it isn't quite clear what he planned to do with him. This happened in 1663. Blood and some other dubious characters tried to force their way into Dublin Castle where Ormonde was based. They were in disguise, but the plot was discovered and most of the gang were arrested and some of them were hanged. However, Blood succeeded in getting away and, disguised as a priest, he managed to reach Holland. However, it should be said, that he did later try and rescue some of his accomplices. However, unfortunately for him and for them, he was unsuccessful and as I said, several of them were tried and executed. One of them was his brother-in-law, William Lackie or Leckie.

"The net result was that Blood was now an outlaw with a price on his head, but this didn't stop him sneaking back into England from Holland. Four years later, our heroic Colonel managed to rescue an old friend of his, a Captain Mason, who was being taken to York for trial and/or execution. This time, Blood was luckier, and he and his men did succeed in rescuing their friend. However, a few of the government's troops were killed and a prize of five hundred pounds was offered for the capture of Blood…"

"Dead or alive?"

"Either way, I think, Harry, but again he was lucky. He managed to get away and then lived quietly for a bit in Romford, Essex under the assumed name of Thomas Allen or Ayliff. Here he worked as a physician, but it seems that he couldn't lead a quiet life for long. Three years later, he made another attempt to capture the Duke of Ormonde while he was on a visit to England from Ireland."

"Did he succeed this time?"

"No, Sophie. Blood intended to grab Ormonde while he was riding in the centre of London. However, this plan also failed as the duke managed to wriggle free out of his bonds and so Blood and his men had to run away immediately. The result of all this was that the price on

Blood's head was doubled to one thousand pounds."

"But, Grandpa, what had Ormonde done to him this time to make him so angry?"

"That I don't know exactly, but some people at the time claimed that George Villiers, the Duke of Buckingham, had put him up to it. They said they had seen Ormonde's son accuse Villiers of using Colonel Blood as the man to do their dirty work, but some historians today claim that Blood was still smarting about his previous failure when he had attacked Ormonde in Dublin ten years earlier."

"And what did Blood plan to do with the duke once he'd captured him this time?"

"Probably hang him at Tyburn where Marble Arch is today or keep him until he agreed to return all of Blood's lands in Ireland back to him."

"Sounds fair enough. But it never happened, right?"

"Right, Harry. And now we come to the most daring incident for which Colonel Blood is known in history, and that also answers your question about plots and the Tower of London. In this story, our hero tried to steal the Crown Jewels."

"Really?"

"Really, Harry. But first let me fill you in on some of the background details to this incredible plot. After Charles II was restored to the throne in 1660, it was decided to store the Crown Jewels in the Tower instead of keeping them at Westminster Abbey. Actually, there weren't too many, as most of them had been broken up or destroyed during the Civil War. A few had been remade for Charles' coronation, and these were now stored in closets on the ground floor in the Martin Tower, one of the towers that made up the outer wall of this five-hundred-year-old fortress."

"So the king felt they'd be pretty safe there?"

"Exactly. Now all of these 'baubles', as Cromwell would have disparagingly called them, were looked after by the official Keeper, Mr Talbot Edwards, a trusted servant of the Crown. He lived with his family, including his wife and daughter, Elizabeth, 'above the shop' as it were, in the top two floors of the Martin Tower."

"That sounds pretty cosy, and no long walks or carriage rides to work either."

"True, but it wasn't very exciting either. You see, Edwards had been given this job, as you would describe it in today's parlance, as an 'unsalaried worker'. However, he was given special permission by the king to show the Crown Jewels off to visitors to the Tower, like seventeenth century tourists, and then keep the fees of about thirty shillings a head for himself. Now all this was going very well…"

"… until Colonel Blood showed up."

"Not exactly, Sophie, but just be patient. It was not Colonel Blood, but the Great Plague which put a spanner in the works. First of all, the number of tourists dropped to zero, and then many of the Tower's soldiers were sent away because it was thought that they too had caught the plague. Fortunately, the Edwards family remained untouched by the plague, and the terrible cry of 'bring out your dead' didn't apply to them directly.

"Then just as they were getting over the plague and business was beginning to pick up again, the Great Fire broke out in the following year, 1666. It spread throughout the south-east part of the city at record speed and even King Charles took an active hand in trying to control it."

"How?"

"He ordered houses to be pulled down in order to create fire-breaks, and things like that."

"But surely Edwards in his thick stone-walled tower was pretty safe, no?"

"No, not really, Harry. Because inside the Tower there was a huge store of gunpowder. The guards and residents like the Edwards were scared that the fire might jump the moat, burn the wooden buildings surrounding the Tower and then a stray spark or the intense heat would explode all the gunpowder in the armoury. In addition to all this, gold from the Goldsmiths' Hall had been brought in for safekeeping, while people whose houses had been burnt down were also taking refuge in the Tower."

"You mean camping out on Tower Green where people had had their heads chopped off?"

"Yes, Sophie, on that same grim site. So, for safety's sake, the gunpowder was moved beyond the eastern wall, as far away from the burning city as possible. The fire burnt itself out after four days and nights, after having destroyed over three-quarters of the old walled city, St. Paul's, eighty churches and well over thirteen thousand houses."

"That couldn't have been good for Edwards' tourist business either."

"It wasn't, but I assume that by the time our story starts, the grand clean-up had started, and life had got back to normal at the Tower. So now, cast your minds back to the spring of 1671, five years after the Great Fire. Imagine our hero, Colonel Blood, looking something like Errol Flynn in an old black and white film of the thirties, with long black wavy hair down to his shoulders; all swashbuckling and aristocratic. He is wearing black clothes and a priest's dog-collar. He meets up with three of his fellow accomplices in, say, one of their houses and they plan what they hope will be the biggest heist of the century, if not of the age."

"The seventeenth century's answer to the Great Train Robbery."

"Exactly...

May 1671. Four men, Blood, Hallowell, Hunt and Parrot are sitting around a table in Hallowell's parlour. A few cheap candles are giving out a flickering light and casting jumping shadows on the map of the Tower of London which Blood has brought with him. Suddenly a gust of wind blows a window open and two of the candles are blown out. The third one falls over on the

328

table and rolls dangerously close to the map.

Blood: For Jesus' sake, move that candle and shut that window!(Hallowell stands the candle up as Hunt closes the window and turns the lock.) Ah, that's better. Now where were we?

Parrot: In the Tower, Colonel (he winks at the others).

Blood: Very funny. That's where we'll be if we fail. So let us now consider the situation very carefully so we won't end up in the Tower. At least, not as prisoners. Now, here's the Martin Tower, between the Brick Tower to the west and the Constable Tower to the east. Here they are, all together on the far corner opposite the Traitor's Gate.

Hunt: And you're sure that's where Edwards keeps the Crown Jewels?

Blood: I found out by asking a few different visitors a couple of days ago, and they all said the same thing. On the ground floor of the Martin Tower.

Hallowell: And Edwards and his folks live upstairs?

Blood: Aye.

Parrot: So what's your plan? I mean you cannot just walk in there and steal those jewels as if you were a magpie, can you?

Blood (refilling his glass with red wine): Gentlemen, my plan is this. It is simplicity itself. As pure as the Emerald Isle and it will also explain why I am wearing this priestly garb this evening.

Hunt: Good. I was hoping you were going to explain the meaning of such clothes to such a sinner as myself (he winks at the assembled men). I was beginning to think that you were in disguise again, you know, being on the run from the king's men once more.

Blood: Well, I'm not at the moment, and you should know that after the plague and the fire, His Majesty has other fish to fry, other than looking for Colonel Thomas Blood.

Hallowell (hesitantly): By the way Colonel, are you really a colonel? (Blood glares at Hallowell who seems to recede into a shell. The others are silent and the question is ignored).

Blood: Now that we have established where the jewels are, and that we can get into the Tower as visitors, we will have to consider the details, namely getting hold of these jewels...

Parrot: ... and getting out with them.

Hunt: Without creating a hue and cry.

Blood: Exactly, my man. Now here is my plan. First of all I disguise myself as a...

Parrot: ... priest. I thought that would be part of it. Just like when you escaped from the Duke of Ormonde's men.

Blood (glares at Parrot): I will start again. First of all I will disguise myself as a simple country parson, a member of the cloth and you, Hallowell, as the plumpest and most smooth-faced amongst us, will accompany me as my ever-loving wife.

Hallowell: Who me? Disguise myself as a blessed woman?

Blood: Of course (caresses Hallowell's face). You've got the softest and most gentle face here amongst us. And besides, you're not taller than me, like Parrot here. Haven't you ever noticed that women are usually shorter than their husbands?

Hallowell: Yes I suppose you're right. But what do I have to do as the parson's wife? Bless everyone and tell them to come to church?

Blood: No, of course not. You will enter the Edwards' home with me and we will play the part of country visitors who wish to see the Crown Jewels. Then you will suddenly feel faint...

Hunt: ... as women are apt to do...

Blood: ... and then ask if you can rest for a wee while in their house, say on their bed.

Hallowell: But why should I come over faint? What good will that do?

Blood: Well, you don't suppose that we'll be able to just walk in and steal the jewels just like that, do you?

Hallowell: No, of course not.

Blood: So my plan is this. The first part is to gain their confidence and trust, and later, say after a few days, we will return and carry out the next part of our plan.

Hunt: What's that? Is Hallowell going to have to

disguise himself as a woman again? Person-ally, I think he'd look very fetching in a bonnet and cloak.

Blood: Be quiet, Hunt. Yes. We do return again as the parson and his wife and I'll be most profuse with my thanks, you know, for having been so kind to my wife who fainted the last time we met. And to show my gratitude, I will bring them four pairs of fine white gloves.

Parrot: But what have gloves got to do with the jewels?

Blood: Parrot, my friend, will you just have some patience and listen? So now for the next act in our little play. When we return for the second time and we have the Edwards' confidence, I will say to them that I have a handsome nephew, a veritable joy to the heart and the soul who would be more than a suitable match for the Edwards' daughter, the comely Mistress Elizabeth.

Hallowell: Very charming. Sounds just like a scene from one of those plays we saw last month in Drury Lane, you remember, the one where the Mistress says...

Blood: Yes, yes, I remember, but that's not what we're here for now.

Hunt: But what's all this love and marriage got to do with the Crown Jewels?

Blood: The answer to your question, my friend, is to cement our friendship with the Edwards family, and by so doing, we will then have a free hand to be in their house and...

Hunt: ... and once we're in there, we'll have a free hand with the Crown Jewels.

Blood: Exactly, my dear friend, exactly.

Hunt:(standing up and bowing) Colonel Thomas Blood. I salute you. You are a genius. You should not only be a colonel, but the Chief Officer of the king's guards!

Blood:(for once blushing at hearing such gushing and fulsome praise) Thank you, thank you. (Stands up and bows to the others).

Hallowell: But how do you know that Edwards is so anxious to have his daughter married?

Blood: Hallowell, don't you know anything about fathers? They always want to have their daughters married off, especially to suitable young men.

Hunt: Hallowell, he's right. And who can be more suitable than the nephew of this learned country parson and his wife?

Blood: Now we've settled that, let's have some more wine to celebrate. Hallowell, ask your servant to bring us some more refreshment. This planning has fair worn me out.

"Hallowell left the room and returned a few minutes later with Rebecca, his servant, a buxom eighteen-year-old wench. Parrot couldn't resist smacking her broad well-upholstered behind, and leaving his hand there as she bent over near him to serve the wine. She stopped, straightened up, looked at him, smiled and then bent over once again to refill the Colonel's glass. She then faced the four men, winked at Parrot, curtseyed and left the room.

"The following week, Blood put his plan into operation. He and his 'wife' were admitted into the Keeper's apartments in Martin Tower. After some pleasant chat about the weather, the rate of rebuilding in the city following the Great Fire, the state of the traffic on the Thames and the king's latest amorous escapades, the 'wife' suddenly swooned into the arms of her devoted and concerned 'husband'. Mrs Edwards then unwittingly played her part in the drama and allowed her female visitor to lie down on her own bed until she felt better. Later, after the 'wife' had regained her senses and composure, the clerical couple left, leaving many thanks and salutations for future health and happiness."

"And, Grandpa, didn't they guess that Colonel Blood and his 'wife' were on the fiddle?"

"No, Sophie, they believed every word he said. But let me continue. A few days later, the Parson and his 'dear wife' returned; Blood again disguised in the dark habit of a Doctor of Divinity, complete with his false beard and a close cap. However, instead of wearing the traditional black gown, he wore a voluminous dark cloak which was to conceal the illegally obtained regalia. Talbot Edwards and his wife were overjoyed to see their new-found friends again. They were even more joyous when Blood, bowing low, offered them four pairs of fine white gloves as a token of their heartfelt thanks for their recent and truly Christian behaviour 'towards my dear wife'.

"As Mrs Edwards was busily trying on one of the pairs, Blood was telling them in his best sanctimonious tones that the behaviour of the Keeper and his wife could easily be compared with that of the Good Samaritan on that rock-strewn road leading down to Jericho of old.

"While everyone was still smiling, Blood coughed modestly, fingered his dog-collar and suggested that since the Edwards were such a noble and Christian family, it would be a goodly and godly act if the fair Mistress Elizabeth Edwards would consent to become the future wife of the parson's nephew.

If the Edwards had been overjoyed at the gift of gloves before, now their joy was boundless.

Mr Edwards: (To Blood) You are like a gift from Heaven. Is that not so, my dearest wife? (Mrs Edwards cannot respond as she is so choked with tears of happiness. All she can do is smile and wipe the tears off her plump red cheeks).

Blood: Since we are all agreed, I think we should meet here again tomorrow and make all the final arrangements. I fear that I cannot stay here any longer as I have some parish business to take care of. You know a parson's life is like that of a shepherd; always on the lookout for his flock and to make sure the weak ones, the little lambs, don't stray too far from the fold.

Mr Edwards: So farewell. We will meet tomorrow in the afternoon.

Blood: Aye, and so we will. And God be with you until then, and even after."

"Grandpa, do you mean to tell me that the Edwards were still buying all that cock and bull story: the marriage, the nephew and all that?"

"Absolutely. They swallowed it hook, line and sinker. They really wanted to get their daughter married off and to this nice man, who appeared to have some money as well. Now listen to the next part of this true and thrilling tale.

"The following day, Blood, accompanied by three accomplices but without his 'wife' who was 'unfortunately sick with a slight fever', returned to the Tower to act out the climax of their criminal play. They arrived earlier than the agreed time and Blood said that his happy nephew, whose role was being acted by Hunt, had unfortunately been delayed, but that he would be more than delighted to see the pretty Mistress Elizabeth in an hour or so.

"Then the parson and his good friends, Hallowell and Parrot, impressed on Edwards about how much they enjoyed hunting and successfully persuaded their host to sell them the box of pistols that he kept in the apartment. This now meant that the Keeper of the Crown Jewels had no means of defending himself.

"As Blood had planned, they now had some time on their hands, so the parson suggested that they go for a stroll until the nephew arrived. They could go and admire the Jewels. 'After all', Blood said unctuously. 'It is no mean thing that the king has thrust such an honour upon you, to personally protect his Crown Jewels'. And he intertwined his fingers together over his voluminous black cloak.

"As expected, Edwards was suitably flattered by Blood's smooth tongue, and with an expansive gesture, ushered his honoured guests downstairs to the ground floor of the Martin Tower:

Edwards: This way, gentlemen. I think we'll leave my wife and Elizabeth upstairs in order to greet your nephew when he arrives and also to prepare our afternoon repast. I think we should see St. Edward's crown first.

Blood: (In a light joking tone) Why? Was it named after you?

Edwards: Oh no. This golden crown was made for our present king's coronation and was made to replace the one that was supposed to have been worn by Edward the Confessor some six hundred years ago. As you can see, with all that gold and all those jewels, it is very heavy and so is only rarely worn.

Blood: Oh yes, I can see that. I'm sure it would certainly give the king a nasty headache if he wore it for very long. Now what are those beautiful things? This one looks like a ball of gold.

Edwards: That is exactly what it is. It is a ball of gold with a jewelled cross on it. It is called the Orb. King Charles held it during the coronation service.

Blood: (Despite himself, becoming more interested in the regalia) But why is it round? Does it have any significance?

Edwards: Well, for a man of the cloth, you do surprise me. I thought that you'd have known that the jewelled cross represents the Christian faith ruling the round globe of the world.

Blood: Oh yes, but of course. That was just what I was thinking when you said that. Now what's this long thing, you know, like a stick?

Edwards: Ah, that is the Royal Sceptre. It is the king's symbol and shows that as ruler of the nation, he is responsible for law and justice.

Blood: Hmmm, it's certainly a very fine piece of workmanship, all that delicate work and jewellery.

Edwards: Now, gentlemen, let me just get the key and I think it is time we went upstairs to meet the ladies. And maybe your nephew will have arrived by now.

Blood: Lead the way, O Keeper of the king's jewels.

"Blood and the other two indicated that it was indeed time to return to the Edwards' apartment. Just as the Keeper was half bent over and pushing the big key into the lock of the heavy wooden door, Parrot and Hallowell threw a heavy cloak over the unsuspecting man's head and stuck a clip over the bulge where his nose was. Edwards' arms started thrashing about like some sort of threshing machine that had suddenly gone berserk and Hallowell found that he couldn't restrain the panic-stricken and suffocating man's arms.

"Hallowell called out to Parrot to help him control the Keeper but to no avail. Edwards kept struggling so much that Blood suddenly pulled out a wooden mallet that he had been hiding under the black folds of his cloak and hit the unfortunate Edwards on the head. Edwards collapsed immediately like a burst balloon and fell to the stone floor, motionless.

"They pulled the cloak off the still figure and bent down to see if he was still breathing. He was, and as soon as some air entered the poor man's lungs, he suddenly showed signs of revival and looked up to see the three men standing over him. He was about to start shouting again when Blood grabbed a sword that had been standing in a corner and brandished it in front of the shocked Keeper. That proved to be too much for him. Holding his hands to his mouth, Edwards suddenly doubled over. He had fainted clean away!

Parrot: Quick, Hallowell! Grab the sceptre and something else before he comes to! I'll take this orb thing and cover it with my cloak.

Blood: I've got the crown, but it's too big to put under my cloak.

Hallowell: So hit it flat with your mallet! That'll make it easier to hide when it's flat.

Blood: Good idea. (Hits crown and knocks it out of shape). Now let's get out of here. Remember, the horses are outside. Let's go. But wait. Shh! Someone's coming!

Parrot: Aye, I can hear footsteps.

Blood: (Whispering) Yes, probably, Hunt. Shh! I think I can hear other voices as well. It sounds like…

Hallowell: Hey! What's this?

Hunt: (Bursts into the room) There's two men upstairs! One of them looks like Edwards and there's another man with him. A guard! Come on. Let's get out of here now! I've had enough!

"And without waiting for the others, he turned round and dashed up the staircase treading on the fallen body of the Keeper as he fled the scene. Edwards started to stir, but was not able to do much, as his movements were noticed by Blood who plunged his dagger into him, leaving the helpless man lying in an ever-growing pool of blood.

"Fortunately for Edwards, the wound was superficial, and in a few minutes Edwards' son who, as luck would have it, had just returned home unannounced from a long sea-voyage, helped to revive his unfortunate father. He started shouting, 'Treason! Treason! The crown is stolen!'

"With that cry ringing in their ears, Edwards' son and Tower guardsman, Captain Beckman, chased after the fleeing robbers who, because of their heavy booty, could not run fast and had not got very far.

"Suddenly, as Beckman and Edwards' son were gaining on the three robbers, Beckman shouted, 'Edwards! Stop! That man's got a pistol!' He threw himself and his friend to the ground, as two pistol shots were fired. The shots did little to help Blood and the other two as he had no time to reload. Within a minute the robbers had been overpowered by Beckman and Edwards' son who were not encumbered by heavy clothes and the stolen regalia. Luckily for Edwards and Beckman, the noise of their chase and the shots had attracted the attention of other residents in the Tower as well as the guards, who now closed in on the mêlée from the nearby Brick and Constable Towers. It did not take long to tie up the three men and recover the somewhat battered Crown Jewels.

Sergeant: How many of them were there?
Beckman: There were four but one of them managed to run away.
Sergeant: Then he must have escaped.
Guard: Aye, he must have done. I saw someone running

in the direction of the Traitor's Gate.
Sergeant: Well, that's where he'll end up. You mark my
words. Now you, Mr Priest or whoever you are,
what do you have to say about all this?
Blood: It was a gallant deed, although it failed. For it
was to gain the Crown.
Sergeant: Gallant deed, by Jesus! Let's see if you'll see
it so gallantly when you're swinging at the end
of a hangman's rope! Come soldier, take some
other men and escort these men over to that cell
over there. We'll deal with them later."

"Grandpa, are you sure this is a true story? Because I for one don't believe a single word of it. Colonel Blood indeed! You are certainly good at making up names for your plotters."

"My dear Sophie. Every single word of what I have told you is true. Go and look up 'Colonel Blood' in any good encyclopaedia and you will see that this story did indeed take place at the Tower in May 1671."

"All right. I surrender," Sophie grinned, holding up her hands. So then what happened to him after this? Did the king order him to be executed or something like that?"

"You can't be further from the truth, my dear. It is true that he was imprisoned in the Tower for some time, but while he was there, he refused to speak to anyone but the king himself. Now Charles, who had a scientific turn of mind, that is, when he wasn't busy with the ladies, seemed quite intrigued by this man and so he ordered him to be brought to the palace at Whitehall for a personal interview. In shackles, of course, and escorted by several armed men for safety's sake. This meeting with the king apparently went very well as far as Blood was concerned. Instead of being hanged as a common thief, the king restored the Colonel's lands in Ireland back to him and also granted him a pension of five hundred pounds a year."

"So he really lived up to his nickname, the 'Merry Monarch'."

"That's right, Harry. Naturally this royal generosity to a known robber caused many eyebrows to be raised. One explanation circulating at the time was that, sometime in the past, Blood had served His Majesty as a secret agent and now the king had found a way of paying him back."

"But didn't Blood fight on Cromwell's side during the Civil War?"

"Yes, and that is another point that muddies up this whole story. Anyway, the truth about this spy-story stuff has never been really unearthed and Blood never mentioned or recorded why the king had been so generous with him. Perhaps the answer is that Charles, who himself had led an exciting life, simply appreciated that aspect in Blood's own career. Fortunately for our dashing Colonel, Charles' good friend, the Duke of Buckingham, looked after Blood's interests at court for a while, that is, until the two fell out with each other.

"It seems that sometime later, Buckingham must have pulled rank and had Blood convicted of some sort of conspiracy at the Court of the King's Bench. As a result, Blood was sent to Newgate prison and charged with *scandalum magnatum*, that is, causing a massive scandal, to the tune of ten thousand pounds. Somehow, Blood was able to find the money and was released, but he died soon after."

"And here endeth the story of the brave Colonel Blood."

"Not so fast, Harry. Some people at the time claimed that this death was just another of the Colonel's little tricks, and so to prove that he was really dead, his body was dug up."

"And was it his body?"

"Yes, Harry. This time Colonel Thomas Blood had not pulled a fast one. One of Blood's friends recognised something special about Blood's hand and so he was quickly reinterred."

"And what happened to his accomplices? Did they hang or was the king generous to them as well?"

"Well, Sophie, as far as we know, Hallowell escaped immediately after being caught and was never heard of again, and the other two, Hunt and Parrot, have since disappeared into the oblivion of history."

"And what about the Edwards family? Were they thrown out of the Tower for having failed in their duty to look after the Crown Jewels?"

"No. It seems that Edwards stayed on at the Tower

and we do know that he applied for a small pension which he received only after months of badgering the authorities."

"I see. The Civil Service doesn't seem to have improved since then, does it?"

"That's true, Sophie. But anyway, Edwards died three years later and was buried in the Royal Chapel of St. Peter ad Vincula…"

"Where Henry VIII's wives, Anne Boleyn and Catherine Howard were buried?"

"Yes, and a simple inscription on his gravestone recorded that he had been the Keeper of His Majesty's Regalia and that he had died at the ripe old age of eighty years and nine months."

"Despite having been bashed on the head with a wooden mallet by Colonel Blood."

"Exactly."

Chapter Fifteen
Titus Oates & the Popish Plot (1678)

Titus Oates

"You know, Sophie, maybe it's because of my love of history, but whenever I see you eating porridge from that box saying 'oats' on it in large letters, I always think of Titus Oates. Titus, like the Arch of Titus we saw in Rome last summer, or Titus as in Titus Andronicus and characters like that."

"So who was this Titus Oates person?"

"He was one of the creepiest and most disgusting men you could have met in London in the late seventeenth century."

"Tell me about him. I must say he sounds somewhat

different from Colonel Blood."

"Oh, he certainly was that all right. He was a really nasty piece of work, and he caused the deaths of a large number of people too. He was, as Lady Caroline Lamb described the poet, Byron, 'Mad, bad and dangerous to know'. I'll tell you what, bring over that big black encyclopaedia from over there on the bottom shelf and we'll see who this Titus Oates really was. Here, page 562. 'Titus Oates: Perjurer and bogus Anti-papist'. And look, here's a picture of our hero as well."

"Why is he standing there in that pillory?"

"Oh, that was only one part of his career. One minute he was up – your 'Mr Popularity of the Year' – and the next minute he was down, pilloried, fined or imprisoned, or all of the above."

"Why? What did he do? I understand he didn't like the Pope or Catholics very much, but neither did a lot of other people, but they weren't pilloried for that."

"That's true, Sophie, but this particularly nasty piece of work hated the Catholics with a vengeance. But anyhow, I'll start this story at the beginning. But before I do, what does the encyclopaedia say about him?"

"It says 'Oates, Titus. 1649-1707. English conspirator and perjurer. Born in Oakham, Rutland, Oates was the son of an Anabaptist minister'… What's an Anabaptist?"

"It's a Protestant sect which believes that people who were baptised as infants should be baptised again as adults. Anyway, that's jogged my memory so now I'll fill you in from here. His father, who was a ribbon-maker as well as a minister, brought the Oates family to London. In 1665, when young Titus was sixteen, he was sent to the Merchant Taylors school and here began the list of the many places he was expelled from."

"Why were there so many?"

"Take a pencil and paper and keep a list of them and we'll see how many come up. First of all, he was expelled from Merchant Taylors after two years, and then he went to a school near Hastings."

"Which threw him out?"

"No, not this one. He graduated from Hastings and went on to Gonville and Caius College, Cambridge, but then he transferred to St. John's College. If I remember correctly, he wasn't too popular at university and… wait a minute, let's see what they say about him in the *Catholic Encyclopaedia*. Here we are, oh, very flattering. Here: 'the most illiterate dunce, incapable of improvement'. Ah, here's some more: they repeat that he was a dunce, and add, 'he ran into debt and being sent away for want of money, never took a degree'. However, that didn't stop him from moving on, because he succeeded in fooling the religious authorities. He must have tricked them somehow, because we next hear about him acting as a priest or preacher of some sort in a place called Bobbing in Kent."

"How long did he stay there?"

"Only for a year. He left with a reputation for being dishonest and he'd also been involved in some sort of fight with somebody, or as it says here, 'he did swear the Peace against a man'. Then he became a curate with his father in Hastings and it seems that what happened next, to coin a phrase, was like father, like son."

"Why? What happened?"

"The pair of them brought some sort of impossible charge against a local schoolteacher and so the Church authorities in Hastings decided to fire the pair of them and sue them as well. Titus ended up being sent to prison in Dover for perjury, but he managed to escape."

"What a shame."

"True. Then he ran away to London where I assume he thought he would be ignored and anonymous in the big city. After that he managed to wangle himself a position as a ship's chaplain, but within a year he…"

"… was thrown out of the Navy."

"Exactly. But Sophie, did this minor setback stop our hero? Oh no. He next became the Protestant chaplain in the Duke of Norfolk's household but began rubbing shoulders with various local Catholics. A year later he himself crossed the floor, as it were, and became a Catholic himself."

"Wait a minute. The picture you showed me a few minutes ago said he was an anti-papist, and now you're telling me he was a Catholic."

"Be patient, my dear, and you'll find out what happened next. So, our Master Oates, now a Catholic hero, was sent to the English Catholic College at Valladolid in Spain, but after five months he was expelled and sent back to London. However, he was lucky, because he was given another chance and was sent off to study at another famous Catholic college, at St. Omer, near Calais in northern France."

"Where we caught the ferry last summer."

"Exactly. And of course, true to form, he was expelled from St. Omer as well. Now we come to an important date in Oates' career. While he was at St. Omer, he came in contact with another disreputable character called Israel Tonge. Now let's see what our encyclopaedia says about him. Ah, here we are. It describes him as 'a city divine, a man of letters, and of a prolific head, filled with all Romish plots and conspiracies since the Reformation'. Now, let us go back to London. It is 1678. Who is the king?"

"Charles II."

"Good. Now Charles II, the 'Merry Monarch', used to like to go for an early morning stroll in St. James' Park. One morning while on one of his strolls, a man called Christopher Kirkby came up to him and..."

"Wait a minute. Wasn't the king surrounded by soldiers and bodyguards and people like that?"

"Apparently not. I think in those days they were much less security conscious than they are today. And besides, Charles knew he was popular with the people. In addition, the king had met Kirkby before, since they were both interested in chemistry."

"Who? Charles II?"

"Oh yes. He may have been a ladies' man, but he was

also very interested in the arts and sciences. So, this Mr Kirkby comes along and starts to bend the royal ear about a Catholic plot which he says is aiming to kill the king while he is out taking one of his early morning strolls. Later, Mr Israel Tonge tells Charles the same thing and adds that he, Tonge, should get all the honours for having uncovered this plot.

"In fact, Tonge didn't only just tell the king about the plot to kill him, but he threw in a few more details as well. He said that all the Catholics and Jesuits together with the French King Louis XIV were involved in this, and that the bottom line was that the French were going to invade England."

"And did Charles believe all this?"

"Let's say he didn't take it too seriously, but instead of checking it out personally, he handed the whole problem over to the Earl of Danby. Now here, Tonge had more luck because Danby hated the Catholics and France. Soon Tonge, together with Oates, who had returned to England in the meantime and had reverted to being a Protestant again, were soon pouring anti-Catholic poison into Danby's very receptive ear. Needless to say, what these two shady characters told Danby was a complete and utter pack of lies, but worse than that, they were dangerous lies."

"Why dangerous?"

"Because Sophie, by the time this plot had been exposed for the fraudulent affair it was, some thirty people had been imprisoned or hanged.

"Now, Sophie, imagine the scene. A richly appointed room at the back of the palace far away from prying ears and eyes. There, our hero, Titus Oates, is being questioned by the king's council. Oates of course, is busy telling all sorts of false and poisonous anti-Catholic lies. Suddenly he pulls out a weapon, a sword or pistol or something and cries out that Sir George Wakeman was plotting to kill King Charles:

Council member: Sir George Wakeman, Oates? You mean the royal physician? Her Majesty Queen Catherine's personal physician?

Oates: Yes, sir! The very same man, sir! (Voice rising) And not only him sir, but also Edward Coleman, sir!

Council member: Have a care, Oates. You're treading on some very dangerous ground there making these accusations against the king's most trusted servants. Very dangerous indeed! You realise of course that Edward Coleman is the secretary to the Duchess of York, the king's own sister-in-law?

Oates: Yes, sir.

Council member: Are you sure about all this? Do you not want to retract what you have just said?

Oates: Oh no, sir. Why, I heard all about it from Mr Israel Tonge, and as you know, my respected sirs, this Mr Tonge is a very honourable gentleman who would certainly not go around spreading malicious gossip like a Billingsgate fishwife.

Council member: Now tell us, Oates, supposing what you are telling us is true, who else is involved in this dastardly plot?

Oates: Well, sir, all I know is that Sir George Wakeman was to be paid fifteen thousand pounds for his services and...

Council member: Fifteen thousand pounds, by George! And by whom?

Oates: By the Catholics, sir.

Council member: And is anyone else involved, that is apart from Edward Coleman?

Oates: Oh yes, sir. Two other men. A Mr Pickering, who is a Benedictine lay preacher and a Mr Grove, who is a Jesuit, sir. They were to be paid fifteen hundred pounds for shooting the king with carbines, sir.

Council member: What, in case the poison failed?

Oates: I don't know, sir. I suppose so.

Council member: But that's terrible. What you are telling us is treason!

Oates: (Sanctimoniously) I know sir. We live in troubled times. But sirs, what I've told you isn't all. There's more.

Council member: More of this treason? Haven't we heard enough?

Oates: Please sir, please hear me out. This is what I know. These Catholics had also planned to hire two Benedictine fellows to stab the king if all that I have just told you failed.

Council member: Are you absolutely sure about all this, Oates?

Oates: Oh, most certainly sir. I even know their names. Coniers and Anderton, sir. And they are both Catholics.

Council member: But Oates, this is terrible. It is the worst thing I have ever heard during all the years that I have had the honour of serving His Majesty.

Oates: I know, sir. And not only that, but… er, I am not sure if I should tell you more. You may not believe me.

Council member: Come on, Oates. Out with it! We wish to hear everything.

Oates: Yes sir. Not only did these Catholics wish to murder the king, sir, but they also wished to kill some other important personages as well, sir.

Council member: Who?

Oates: They planned to kill the Prince of Orange, sir, as well as the Bishop of Hereford and the Duke of Ormonde. And I believe there were more, sir, but I cannot remember any more names at this moment.

Council member: Well, Oates. I think you have remembered more than enough for one day. We will speak again in a few days' time and see if you can remember any other names in the meanwhile.

Oates: Yes, sir. Will that be all? May I go now? You see, I have to help out at the new church just east of St. Paul's.

Council member: Yes, Oates, you may go now. But please do not talk to anyone about what has passed between us in this chamber today. Can we trust you?

Oates:(Bowing very low, smiling obsequiously) Oh yes, sir. You know you may count on me. (Leaves the chamber, thinking of the reward he hopes to gain)."

"So was Oates well rewarded for this day's work?"

"He most certainly was. He became an instant hero and was wined and dined by everyone including the nobility. In addition, Parliament awarded him a salary of twelve pounds a week, which was a fair sum in those days, as well as various other financial gifts from the Treasury. He then started to put on airs and graces and said that he had earned his doctorate, which of course he never had, at Salamanca in Spain, a city that he had never been to. He even paraded around dressed up as a clergyman. In fact, he went the whole way."

"But didn't anyone call his bluff?"

"Not at this point. That came later."

"But didn't anyone see that this man was a fraud?"

"No, Sophie. You see, sometime after he had made all these terrible accusations, some letters which Edward

Coleman had written were found and these had been addressed to Louis XIV's confessor."

"So Coleman looked like a baddie after all."

"Exactly."

"So, therefore, it was assumed that all of Oates' other stories were true."

"That's right. Coleman was indeed found guilty and later executed, the first of quite a large number of people who paid with their lives for Oates' lies."

"And Sir George Wakeman? What happened to him?"

"He denied all connection with Oates' stories about him trying to poison the king, and fortunately for him, he was believed. You see, he had been a firm royalist all his life and he also had some influential friends. He was tried, but acquitted and as far as he was concerned, that was the end of it."

"Grandpa, what caused Titus Oates to fall? Was it a woman?"

"No, Sophie, it was hubris, extreme arrogant pride. You know the saying, 'pride comes before a fall'? That's what caused Mr Titus Bloated Oates to fall. And it all started with a murder. In October 1678, the body of Sir Edmundbury Godfrey was found on Primrose Hill, London. The corpse had been pretty well disfigured, and as they say today, it looked as if the good man had really suffered from GBH."

"Grievous bodily harm."

"Exactly."

"Grandpa, who was this Sir Edmundbury Godfrey?"

"He was a Justice of the Peace – or JP for short – a judicial officer who had been present when Oates had been spilling the beans about the Catholic plot to kill the king. Before long, it was put out that he'd been killed by the Catholics, and this was the excuse the authorities had been waiting for."

"Why?"

"If you look in the *Catholic Encyclopaedia*, you will find a list of over two dozen Catholics who were executed over the next year starting with Edward Coleman. You'll also notice that these people were not just simple souls but also included several members of the aristocracy such as Viscount Stafford and the Bishop of Armagh in Ireland. In fact, this was the beginning of the Popish Plot and many people jumped on the bandwagon in order to exploit it. Such people also included the Whig party who now had an excuse to blame the Catholics for all sorts of things."

"And how did Oates suffer in all this?"

"At first he didn't. He was extremely popular, and he and other disreputable characters all happily perjured themselves in court at the expense of some very unfortunate Catholics."

"Wait a minute. So now we have a plot within a plot."

"Exactly. Let's try and see what happened. But we'll have to retrace our steps a little. So, as all good stories begin, once upon a time, or, on one wet and dark stormy night, two drunks stumbled across a body in a ditch north of the City of London. At first, it seemed as if the man had been killed in a sword fight as a sword was still sticking out of the body. However, at the autopsy it was declared that the dead man, Sir Edmundbury Godfrey, had been beaten up with a club or some such weapon and had died as a result of severe blows to the chest. The sword and the broken neck were just added afterwards to try and fool any future possible investigation.

"Yes, and it was also noted at the autopsy that the murdered man hadn't eaten anything for some time before he was killed, and that his shoes were clean even though the body was found in a muddy ditch. Now, Sophie, how do you account for that?"

"The victim had been murdered in a clean place and then his body had been dumped later in the muddy ditch where the two drunks had found it."

"Brilliant. I suppose you learned all that from watching those 'C.S.I.' programmes on the telly. But now, to continue with the next problem in this story: how and why had Sir Edmundbury been murdered? We know that he was a bachelor; was fifty-seven years old, and was said to be the best JP in England. He was also an active churchman and had been knighted for his services during the Great Plague. So the question is, why had he been murdered?"

"Maybe it was suicide?"

"What? Kill yourself with a long sword and then violently break your own neck and transport yourself to a ditch outside London, making sure your shoes stay clean, to boot? No. Suicide doesn't seem very likely. No, the reason or motive for this particular mystery must be tied up with our despicable friend…"

"Titus Oates."

"Exactly. Oates claimed that five Catholic lords had banded together in order to kill the king, and one of the first men in authority he had spoken to about this was Sir Edmundbury Godfrey JP. When King Charles heard this, he literally laughed in Oates' face, since he knew that the alleged leader of this Papist plot was an old man who stayed home most of the time as he suffered from gout. The whole idea seemed completely ridiculous to the king, especially as all the men involved were highly respected, including one who was a Fellow of the Royal Society. Nevertheless, maybe for safety's sake, he had them all arrested, but he also had our obnoxious friend, Mr Titus Oates, arrested and imprisoned as well, for perjury."

"And was that the end of Oates and his Popish Plot?"

"Not quite. Unfortunately, the House of Commons ordered him to be released, and so, with a self-styled 'Captain' William Bedloe, he continued to perjure himself. This time his victim was the Chief Justice, an honourable gentleman with the Dickensian-sounding name of Scroggs, who had acquitted Sir George Wakeman and a few others.

"Oates also decided that if the king and his chief advisers wouldn't listen to him anymore, then he'd take his stories elsewhere. This he did. He went to see Sir

Edmundbury and swore a written statement giving all the details about this Papist Plot. Sir Edmundbury then passed on this information to his colleague Edward Coleman. When Oates saw that the authorities were still not acting on his information, he returned to Sir Edmundbury about three weeks later with even more details about this devilish Catholic Plot."

"He didn't give up easily, did he?"

"Oh no. Oates was a very determined perjurer. However, by now, this good J.P. was really worried, especially as his friend, Coleman, seemed destined to be the victim of an extreme anti-Catholic witch hunt. Coleman was then arrested, and this was brought about by another nasty character called the Earl of Shaftesbury. This rather short man was a really devious and treacherous person who was determined to bring about a violent anti-Catholic wave of trouble. One of the reasons for this is that his political party, the Country Party, wanted Charles II's illegitimate son, the Duke of Monmouth, to succeed the king instead of his brother James, who was a known Catholic. As you know, James eventually did succeed his brother and became the very unsuccessful James II."

"And where does Oates fit in with all this political and religious messing about?"

"Sophie, I'm coming to that. Oates was working for Shaftesbury who was using him to stir up trouble. As Shaftesbury admitted later, 'I will not say who started the game, but I am sure I had the full hunting of it'. And as we know, Oates and the earl were successful. Coleman was tried for high treason and executed, and Oates and Bedloe were seen as heroes. Then, to top it all, Oates was voted a twelve hundred pound a year allowance from Parliament."

"So Oates came out again on top."

"Yes, unfortunately you are right."

"But Grandpa, you still haven't told me yet who murdered Sir Edmundbury Godfrey."

"I can't tell you that."

"Why not?"

"Because there is no clear answer. If you look in that book, *Historical Enigmas*, you will see that Hugh Ross Williamson points the finger at Philip Herbert, the seventh Earl of Pembroke."

"Why? How was he involved?"

"Pembroke was a leading member of the pro-Protestant Country Party, which was opposed to much of the court and the government. He was known to be a very violent creature and had killed at least six people, if not sixteen, and had got away with it. However, in February 1678, this twenty-year-old aristocratic ruffian was brought before Sir Edmundbury Godfrey J.P. for killing one of his drinking chums by kicking him in the chest. Sir Edmundbury was forced to let him off on a legal technicality, and then left the country knowing that Pembroke was thirsting for revenge. He returned to England about six months later in September, and as part of his duties, heard Oates' deposition about the

Popish Plot. Knowing what we know about the good Justice, he probably told Oates what he thought of him and his plot. Therefore, it is probably no coincidence that he was found dead a month later.

"It was never proved that Pembroke, working for the Country Party, was the actual murderer, but two years later, in 1680, a man called Smeeth was murdered by Pembroke by being kicked to death. This time, King Charles had all the petitioners for Pembroke sign their names, and lo and behold, they were nearly all members of the Country Party. This seemed to prove that the party had vested interests in silencing Sir Godfrey, and the murder of this man was all that was needed to exploit the wave of anti-Catholic feeling that was sweeping the country. In fact, in comparison it seemed a little bit like an earlier English version of that anti-Communist wave that hit America at the beginning of the 1950s."

"You mean McCarthyism?"

"Yes. Many Catholics were imprisoned and about three dozen were executed on the word of Oates and his accomplices. The House of Commons tried to pass a law that the Catholic Prince James wouldn't be able to succeed his brother as king, but then Bedloe died in 1680 and Oates perjured himself…"

"… again."

"Exactly, by saying that Viscount Stafford, one of the Catholic lords originally accused of plotting to kill Charles, had bribed certain witnesses to actually do the deed. Poor old Stafford was found guilty and executed.

Charles dissolved Parliament and said it would meet again in two months' time in Oxford and not in London. This would allow the atmosphere to cool down and, as a result, the anti-Catholic plot began to fizzle out."

"And what happened to Titus Oates?"

"A year later, that is, in 1681, Oates tried to blacken the name of a Mr. Israel Backhouse, the master of Wolverhampton Grammar School. But Oates' plan misfired, and the good man was acquitted. Then in 1682, Oates was found guilty of perjury and his government pension was reduced to two pounds a week. He was sent to prison for calling the future King James II a traitor, and sometime after, Judge Jeffries…"

"The one who ran the 'Bloody Assizes'?"

"Yes, the same one, fined Oates a hundred thousand pounds for the crime of *scandalum magnatum* that is, scandal on a grand scale. Oates was tried for perjury, found guilty and condemned to be degraded, whipped and pilloried. Jeffries also gave him a life-sentence and said that Oates 'deserved more punishment than the laws of the land can inflict'."

"Good. So Oates got his just deserts in the end."

"Wait a minute. For then the wheels of history took another turn. Charles II died in 1685 and his Catholic brother, James, became king. Four years later he was chased out of the as a result of the Glorious Revolution and replaced by the Protestant William III. This meant that Judge Jeffries was thrown into the Tower because of his part in the Bloody Assizes, you know, the series of trials where he had tried over fourteen hundred rebels against King James and nearly three hundred of them were found guilty…"

"… and were hanged, drawn and quartered."

"Exactly. But then the judge died soon after in the Tower of 'flu or some such disease. Oates, who was never backwards in coming forwards, saw this as an opportunity to be released and appealed his sentence and was freed. In fact, he was given a royal pardon and a pension to go with it."

"Shame!"

"True, but this was later taken away from him. Then after King William's wife, Mary, died, Oates was awarded five hundred pounds by the Treasury to pay off his debts. And then, to cap it all, he was also granted three hundred pounds a year for both him and his wife. Then Oates became involved with the Baptists and, true to form, they expelled him because he had tried to swindle a fellow Baptist. Unfortunately, this didn't stop him for long, because he attempted another bogus plot, which failed."

"He never gave up, did he?"

"It seems not. He died in 1705 and all I can say is good riddance to him."

"I bet the Catholics were pleased about that."

"I'm sure they were. But they were still a long way from being regarded as equal citizens in this country, but that's another story."

Chapter Sixteen
Kill the King:
The Rye House Plot (1683)

The Rye House Conspirators

"Sophie, here's a letter for you, and I see it's from Rye House. Who do you know there?"

"Judy. Judy Holmes. You know, the girl who left school in the middle of the last term because of her father's job in Hastings."

"You mean her house is so called because she lives at Rye, near Hastings?"

"Yes. Why?"

"Because I was thinking of another Rye House, but this one's at Hoddesdon in Hertfordshire."

"All right Grandpa, I recognise that tone. What happened there? Who got killed there?"

"Sophie, I'm shocked."

"Well Grandpa, you must admit, most of your stories do have dead bodies lying about at the end of them."

"My dearest granddaughter, that is an unfair accusation. Some of them do end happily. I mean, look at King James I. He survived a good number of plots against him."

"All right, so who are we talking about now?"

"King James I's grandsons."

"Who? Charles II or James II?"

"Both of them to be exact."

"Why? What did they have to do with your Rye House?"

"They didn't have anything to do with the place. The plotters tried to involve them in their plot and…"

"Wait a minute, Grandpa. This is getting a bit too complicated for me. Please start from the beginning. I can tell by the way you're playing with your chocolate bickie that you're dying to tell me a story, so I'll be a good girl and sit down and keep quiet."

"All right, my dear. So, the situation was like this. It was 1683. Charles II had been king for over twenty years. I suppose, taken all round, he hadn't done a bad job. He'd got himself some good publicity as you would say today. He had helped during the Great Fire of London in 1666 by personally taking over trying to contain the blaze and not by just sitting on the throne and ordering everyone else to do the dirty work.

"He had also gained another sort of publicity by having lots of mistresses, at least a dozen of them, including Nell Gwynne. These good ladies had produced about twenty illegitimate kids, the first and foremost being James Scott, who later became the Duke of Monmouth. But I'll tell you more about him later.

"And in addition to increasing the population of England, he was also very interested in science. In fact, he was so interested that he even had his own laboratory as well as founding the Royal Society and the Observatory at Greenwich. And like our present queen, he would often be found with a few dogs at his heels, but in this case, they were King Charles spaniels and not corgis. He also kept Arab racehorses and he himself rode in races at Newmarket, his favourite horse being called 'Old Rowley'. This was a name that some people also used for the king himself. Other less Christian souls said he was so-called because their 'Merry Monarch' was said to roll from one of his mistress' beds to another, but that last point isn't really relevant to our story. So, let's just say that he was a friendly fellow whose favourite expression was 'odd's fish' and that after having led a tough life during his period of exile during the Civil War he wasn't really keen to rock the ship of state too much.

"So that was the situation at the beginning of the 1680s when the Whigs, the early Liberal party, under the leadership of the Earl of Shaftesbury, introduced a Bill into Parliament that would prevent the king's brother, James, Duke of York, from succeeding to the throne when Charles died."

"What was wrong with James?"

"Nothing, except that he was a fervent Catholic. The country had recently experienced Titus Oates and his Popish plot, and James had married Mary of Modena, England's only Italian-born queen who also happened to be a Catholic as well."

"So what?"

"So what? If the good lady had a son, then he'd also be brought up as a Catholic and that didn't sit well with the general atmosphere at the time. However, Charles managed to block this Whig law a couple of times, but in 1681, Parliament succeeded in passing it first through the House of Commons and then through the House of Lords."

"So what did Charles do then?"

"He simply dissolved Parliament and used the military to threaten the Whigs to toe the line. The situation became pretty tense and there was even fear of another civil war breaking out."

"Between Charles and his royalists and the parliamentary side?"

"Exactly. Fortunately, this didn't happen but Charles, in an effort to cover himself, then made a secret treaty with the French in case such a war should break out in the future."

"That sounds a bit steep. An English king signing a deal with a foreign king in order to keep his own people in line."

"That's true, Sophie, but you must take Charles' own background into account. Remember, he'd had a French mother - Henrietta Maria - and that he had fled to the Continent after the Civil War and then lived like a poverty-stricken refugee for about ten years. When he returned to England in 1660, he said that he was determined not to go on 'his travels' again. And if that was how he was going to keep his kingdom, then so be it.

"At the same time, the authorities in London sent out patrols to keep the streets quiet and orderly. That is, they made sure that people were not lighting bonfires and burning straw dummies of the Pope."

"Like Guy Fawkes."

"Exactly. So you can see, the king was quite concerned about having the rowdier elements of society keep the peace, and he also made sure, like with this deal with Louis XIV, that he'd be able to cover himself if things got really out of control. But there was something else too. It wasn't only the question of James' succession that annoyed the Whigs, because the king in fact had somewhat spoiled their plans with another aspect of this problem."

"What had he done?"

"In 1681, the Whigs had invited the Protestant ruler of Holland, William III, over to London for a meeting. The aim of this was to see about setting him on the throne instead of King Charles' brother, James. And then, while William was in England, Charles invited him over to Windsor at the same time. Now, according to the rules of protocol, William had to be with Charles and not the Whigs. As a result, the Whigs, as no doubt you would phrase it, really went off Dutch William and thought that he was getting too pally with the king, so they transferred their support to someone else, to…"

"The Duke of Monmouth?"

"Exactly. Technically he was the king's eldest son, even though he was illegitimate."

"But so was Henry VIII's first son, Henry Fitzroy, no?"

"Very true, Sophie. But it wasn't the question of illegitimacy that prevented Fitzroy from becoming king. It was just that he died about ten years too early. Anyway, Shaftesbury, the leader of the Whigs, decided to throw in their lot with Monmouth, especially after the latter had helped him with a certain legal problem."

"You mean you scratch my back and I'll scratch yours?"

"Exactly. So by now Charles was getting more than a little fed up with his favourite son, so he transferred some of Monmouth's offices to two of his other illegitimate sons. In fact, things came to such a head that in the end, after Monmouth had gone on a royal trip around the country, that Charles put his royal foot down and banned him from coming to court at all."

"I bet that kept him happy."

"It didn't. So now the situation was ripe for Monmouth and anyone else…"

"And Shaftesbury?"

"No, he'd gone into exile in Holland – now it was time for Monmouth and anyone else who had a grudge against the king to get together and start plotting."

"Welcome to the 'Rye House Plot'."

"Exactly. In the summer of 1683, Algernon Sidney, a political theorist, Lord William Russell, Monmouth and a few others got together with the idea of getting rid of the king altogether."

"You mean murdering him?"

"Yes and no."

"Yes and no?"

"Yes to murdering him and no, because it wasn't just Charles they wanted to get rid of, they also wanted to get rid of his brother, James, as well."

"But, Grandpa, surely that would have meant that the murderers would have had to catch both Charles and James together, at the same time and at the same place."

"Exactly. And that place would be …"

"Rye House."

"Exactly, Sophie. Rye House in Hoddesdon, Hertfordshire."

"So how did the plotters plan on carrying out their evil deed?"

"Oh, that was quite easy, at least, as they thought it would be. Just imagine it. You are one of the plotters, say Lord William Russell, and you meet up with the others in a nice town house in London belonging to a Whig sympathiser, say, a Mr Shepherd who is a wine-merchant in the city. The house would probably be somewhere in the area of today's West End, say, at Covent Garden or perhaps somewhere near Holborn. You are all sitting around a medium-sized polished oak table and a large map of England is spread out in front of you, together with some cakes and several glasses filled with good red port:

Sidney: So, Russell, my old friend, what say you about your Whig ideas now, eh?

Russell: Sidney, they have not changed. Since that Titus Oates fellow convinced me that there is indeed a Popish Plot and the Catholics are determined to take over the country again, my mind has remained quite resolute on that score.

Essex: But Russell, old man, that Titus Oates character was proved to be a fraud. Spent all his life being thrown out of one religious institute or another.

Russell: I know that, Essex, but even if he was a fraud, the situation that he exposed is real.

Essex: What do you mean by that?

Russell: I mean that it is now 1683. The king, that

womanising fop, has reigned now for well over
twenty years. Who is next in line, pray tell me?

Hampden: *His brother, James.*

Russell: *That's right, John. And he is as Catholic as the*
Pope, no? Even more so, if you ask me.

Hampden: *You're right there, Russell. Especially if you*
take his wife into account.

Howard: *Ah, yes, the Italian, Mary Beatrice of Modena.*

Russell: *Right again. You can't be more Catholic than*
that woman, that is apart from 'Dismal Jimmy'
himself.

Essex: *'Dismal Jimmy'?*

Russell: *Well, Essex, that's what Nell Gwynne called the*
king's brother.

Howard: *Aye, she should know. No one could be nearer*
the royal family than that wench.

Russell: *Near? Intimate I would say is a better word.*

Essex: *Will you gentlemen stop discussing Nell Gwynne*
and her intimacy with the king and let us see
what we can do about this situation?

Sidney: *I'll tell you what we can do. We must simply*
remove the king and his brother from the scene.

Russell: *You mean kill them?*

Sidney: *Yes, I do.*

Howard: *And how do you propose to do that? Stroll into*
the palace with a cocked pistol or a drawn
sword? The king may be a good-natured soul,
but he's certainly no fool. And don't forget, there
are guards around him most of the time.

Sidney: My lord Howard, do you take me for a fool? I know all that and that is why I propose we use a different venue for our scheme.

Howard: Is that the reason that you have this map of England unrolled in front of us on the table?

Sidney: Yes. Now you fellows, look here. What is the king's favourite sport?

Essex: Wenching.

Sidney: Possibly. But think of another.

Howard: Hunting.

Russell: Horse-racing.

Sidney: Right. And where is his favourite venue for this?

Essex: Newmarket, in Suffolk.

Sidney: Right. Now what I propose is that we get rid of our 'Merry Monarch' and his dismal brother somewhere here in the country outside of London...

Essex: Where we will not be seen.

Sidney: Exactly.

Russell: And where, I pray you, should this cleansing action take place?

Sidney: Well, gather round and look closely at this map. Here is London and here is Newmarket.

Howard: So you are saying that it should be done somewhere between the two?

Sidney: Right.

Howard: What about in Cambridge?

Russell: Too crowded, eh, Sidney?

Sidney: Right. It would be too much like London. No, I

suggest we choose a small quiet and secluded place. Then, when it is over, we'll be able to disappear more easily and no one will be any the wiser. What say you?

Essex: But, Sidney, consider you this. If we were to carry out our plan in London, wouldn't we have a better chance of getting lost amongst the crowds instead of sticking out as strangers in the countryside?

Sidney: Perhaps. I hadn't thought about that. I suggest we all give this some serious thought. I propose that we sleep on it and all meet up again at my house near the Strand next Monday evening. Is it agreed?

"It was. The following Monday the same group of Whig malcontents met at Algernon Sidney's house near the Strand. As before, a centrally placed table was covered with a map of the south of England, and after a glass or two of wine, the discussion got under way:

Sidney: Well, gentlemen, I have given this matter much thought and I am still convinced that the best place to carry out our plan is to do so outside the bounds of the City of London.

Russell: So have you any suggestions where?

Sidney: Now that is my next point. As I said last week, I suggest that we carry out the plan somewhere between London and Newmarket. And that place should be here. Look carefully, gentlemen. At this small and isolated hamlet here in Hertfordshire called Hoddesdon.

Howard: Why there?

Sidney: Because, my dear Lord Howard, it is ideal for our purpose.

Essex: But Sidney, where in Hoddesdon? You told me about this place yesterday, but you weren't specific about the exact venue.

Sidney: So now I will be. Rye House.

Russell: What's Rye House?

Sidney: That's what I was coming to next. Rye House is a fairly spacious country-house that stands alongside the London-Newmarket road.

Howard: But there are many houses like that.

Sidney: I know that. But this one is especially suitable for our purpose for two reasons. The first is that it is very near to an extremely narrow part of the road, which will make it easier to achieve our aim...

Essex: And secondly?

Sidney: And secondly, the house is owned by a Mr Richard Rumbold...

Russell: Who is he?

Sidney: He is an old soldier who some thirty years ago served under Cromwell. He was also one of Cromwell's guards in Whitehall and actually witnessed the execution of Charles I.

Howard: So in other words, you are saying that this

Rumbold fellow is a confirmed Parliamentarian?

Sidney: Aye. It seems that way.

Russell: So now, gentlemen, let us take this a step further. Assuming we succeed in our plan and rid the country of the king and his brother, what do we do next?

Howard: No problem. Monmouth becomes king.

Russell: I agree with you there. It's obvious that Monmouth is the next in line. After all, he is the king's eldest son, even though he is illegitimate.

Sidney: My lord Russell. I beg to differ with you. I see no reason why Monmouth should succeed the king. In fact, I don't see any reason at all why he or anybody else should succeed the king just because he's got blue blood flowing through his veins.

Essex: And pray, my good Sidney, who should succeed the king, if not someone of royal blood?

Sidney: Anybody.

Howard: Anybody?

Sidney: Aye. Anybody suitable that is. I mean, why cannot we go back to having a republic or commonwealth as we had in the times of Oliver Cromwell? Did we not have law and order then? Did we run around like heathen savages for eleven years?

Essex: That's true, but...

Sidney: Has it been ordained from on high that this

country must be ruled by a king, or even a queen?

Essex: But Sidney, this country has always been ruled by a monarch.

Sidney: Almost my dear Essex. And anyway, there are precedents for countries being ruled by ordinary men. Think of the Bible. Until King Saul ruled over the Holy Land, the country was ruled by wise men, priests and prophets, no?

Howard: What you say indeed is true, but...

Sidney: Then who says we need a king to lead us? My lord Russell, just because you and your friends, like Robert Ferguson and Sir Patrick Hume, are close to the Duke of Monmouth, does that mean he should rule us?

Russell: Well, I was just going to say that...

Sidney: Was I severely wounded fighting at Marston Moor or exiled for seventeen years on the Continent just to allow that spoiled and selfish son of the king and his mistress, Lucy Walter, to become sovereign over us all? Pray, answer me that.

Russell: Sidney, my friend. I did not realise that you felt so strongly, so passionately, about the idea of republicanism. But I will tell you this. This noble country of ours has been ruled by a king or queen for so long that the monarchy is as much part of its structure as the land itself, with its rivers, forests and fields. I know that we were ruled for eleven years by Oliver Cromwell and his unfortunate son, 'Tumbledown Dick', but did the people wish for this state of affairs to continue?

Sidney: Well, I must admit that...

Russell: Just so. And so, when General Monck invited the present king back from exile, how was he received? I can tell you. It was with great joy by the majority of the people. I admit I was not one of them, but I cannot deny that this country needs a king, and if a king will bring us stability, then the Duke of Monmouth it should be.

Essex: You know, gentlemen. This discussion could go on for a long time. So how about we adjourn it for a while and go into the city to seek some amusement to clear our heads? I for one know a very pleasant and amiable establishment just off Drury Lane.

Sidney: As you say, my lord. After all, we not only have to look after our minds, but also our bodies, eh?

Russell: Just so.

"And so after finishing off the remainder of the port and rolling up the map and hiding it behind a particularly well-embroidered arras, the would-be executors of this regicidal plan set out for an evening's amorous sport, leaving their discussion unresolved."

"And Grandpa, did they ever solve their problem?"

"No, Sophie, they did not. It is true that they had

further meetings and probably discussed the technical details of exactly how, where and when to kill the king and his brother, but all their future plans fell through."

"Why? Did they chicken out in the end?"

"No, my dear. They did not, as you so delicately phrase it, chicken out. As with many of the plots we have talked about, they were betrayed. It seems to me that the more time you spend plotting, the greater the chances are that someone will spill the beans. If you remember, Guy Fawkes and the men with him took over a year and a half to put their plan into action, and you know what happened to them, don't you?"

"So Grandpa, who spilled the beans this time?"

"That I don't know. It's possible it was one of the plotters' servants, for after all, many of these men were aristocrats and their houses were always full of servants of one sort or another. Or simply one of the plotters just got cold feet and, as they say, blew the whistle. But in the end, the king and his brother were saved by a stroke of good luck."

"What happened?"

"Well, it's true that they did attend the races at Newmarket and probably had a good time there. But then a fire broke out at the racecourse and the king and his brother left early to return to London. Somehow this threw the plotters off their guard, for obviously they had not planned for this, and as a result the whole thing fell apart.

"Several men were arrested immediately and three

were sentenced to be hanged: Lord Russell, Algernon Sidney and the Earl of Essex. That is, Russell and Sidney were hanged, but Essex met his end in an equally grim and bloody way. He was certainly arrested and imprisoned in the Tower of London, but one day in July 1683, he was found in his cell with his throat cut. It has never been proved if this was some form of judicial murder or suicide.

"Personally, I tend to think it was suicide, since judicial murder doesn't strike me as Charles II's style. Anyway, in addition, a few others were charged with 'forming a council for the purpose of insurrection' and executed.

"Another one of the condemned men was Robert Baille, who was allegedly not only against the king and his brother, but also against the English domination of the Scottish Presbyterian church. Like the others, he was arrested and held for six months and then sent to Edinburgh. There he was tried, found guilty and hanged, drawn and quartered. However, unlike some of the others, the evidence against him wasn't conclusive, so since then he has been seen as a martyr in some quarters."

"And what happened to the Duke of Monmouth? As far as I know, Grandpa, he never did become king, did he?"

"No Sophie, he didn't, but he certainly tried. Despite his well-placed connections, the highest if you wish, James Scott, the Duke of Monmouth, came to a really sticky end. Even though he had served as a captain in the king's guards and became the Captain General of the English army, Charles banished him from the country following the anti-Catholic riots. However, Monmouth wouldn't be told what to do and returned home and became involved with the anti-Catholic Whig party and their plots. After the Rye House plot fell apart, he was pardoned by his soft-hearted father, but later banished again from court. This time he took refuge in the Netherlands."

"That doesn't sound so sticky."

"Be patient, my dear Sophie. So anyway, Monmouth remained in exile for over a year, that is, until Charles had died and James was ruling as King James II. Then Monmouth decided, during the early summer of 1685, that the time was ripe for him to seize the throne. He landed at Lyme Regis in Dorset with just over eighty supporters, but he quickly raised an army of about four thousand simple farmers and country-folk from the West Country, who hailed him as King Monmouth. However, none of the local gentry supported him, even though the Duke of Argyll had done so earlier.

"A month later, in July, his army of untrained peasant soldiers was completely smashed by James I's forces at Sedgemoor in Somerset. Monmouth had decided to surprise the king and attack his forces at night, but as luck would have it, one of his soldiers accidentally gave the game away when he fell into a ditch and accidentally fired his gun. In the following battle, one thousand rebels were killed as opposed to three hundred of the king's men. Monmouth fled to the New Forest, but he was captured almost immediately and brought to London as a traitor. Unfortunately for him, his Uncle James was less forgiving than his father and ordered him to be executed.

"But Monmouth wasn't finished yet. He wrote a letter to the king in which he squarely put the blame for the whole affair on others. James wasn't particularly impressed but still granted the young man an interview. Monmouth then offered to convert to the Catholic faith, but the king's priests said that he wasn't really sincere. That was the last straw as far as Monmouth was concerned. He was executed a week after the Battle of Sedgemoor. Jack Ketch, the executioner, had to make 'five chops' as the records say, before his head finally rolled off the block onto the straw below."

"As you said, Grandpa, a sticky end."

"Yes, and *that* was the end of the Rye House Plot, although it didn't do James II much good in the end. He was driven out of London three years later due to his Catholic beliefs and died a dozen years later in exile in France."

"So neither Charles II or James II were killed at Rye House. They both ended up dying in bed."

"Exactly."

Chapter Seventeen
Kill 'Farmer George' –Three Times!

King George III

"Grandpa," Sophie announced, coming into the room with her best friend, Jane. "We've just been to see the film, *The Madness of King George*…"

"But that's an old film. It came out in 1994. I thought you two were into more modern stuff."

"We are, Grandpa, but our history teacher thought that it might help us appreciate the costumes and way of life in Georgian England better."

"And did it?"

Both of the girls shrugged.

"But it was so sad to see how they treated poor old 'Farmer George' in those days," Jane said. "It was so sad that they didn't really know how to look after him when he was ill."

"Yes, Grandpa," Sophie added. "And while we were watching it, I was wondering, you know that George III was on the throne for such a long time, sixty years, wasn't he? Well, did anybody try and bump him off?"

"Yes, Sophie, you're right. He was king from 1760 until 1820. And as for someone trying to shoot him, yes, there were at least two attempts when someone tried, as you indelicately phrased it, to bump him off. A man and a woman or, to be more accurate, a woman and a man."

"What, a woman as well?"

"Oh, yes, there have been quite a few female assassins in history, Sophie. I can think of at least five. First of all, there was Mistress Marcia who tried with others to kill Commodus, the Roman Emperor; then there was Charlotte Corday who, during the French Revolution, stabbed the writer, Marat…"

"Professor Warkworth, I read that. He was in the bath at the time, no?"

"Yes, Jane, you're right. And then there was Violet Gibson," the professor counted off number three on his fingers. "An Anglo-Irish aristocrat who tried to shoot Mussolini in 1926, and she was followed by Idoia Lopez Riano, '*La Tigresa*'."

"Ooh, that's an exciting name."

"Yes, Sophie, but she wasn't really such an exciting woman. You see, she killed over twenty people while claiming that she was a fighter for the Basque independence movement. And the last one I can think of at the moment was Sara Jane Moore, a woman who tried to assassinate President Gerald Ford in 1975."

"And Professor Warkworth, who tried to kill King George III?"

"Her name, Jane, was Margaret Nicholson or, as she was probably known then, Mistress Margaret Nicholson."

"And what did she do, Grandpa? Did she succeed?"

"Well, before I tell you that, just imagine a sunny day in August 1786 in central London, that is, about two hundred and thirty years ago:

'Look, here's the king's carriage! And it's stopping!'
'Aye, right here.'
'Look! He's getting out. I wonder why?'
'He often does that. He does it to show that he's a man of the people. Y'know, shaking hands with us common folk and stuff like that.'
'D'you think he'll shake my hand if I go over to him?'
'Well, you'd better wash it first. But look, there's a young woman walking over to him. What's she giving him? It looks like a scroll of paper to me.'
'Yes, you're right. I think she's giving him a petition of some sort.'

'Aye, maybe to get her father or husband out of prison or something like that.'

'No, no, look, she's just raised her arm! It looks as if she's trying to stab the king!'

'Aye, she's holding a long knife or dagger of some sort!'

'No, that's no dagger. That's a dessert knife! Look, she's trying to stab him again in the chest!'

'Isn't anyone trying to stop her?'

'Yes, there are some of his servants and guards who have grabbed her and someone else is shouting, 'Treason!'

"And that, Sophie and Jane, is what happened when Margaret Nicholson tried to assassinate King George III. She lunged at him twice with her ivory-handled dessert knife, didn't hurt him at all, and was then caught and arrested."

"But why did she try and kill him, Grandpa? What had he done to her?"

"He personally hadn't done anything to her, but the people then said that she was mad and even the king was supposed to have said, 'the poor creature is mad; do not hurt her, she has not hurt me.'"

"Professor Warkworth, did that save her? Because in those days, killing or trying to kill the king was considered to be treason, wasn't it? A capital offence."

"Yes, Jane, you're right, but in the end, it did save her. They held an inquiry into who she was and why she had tried to kill the king, and this is what they found: Margaret Nicholson was thirty-six at the time and had come to London from County Durham in the north. Her father had been a poor barber and, to make ends meet, she had worked as a servant girl for various lords from a very young age."

"But Grandpa, wasn't that the usual behaviour for young girls then?"

"Yes, but it seems that one of her employers fired her after she had fallen in love with a fellow servant."

"Why? There's nothing wrong with that, is there? Y'know, a bit of kissing and stuff under the stairs."

"Sophie, a 'bit of kissing and stuff under the stairs' as you call it could lead to unwanted babies and no aristocratic employer wanted that, so she was fired."

"Poor thing."

"Perhaps, but to continue with her story, she must have found it hard to find work after that and at some time, although we don't know when, she did what all poor girls did in the north of England…"

"She came to London to find work."

"Exactly, Jane. Margaret found a lodging house in Wigmore Street and began to take up needlework and repair clothes. But it seems that during this period she began to show signs of insanity."

"What do you mean, Grandpa?"

"Well, after they had arrested her, the king sent some officers, well, constables, that is, the early equivalent of today's policemen, over to her lodgings and they found all these weird and wonderful letters which said that she was the heir to the throne."

"But Professor Warkworth, wasn't King George famous for having loads of kids already?"

"Yes, Jane. He had fifteen altogether, including his fifth daughter who was named Sophia."

"So Grandpa, what made Margaret think that he was going to accept her when he already had so many?"

The professor shrugged. "I don't know. All I know is that she was obviously mentally disturbed when they arrested her."

"What, just because of that?"

"No, because of other things as well. Margaret also said that she was the mother of Lords Loughborough and Mansfield when, in fact, both of these two were older than her. In addition, they found that she had previously sent petitions to the king and, all in all, they concluded that she was insane. She said later that she hadn't aimed to kill the king, but just to scare him, and her landlord said that she was sober and hard-working but, in the end, none of this helped her."

"They strung her up?"

"No, Sophie. They sent her to the Bethlehem Royal Hospital, that is, the Bedlam lunatic asylum, and she died there over forty years later."

"So really, Professor Warkworth, this is a very sad story, isn't it?"

"Yes, Jane, it is. But there is a positive aspect to it as well. First of all, the king, who wasn't really much of an exciting figure, became more popular because of the kind way he had treated her and secondly, because of what happened, there was a change made in the law. In 1800, a new plea could be entered into an accused person's defence, the plea 'not guilty by reason of insanity'. And, interestingly, it was this same plea that was used for the next person who tried to assassinate the same King George, four years later. A man called John Frith."

"Who was he, Grandpa? Another man suffering from delusions of power?"

"You are half-right, Sophie. This John Frith was certainly suffering from some delusions, but not of power. He believed himself to be St. Paul."

"Why, what did he do?"

"Well, one day, on 21 January 1790 to be exact, John Frith threw a stone at the king's carriage as it was on its way to the State Opening of Parliament."

"Grandpa, that's not going to kill him."

"I know that, Sophie, but trying to harm the king or queen was, and in fact still is, considered as treason and so it was dealt with as such. He was put on trial when he claimed that he had been illegally deprived of his livelihood as a lieutenant in the Army. He blamed James Amherst, a senior officer who, Frith claimed, had sent 'supernatural agents' to whisper in his ear and who had 'fabricated evidence of insanity against him.

"But, Professor Warkworth, what has this to do with throwing a stone at the king?"

"I'm not sure, Jane, but I believe Frith did so in order to gain some publicity. You see, when he was put on trial, he claimed that he was the Messiah and also, for some reason, he couldn't sleep near large buildings."

"He sounds completely nuts to me."

"I think you're right, Sophie, and so instead of hanging him for treason, they sent him to Newgate Prison where he was later declared unfit to plead in court because he was insane. He stayed there for one year and then was transferred to the Royal Bethlehem Hospital, Bedlam, where he died soon after."

"But what has all of this got to do with St. Paul?"

"I don't know, Jane, but all I know is that the third person who tried to kill George III also suffered from some religious delusions. His name was James Hadfield and he believed in the Second Coming of Jesus Christ. He believed that if he were killed by the British government, this would speed things up."

"So, Professor Warkworth, he was also insane then?"

"Oh, yes, Jane. He most certainly was. And not only that, but he conspired with a Mr Bannister Truelock to kill the king and then he would be hanged, and so suffer martyrdom as a result."

"Grandpa, who were these men, James Hadfield and Bannister Truelock? Were they just poor down-and-outs?"

"Yes, Sophie, in a way. Truelock was a shoemaker and a religious fanatic, and Hadfield was also a religious fanatic and a badly wounded ex-soldier. He had fought in the British army in Belgium against the French and had been badly wounded by being struck several times on his head with a sabre. It was after this, when he came back to England, that he started believing in the Second Coming and contemplating how to achieve it."

"So what did these two do, Professor Warkworth?"

"One evening in May 1800 when the king was at the Theatre Royal in Drury Lane… no, wait a minute, I'll read you out bits of what Mr Michael Kelly, the musical director, recorded at the time. That will be a more accurate description of what happened. I've got his book here on the bottom shelf. Yes, here it is, this fat green tome. *Reminiscences of Michael Kelly.* Here we are:

> *When the arrival of the king was announced, the band as usual played 'God save the King'. I was standing at the stage-door opposite the royal box to see His Majesty. The moment he entered the box, a man in the pit next to the orchestra on the right hand stood up on the bench and discharged a pistol at our august monarch as he came to the front of the box.*
>
> *Never shall I forget His Majesty's coolness – the whole audience was in an uproar. The king, on hearing the report of the pistol, retired a pace or two, stopped, and stood firmly for an instant; then came forward to the very front of the box, put his*

opera glass to his eye, and looked around the
house without the smallest appearance of
alarm or discomposure.

"So there you have it. Your king – as cool as a cucumber."

"And Grandpa, what happened to Truelock and Hadfield afterwards?"

"Since Bannister was charged only with urging Hadfield to do the dirty deed, he was sent to Bedlam…"

"Where Margaret Nicholson was?"

"Yes, but Hadfield had a tougher time. He was grabbed by some of the players in the orchestra and they bundled him downstairs into the music room under the stage. The Duke of York and Mr Richard Brinsley Sheridan, the theatre manager…"

"And playwright."

"Yes, Jane, and playwright. Well, these two and Sir William Addington, a Bow Street magistrate, examined Hadfield to see who and what he was. In the meanwhile, the audience upstairs were demanding that Hadfield be brought up onto the stage to be seen. Kelly didn't want that as he was afraid that riots would break out, so he went up onto the stage and calmed everyone down. He told the audience that Hadfield was safe under lock and key and that if he were allowed to get up onto the stage, he might seize the chance to escape."

"Did the audience buy that?"

The professor nodded. "Yes, Sophie, they did."

"What was the king doing all this time?"

"He stayed to see what was happening, Jane. His Lord Chamberlain kept telling him to go back to the palace, but he insisted on remaining behind as everybody in the audience was shouting 'God save the King' and waving their hats. Kelly wrote in his book that the queen and the princesses were crying and 'it was a sight never to be forgotten by those present'."

"Grandpa, what happened to James Hadfield afterwards? Did they hang him?"

"No, they didn't. What happened was an interesting case in British law. Of course, he was put on trial for treason, and he was defended by Thomas Erskine, a very famous barrister of the time. I think to summarise the trial, it went something like this:

Judge: Mr Erskine. How does the defendant plead?

Erskine: He pleads that he is not guilty and also insane, Your Honour. As such, he cannot be held responsible for his deeds.

Judge: His deeds, as you phrase them, include attempting to kill His Majesty, King George III, and that of course is a treasonous act.

Erskine: I am very well aware of that, my lord, but if you have no objection, I would like to call upon my first witness.

Judge: Please do so.

Erskine: I call on Mr Joseph Craig, a musician who was playing in the Drury Lane Theatre orchestra on the night in question. (After the witness is sworn in, he is questioned by Mr Thomas Erskine). Mr Craig, please describe the scene that you saw on Thursday 15 May 1800 at the Drury Lane Theatre.

Craig: *I was sitting in my place on the stage when I saw the accused, er, Mr Hadfield come to the front of the theatre and point and even shoot his pistol – it was a flintlock pistol, I noticed – at the king in his royal box. Naturally I was quite shocked at this.*

Erskine: *Quite. And what did you do next?*

Craig: *I saw Mr Hadfield drop his pistol, and then several other players and people present, including myself, rushed over to where Mr Hadfield was standing and we dragged him over the rails into the music room below the stage.*

Erskine: *And then what happened?*

Craig: *The Duke of York and Mr Sheridan, the manager, came in and Mr Hadfield looked at the duke and said, 'God bless Your Royal Highness, I like you very well. You are a good fellow. This is not the worst that is brewing'.*

Judge: *Mr Craig, were those his exact words?*

Craig: *Yes, Your Honour.*

After several more questions, Mr Craig stepped down and a Mr Wright, after being sworn in, took his place as the next witness.

Mr Erskine: Mr Wright, please tell the court what you were doing at Drury Lane Theatre on the aforementioned night.

Wright: I was sitting in the first row in front, nearest to the orchestra, waiting for the performance, when suddenly I was shocked to hear the report of a pistol. I then saw His Majesty turn around in his royal box and then I jumped forward and caught the accused Mr Hadfield by his collar.

Erskine: And is that all?

Wright: No, sir. A young lady, who was standing behind me, pointed to the ground where Mr Hadfield's pistol lay. I picked it up and I believe it is here now in court.

Erskine: Thank you, Mr Craig. You may step down.

Then Mr Law, one of the counsels for the prosecution, called on the Duke of York to be called to the witness stand. As soon as James Hadfield saw him take his place, he shouted out, 'God bless the duke. I love him!'. The prisoner was immediately sat down in the dock and Mr Kirby, the Keeper from Newgate Prison, was told to keep his prisoner under control for the duration of the proceedings.

The Duke of York: All I know about this miserable affair, sir, is that my brother, the king, was at Drury

*Lane Theatre that night and that this man
attempted to assassinate him. I was quite
surprised by all this as I know the accused to be
a good man, and one who had served as one of
my orderlies. Since then, he has told me that he
will probably hang for this crime and that he
regrets that his wife will also have to suffer.*

*Erskine: If you knew him to be a good man, can you
think, Your Grace, why he decided to perform
this extreme act?*

*The Duke of York: No, I cannot. All I know is that when
I was dealing with him after the shooting and I
asked him this same question, he replied that he
was tired of life and that he should be killed.*

"After this, although Hadfield was expected to be
held not responsible for his actions and that he would
receive a verdict of 'not guilty for reasons of insanity',
this was not to be."

"Why not, Grandpa? Everyone had seen him try and
kill the king."

"I know that, Sophie, but if he had received this
verdict, then technically he could have been allowed to
resume his everyday life."

"So, what happened, Professor Warkworth?"

"In the end, Parliament rushed through an Act which
allowed the courts to send people like Hadfield to the
'incurable' ward at the Royal Bethlehem hospital. He
was deemed a 'criminal lunatic' and was sentenced to

remain there 'until His Majesty's pleasure be known'."

"And was it known, Grandpa?"

"Yes, Sophie. Hadfield spent the rest of his life there until he died forty years later. Apart from one brief escape in 1802, he spent his time with his pet cats, dogs and squirrels, seeing visitors and writing poems. In 1833, the governors of the prison bought him a wig to cover the scars on his head that he had received from the time he had served in the Army and when he died in 1841, they discovered some nasty wounds to his brain during his autopsy."

"So Professor Warkworth, it was probably those wounds that had caused his madness."

"Yes, Jane. You are probably right. But whatever it was, by trying to kill the king and then being deemed insane, this trial was one more important step on the way to recognising the criminally insane and dealing with them in a more humane manner."

Chapter Eighteen
The Cato Street Conspiracy (1820)

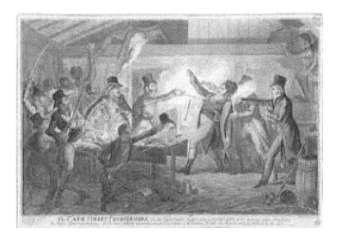

The Cato Street Conspiracy

"Grandpa, do you know where Castlereagh Street is?"

"No. Why?"

"Because I've been told that there's a good shop there where I can buy a new computer keyboard."

"I see. Wait a minute. I think it's somewhere near Oxford Street and Edgware Road. Have a look on your mobile. It should be there."

"Ah, here it is, Grandpa. Just off the Edgware Road. But it's nearer the Marylebone flyover than Oxford Street. Here, it is, just near Harrowby Street."

"Wait a minute, Sophie. Is there a street named Cato Street marked there? Just next to it? Look carefully now. That print is too small for my eyes."

"Cato Street, you said – I'm looking. Yes, here's Cato Street. How did you know?"

"To be honest, I didn't. I just guessed. But I thought that if there's a Castlereagh Street and a Harrowby Street in the area, then there'll probably be a Cato Street as well."

"OK. I know that I am letting myself in for a history lesson, but what's the connection between Castlereagh, Harrowby and Cato?"

"Well, my dear Sophie, it's like this. Castlereagh was the Foreign Minister in the 1820s, and Harrowby was a lord who lived at the same time, and Cato was..."

"Another lord."

"No. He was nothing of the sort. In fact, quite the opposite is true. Cato was the name of two Roman statesmen whose name was used as the site of the Cato Street massacre."

"Excuse me, Grandpa. You have completely confused me. What is the connection between two nineteenth century politicians, two Roman statesmen and a massacre? And anyway, who carried out the massacre, Castlereagh, Harrowby or Cato? My guess is that it was Cato since the Romans were quite a bloodthirsty lot."

"Well, I'm sorry to tell you, my dearest granddaughter, but you are quite wrong. None of these gentlemen were murderers. The connection is that some other guys, as you would call them, wanted to murder Castlereagh and the British cabinet in Cato Street."

"What? Where I'm going tomorrow?"

"The exact same place, or at least in that area."

"So what happened?"

"Well, in a way, it was bit like a repeat performance of Guy Fawkes and the Gunpowder Plot, but over two hundred years later."

"Why? Did they want to blow up the Cabinet with gunpowder?"

"Oh no, not with gunpowder. They planned to assassinate the members of the Cabinet personally."

"Hmm, that sounds a bit bloodthirsty. And what about the king? It was George III who was sitting on the throne then, no?"

"No. He had died at the beginning of the year, in 1820 that is, so his son, George IV, who had been acting as regent for the past few years, was now king in his own right."

"So from the way you are talking, I take it that this massacre didn't exactly work out. What happened? Were these guys Catholics who were fed up with being discriminated against?"

"No, no, Sophie. They weren't Catholics and I doubt if they thought very much about religion at all. No, these would-be assassins were all radicals and reformers, that is, they hoped to bring about major changes in society. They believed in attacking all the economic, political and social ills of society as they understood them. But unlike other groups or individuals who wanted to change the British way of life, these radicals were very extreme and demanded sweeping and immediate changes. As far as they were concerned, the means, however violent, justified the ends."

"Grandpa, they sound a bit like some of the characters we learned about when we studied the French Revolution."

"Perhaps you're right in a way. And in fact, many of the English radicals took the French Revolution as their model. Remember, only thirty years had passed since the French had chopped off the heads of King Louis and Marie Antoinette, so there were still people around who remembered these things at first hand and not just from dusty old history books.

"Oh, and one other thing. Often these radicals were not combined politically and they were usually to be found in small groups, some moderate and some very extreme."

"What? Like the Bolsheviks and Mensheviks in the Russian Revolution?"

"Exactly."

"So, Grandpa, I suppose then it was the extreme radicals whom we're talking about here."

"Of course. And their leader had the lovely non-violent and pastoral name of Thistlewood. Arthur Thistlewood."

"So, tell me about him. I know you're dying to and I'm not going to Cato Street or thereabouts till tomorrow."

"You cheeky thing. But yes, you're right. I do want to tell you, but first put on the kettle and then we'll learn about the grim story of the Cato Street Massacre."

Twenty minutes later, after he had finished his 'Lord Nelson' mug of tea and two chocolate digestive biscuits, the professor sat down with a hefty volume about the reign of King George IV. "Right now, where were we? Ah yes, the Cato Street Massacre... Radicalism and Jeremy Bentham."

"Jeremy Bentham. Who's that?"

"Oh, he was quite a character. He believed that all laws should provide the greatest happiness for the greatest number of people, and he wrote a lot about this in order to spread the word of his radical ideas. And, oh yes, if you want to see him today, you can still do so."

"How?"

"Because his skeleton and mummified head, or at least a model of it, is in the museum at University College London."

"What? Where you used to teach?"

"Yes, that's it."

"Sounds pretty grim to me. But anyway, if we're being grim, let's get back to the Cato Street Massacre. In 1820, no?"

"No, not really. This particular plot started much earlier, in the latter half of the eighteenth century to be precise. For it was then that Thomas Spence, one of the chief advocates of these revolutionary ideas, was born. He came from Newcastle in the mid-1750s and grew up to be a schoolteacher. He moved to London in 1792, but by the time he was twenty, he was already talking about ideas like nationalising the land for the public good. This, as you can guess, was pretty extreme."

"Because all the land belonged to the gentry?"

"Yes, or at least most of it. And as you can guess, they were very loath to part with any of it, and especially to the poor. And so, Spence came to London and started selling, or at least trying to sell, copies of Thomas Paine's book *The Rights of Man* on street corners. He was very quickly arrested and bundled off in the eighteenth-century version of a paddy wagon. Fortunately for him, he was released soon after and he opened a shop in Chancery Lane, you know, near where the City and the Law Courts are today. Here he sold all sorts of radical pamphlets and books, and in fact he even started his own periodical. It had the delightful title of *Pig's Meat*."

"*Pig's Meat*?"

"Yes. Actually, its full title was *Pig's Meat, or Lessons for the Swinish Multitude*. This of course was too much for the authorities, who arrested and jailed him for about a year. However, this didn't seem to deter our hero, for after his release he carried on doing the same thing and, in 1801, he was re-arrested and imprisoned for selling seditious literature. After his release he then opened a shop in Oxford Street."

"In Oxford Street! He must have come into the money."

"Not really. The Oxford Street of those days was not like the Oxford Street of today."

"So what did he sell? Souvenirs from London? Ladies' fashions?"

"Very funny. Actually, he sold hot drinks, as well as handbills and things like that. He wasn't too successful and ended up selling things from a barrow. And in addition to all this, he was one of the first feminists."

"What?"

"Yes, he advocated women's rights and even put forward the idea to make it easier for the working man and woman to get a divorce."

"I can just imagine the establishment being delighted with those sorts of ideas."

"Exactly. Especially as the authorities were feeling particularly jumpy because of the French Revolution and all the radical ideas that were coming over from the Continent."

"But, Grandpa, but did he do anything more exciting or practical than printing handbills and selling hot coffee or whatever?"

"Oh yes. He became recognised as the Head of the radicals who prophesied revolution. He and other men, including a fellow radical called James Watson, would go to different pubs at night and try and spread the good word."

"Yes, and have a quick one at the same time."

"Maybe that as well. Anyway, they'd chalk all sorts of graffiti over the walls like 'The Land is the People's Farm' and 'Spence's Plan and Full Bellies' with the result that he was nearly arrested again. Actually, Spence and seventeen other radical writers were later arrested in about 1809, but by then he was nearly sixty years old and I suppose the authorities considered that he was past being a major troublemaker. He died in 1814 and was buried by forty 'disciples', as they called themselves, and they promised to keep his ideas alive. As a result, they established the Society of Spencean Philanthropists."

"Grandpa, this is beginning to sound like a long story."

"Well, I warned you that it would be, but this is the end of chapter one. For this society was to continue for only another six years, but among its members were the men who organised the Cato Street conspiracy."

"Ah, so that's where you've been leading me to – Cato Street."

"Exactly."

"So tell me, Grandpa, who were some of those wicked conspirators?"

"Well, their leader, as I mentioned before, was Arthur Thistlewood, and the other members included John Brent, James Ings, William Davidson and Richard

Tidd."

"And what are you going to tell me about these men? I'm sure you're dying to tell me."

"Now how would you know that? But yes, of course I am. Isn't it always the 'baddies' as you call them who are the most interesting? I mean why do people remember Guy Fawkes and not some saintly do-gooder of the seventeenth century?"

"Yes, it's like the 'baddies' in the Walt Disney cartoon films are much more exciting than the heroes."

"Hmm, you might be right there, but let's get back to the story of the Cato Street Massacre. So cast your mind back to just over two hundred years. You are in a dark and dank smelly room, somewhere in a murky and mucky part of London, far away from the prying eyes of the authorities."

"It's 1820, yes?"

"No, it's a few years before that. 1816 to be exact."

"OK Grandpa, let's hear the details then."

"Picture the scene: a small back room at 'The White Hart' pub in Camden, North London. A couple of half-burnt-out candles cast a flickering light over the room as dusk descends over the capital. Four men are sitting around a table with glasses of beer at various stages of being finished off. Among a few sheets of paper, some more empty glasses and bottles litter the table. It is obvious that the man sitting with his back to the window and facing the other men is the leader of this group. He has a long and thin face, a high forehead, bright piercing eyes, a sharp nose and thin lips which, when not being used for talking, remain tightly pressed together. His hair is cropped short except at the front which is tousled and curly. His long side-whiskers stop at the line of his thin mouth.

"Despite his personal poverty, he is wearing a more or less clean white cravat which sharply contrasts with his brightly coloured waistcoat and dark blue jacket. He is absent-mindedly playing with a pencil, occasionally writing the odd word on a piece of paper in front of him. This contains a few sketches of something that looks like a football field.

"He looks up at James Watson who is sitting opposite him and scribbling a few figures down on another piece of paper:

Thistlewood: Come on, James. What's the problem?

Watson: It's this field, Arthur. I'm just wondering if there's going to be enough room for all the people we want.

Thistlewood: Why? How many people do you think will attend?

Watson: Well, it'd be good if ten thousand come.

Preston: What! Do you really think that many will come? You really live in hope!

Thistlewood: Well, we can all dream, Thomas.

Hopper: Aye, you can do that well enough Arthur. But it's not dreams that are going to move our movement and anyway, what will the government do if ten thousand do indeed come? Now you tell me that.

Thistlewood: Well, I'll tell you this, John Hopper. If some sort of parliamentary reform doesn't go through soon, or if the present economic situation doesn't improve, a meeting in a field organised by men such as us, the Spencean Philosophers, will be a very minor affair in contrast to what will happen in the future.

Watson: And Arthur, where are you planning to hold this grand open-air meeting of yours?

Thistlewood: Spa Fields.

Preston: Spa Fields? Where's that?

Thistlewood: Islington way. North London.

Hopper: And when is it going to be held?

Thistlewood: Oh, I think sometime this November or December, and then... (Sharp knocks heard on the door. The four men immediately roll up any pieces of paper in front of them and hide them in their jackets.)

Watson: Who's there?

(Voice from outside): Castle. John Castle.

Thistlewood: Well, come on in, lad, and make yourself at home. Here Thomas, pull up that chair for John. (Castle settles himself down and looks at Watson, Preston and Hopper. It is obvious that he has met Thistlewood in the recent past). Gentlemen, allow me to introduce you to Mr John Castle. He is joining us and will help us *with our organisation of this forthcoming meeting at Spa Fields. I've already told him of what we are aiming at and I'm sure now, John, that if you listen carefully, you'll understand what we are planning to do. And so, gentlemen, as I was saying, we plan to have this big meeting sometime in November or December, but right now, we have to think about getting some speakers, that is apart from ourselves. Have you gentlemen any ideas?*

Preston: What about 'Orator' Hunt?

Watson: Who? Henry Hunt?

Preston: Aye, that's right. He knows how to talk. By Jove he does! I've heard him talk down in East Grinstead in Sussex and I've also heard him talk at meetings in Birmingham and Blackpool. And you know what? There were over forty thousand people, yes, forty thousand people at one of those meetings in the north. Aye, and some people say there were even more!

Hopper: That's right. And I've heard that there were over twenty thousand people who came to listen to him at Nottingham, too.

Thistlewood: So, it's settled then gentlemen. We'll see if we can persuade 'Orator' Hunt to talk for us. I know for a fact that his ideas and ours match and...

Preston: Aye, and he fell out with the landowners in Wiltshire over some of his ideas. You know, dividing up the farmland for the common good and...

Castle (with a pen and paper at hand): What did you say this Hunt fellow's first name is?

Preston: Hunt. Henry Hunt.

Castle: And did you say that he got into trouble with the Law in Wiltshire?

Hopper: Oh, aye, he had some sort of argument with Lord Bruce and...

Watson: Hey! What are you scribbling there?

Castle: Nothing special. Just about the plans for the Spa Fields meeting. Er, I don't want to get them wrong now, do I? But please tell me more about this Mr Hunt. He sounds a most interesting character.

Hopper: Ah, so as I was saying, he had some sort of argument with this landlord feller, Lord Bruce, and so as a result, he moved to East Grinstead in Sussex. And it was soon after this that he gained his reputation as a great orator.

Preston: So he's definitely the man we want for our meeting. (All nod in agreement and Castle puts his notebook away).

"The rest of the meeting was spent finalising details, and by ten o'clock the men decided to disperse separately so as not to attract attention. Thistlewood left the building with Watson, and a few minutes later they were followed by Castle, who left on his own. Hopper and Preston blew out the remaining candles, checked they hadn't left any incriminating pieces of paper about, and then they left. This they did in groups of two and three and then they split up as soon as they had gone a few yards. It was not good to be seen together. The government was in a jittery mood and if any well-known radicals were seen in groups, it would be too inviting for the authorities not to start asking any questions."

"And chucking them into jail."

"Exactly, Sophie. Any excuse for the government to do that. But to continue, at another meeting, held about ten days later at 'The Mulberry Tree' public house in Moorfields, Arthur Thistlewood was able to confirm to the other four men that 'Orator' Hunt would indeed attend the meeting at Spa Fields and that both he and James Watson would address the crowd. Watson blushed slightly, but this was not noticed as the poor light in the room covered up any outward signs of his embarrassment. Thistlewood also informed his fellow Spencean Radicals that the date of the meeting had been fixed for 2 December 1816.

"The weather at the beginning of December was typical for a London winter. The sky seemed low and heavy and grey clouds threatened to drench the city. A light wind blew the few remaining scruffy autumn leaves about over the scrubby grass of the field, but the men standing on the simple wooden platform were not at all interested in the vagaries of nature. They were more interested in seeing how many people would turn up. Thistlewood and the others had distributed handbills in all the local pubs and had also tacked notices to trees in the area. Now they would see if their efforts would bear any fruit:

Watson: Not many people, Arthur. Just look down there.

Thistlewood: It's early yet, lad. Be patient. Look, there's a whole crowd of people coming from over there behind those trees.

Preston: Look in the other direction. There's even more people coming over from the north. By the way, where's Castle? He said he'd be here by now.

Thistlewood: Don't know. Maybe he got held up. (Suddenly Thistlewood puts his cupped hand to his mouth and shouts) Henry! Henry Hunt! We're over here! Oh, I am glad to see you.

Hunt: And I'm glad to see you. And I'm also glad to see the place filling up. As I was walking over here, I noticed quite a lot of people making their way here.

Thistlewood: Good, good. We'll have a full meeting yet. Never you fear about that.

Hunt: I'm with you there, Arthur. You know, I feel exactly now as I did before I appeared at that big meeting at Birmingham a few months ago. And you, James Watson. Don't you look so nervous. Once you start speaking here, you'll forget the butterflies in your stomach. Fear not, lad. We'll have the government granting our demands for reform before long. Just you mark my words.

"By now, Spa Fields Islington had filled up and Thistlewood moved to the centre of the platform. He held up his hands as high as he could and a wave of muffled silence moved over the crowd like a wave, starting from the front by the platform.

Thistlewood (holding up a large megaphone): Ladies and gentlemen, we are meeting here together on this cold December day in order to demand parliamentary reform from a government that has proved itself deaf to all our pleas up till now. How much longer can we, the working people, the backbone of this country, continue to work and toil and yet not be represented in Parliament? How much time can we, the working people, be expected to remain silent when it is because of our work, our sweat, and our hardship that this country is so great? And yet, despite all this, we, the working people, have not been given the vote. I ask you, and I ask you now, how much longer can we…

"But his questions were not answered as they were drowned out by a roar of applause and shouts of approval. Thistlewood smiled at the crowd. He was in his element. 'Orator' Hunt patted him on the shoulder and whispered 'well done' in his ear. James Watson was also smiling; his nervousness had disappeared. Now he was bursting to have his say. Thistlewood gave him an encouraging pat on the back.

Hunt: It's going well Arthur. Just as I said it would. You were wrong to be worried.

Thistlewood: I'm glad, Henry. We've done well so far. But hey, what's going on over there? Something's happening at the back of the crowd. There, near the trees.

Watson: I can see men, men and horses. Arthur, it's the militia! The government has brought out the militia to break up the meeting!

Preston: But why? Nothing's happened yet. We haven't broken any laws.

Hopper: Come on. Let's get away quickly or we'll be arrested. Look, they're coming over here!

Thistlewood: We can't leave. We called these people here. We can't abandon them here now. If we do, we'll lose them forever.

Watson: But look at the troops! They're coming nearer all the time!

"Within a few minutes, a ring of armed soldiers had surrounded the platform while others were roughly breaking up the crowds. A soldier pushed a poorly dressed woman standing by one of the supports of the platform: 'Come on darlin'. Move it! Get on 'ome and serve your 'usband 'is supper. This ain't a place for women'.

"As the ring around them tightened and grew more threatening, Thistlewood signalled for Hunt to disappear. 'Quick, go away Henry! You're not really a member of our society and there's no need for you to get caught up in any of this. It's better you go'. But before the Orator could reply, John Stafford, the Chief Clerk at Bow Street Magistrates Court climbed his way up on to the platform and stood there, arms akimbo, accompanied by four armed militiamen.

"He faced Arthur Thistlewood and pulled out a large piece of paper from his long dark blue coat. The Spencean leader just had time to notice the royal coat-of-arms of King George III at the top of the page before Stafford's voice boomed out: 'Arthur Thistlewood, on orders from the British government and the Bow Street Magistrates, I am arresting you for disturbing the peace of the realm of His Majesty, King George III'.

"As Thistlewood was about to reply, a scuffle broke out at the back of the platform behind John Stafford. This was followed by a ghastly cry: 'Help! Help! He's stabbed me!' and suddenly Officer Joseph Rhodes fell onto the platform, a bloodstain spreading rapidly over the front of his blue uniform.

"That was the end of any further words between the radical leader and the representative of His Majesty's government. At a sign from Stafford, Thistlewood, Watson, Hopper and Preston were quickly surrounded. 'Orator' Hunt was read out a strongly phrased warning and brusquely dismissed. It was clear that it was Thistlewood and his fellow Spenceans who this well-organised and well-equipped government raid were after.

"As the bewildered group's hands were being bound prior to them being led away to a waiting carriage, another group of militiamen headed by the Lord Mayor were cutting off another group of radicals from marching onto the City of London. Fights and scuffles broke out as the two groups met, but eventually the well-trained officers and men prevailed, and the rioting came to an end as the sun set over the battlefield in North London.

"Soon after, the four radicals found themselves in court. For some reason, known only to themselves, the authorities decided to charge James Watson first and not Arthur Thistlewood, the acknowledged leader. Perhaps it was because it was Watson and not Thistlewood who had been picked to address the Spa Fields meeting. However, these fine points of the English legal system did not really interest the four Spencean Philanthropists.

"Imagine the surprise of the four men in the dock when the clerk of the court called in the government's main witness for the prosecution: 'Call in John Castle! Call in John Castle!'"

"Do you mean that the government had planted him there as a spy?"

"Yes, Sophie. That was a typical government move to keep an eye on such Radical groups."

"Ah, like that Gifford guy who was planted in Babington's plot to bump off Elizabeth I?"

"Exactly. So now lest's jump back to the 1820s.Within three minutes a smug-looking witness was ushered into the courtroom. After being sworn in, the judge reminded the four men that they were being charged with high treason and 'it grieves me to add that because Officer Joseph Rhodes was not actually stabbed and fatally wounded by one of you, that I cannot add the charge of wilful and malicious murder'.

"The trial proceeded as smoothly as the government had planned, that is, until the judge called on the lawyer for the defence to question the chief witness for the prosecution:

Lawyer: Now come, come, Mr. Castle. You claim that you are an honest upright citizen, a pillar of society, nay a model citizen that each and every one of us should look up to. Pray do not blush so much sir in embarrassment. I am sure that such a man as yourself is used to being referred to in such glowing terms.

Castle: Yes, sir. Of course, sir.

Lawyer: And am I not correct in supposing that you have been such an upright citizen throughout all of your life?

Castle: Er, yes sir. That is true, sir.

Lawyer: And so, Mr. Castle, let me just briefly summarise your upright and noble career here in this courtroom for the benefit of those who have not had the fortune to acquaint themselves of yourself beforehand. (At this point the judge leans forward as do most of the other people in court to hear the lawyers next words. It is clear from the lawyer's tone that he is about to surprise all those present). Mr. John Castle, you were born in Yorkshire in or about the year 1785 and moved to London about twenty years later. Am I right?

Castle: Yes, sir.

Lawyer: And am I also right in saying that when you came to London, you were gainfully employed by a Mrs. Thoms?

Castle: Er, yes, sir.

Lawyer: Speak up, man.

Castle: Er, yes, sir. That is correct, sir.

Lawyer: And did this Mrs. Thoms run a hotel of some description?

Castle:(More confidently now) Yes, sir.

Lawyer: And Mr. Castle, isn't it more accurate to describe this aforementioned hotel as… as, how can I phrase it without sounding distasteful, as a brothel?

Castle: (Mutters) Yes, sir.

Lawyer: Speak up, man. His Honour must be able to hear your replies as well as myself. Please repeat your answer.

Castle: Yes, sir. You are right sir. But I left it pretty soon after I saw what sort of place it was.

Lawyer: Oh, I am glad of that. I would hate to think that you spent more than a minute of your life in such a place, once you realised where you were being employed.

Judge: Mr. Lawrence, I would like to know where these questions are leading us, if indeed they are not leading us up the proverbial garden path, which I fear is the truth of the matter. After all, we are here today in order to render judgment on the nefarious activities of Mr. Thistlewood and his subversive cohorts, and not to conduct an enquiry into the chief witness for the prosecution's past employment record.

Lawyer: Yes, Your Honour, but I am sure that if you are patient and bear with me for a few more minutes, you will see that I am not leading you up the proverbial garden path, but into a very disgusting, er, how shall I phrase it, a veritable slough of despond, that is, if I may borrow a phrase from Mr. John Bunyan's excellent book The Pilgrim's Progress.

Judge: Very well then, but please make some of your own progress with your pilgrim and refrain from wasting the court's time. After all, we have a full day's work ahead of us here today.

Lawyer: Indeed, Your Honour. So now, Mr. Castle, as you were saying, you left Mrs. Thom's brothel in King Street, Soho and then you formed a business relationship with a Mr. Daniel Davis, is that not so?

Castle: (Mutters) Yes.

Lawyer: *Speak up, man. We all wish to hear you here today.*

Castle: Yes, sir.

Judge: *(Interrupting) And what kind of business was this?*

Castle: Money, Your Honour.

Lawyer: *Of course it was money, man. All business ventures are based on the exchange of goods, services and money. Now Mr. Castle, can you be somewhat more specific and inform the court about what aspect of money and business you were involved?*

Castle: Making money, sir.

Judge: *Of course you were. That's the whole aim of business. Mr. Lawrence, please instruct your client to elucidate and enlighten us on his business ventures and give the court a few relevant details.*

Lawyer: *Mr. Castle. You've just heard His Honour. Please inform the court exactly how you made your money in business.*

Castle: (Mutters and coughs at the same time) We forged banknotes, sir.

Lawyer: *Excuse me. I didn't quite catch what you said. Did you say that you were engaged in the business of forging banknotes?*

Castle: Yes, sir.

Lawyer: And how were you punished for this disgusting criminal activity?

Castle: I wasn't, sir.

Judge: Mr. Lawrence, did I hear Mr. Castle correctly when he said that he remained and indeed remains unpunished for this terrible offence?

Lawyer: Yes, Your Honour. That is indeed the situation. It says here that the charges were dropped against this witness on condition that he agreed to give evidence against his business partner, or his partner in crime, Mr. Daniel Davis.

Judge: Indeed! And what else does it say in the records in front of you?

Lawyer:(Reads) 'As a result of the evidence that Mr. John Castle produced in court, Mr. Daniel Davis was found guilty as charged and the maximum sentence was duly carried out'.

Judge: Execution? Hanging?

Lawyer: Yes, Your Honour.

Judge: I see. (Turning to the prosecution) And Mr. Brookes, how long have you known about Mr. Castle's abominable past?

Brookes: Not long, Your Honour. I was just informed very recently by Mr. John Stafford, the Chief Clerk at Bow Street that Mr. Castle had been planted in this Spencean Society and that is how we obtained such reliable information about what these men were planning to do.

422

Judge: You have just used a key word there, Mr. Brookes, reliable. For I feel that, in all honesty, I must ask the jury to question the reliability of this witness. After all, we have just heard about Mr. Castle's criminal past, that is, his record of consorting with loose women and brothels as well as forging His Majesty's banknotes. In conclusion, I think that all these aspects of this witness' career should indeed be taken into consideration.

"They were. As a result, James Watson, the first of the accused, was not convicted of any crime and he and the other three were released since the authorities deemed it that they had all been arrested for the same offence."

"And so, Grandpa, was that the end of Thistlewood and his Spencean Society? And where does Cato Street fit in all this?"

"Oh no, my dear. Soon after this, Watson and Thistlewood fell out because Watson believed in more peaceful means of persuasion while Thistlewood was convinced that parliamentary reform could only be brought about through violent action."

"So then what happened?"

"Watson started to write pamphlets and distribute them around. His idea was to establish Unions of Non-represented People and he hoped that the people would pay him a penny a week to cover his costs."

"And did they?"

"No, Sophie, they did not. In December 1818 he was imprisoned for debt and was released the following year, the year of the Peterloo Massacre."

"The what?"

"The Peterloo Massacre."

"Sounds a bit like Waterloo to me."

"Good. That's what it was supposed to sound like."

"Why?"

"So, Sophie, let's begin at the beginning. By the summer of 1819, the demand for parliamentary reform was so great that between sixty to a hundred thousand people met at St. Peter's Fields, Manchester to hear 'Orator' Hunt speak out about it. The authorities became very nervous and called out the militia. Things then got out of hand, and the troops, Hussars they were, charged the crowds which had remained pretty orderly up to that point and plunged into them with sabres drawn. Naturally, people were trampled on and many demonstrators were cut down where they stood."

"Sounds pretty grim to me."

"It was, Sophie. It was very grim. Eleven people were killed and about four hundred were wounded. The whole affair caused a fantastic amount of resentment against the government, especially against Henry Addington, the Home Secretary. The government then proceeded to rub salt into some very open wounds and passed the Six Acts. These laws prohibited meetings of over fifty people; gave magistrates the right to search private houses for arms; increased the tax on cheap papers and pamphlets and prompted the passing of several other very restrictive and anti-democratic laws."

"And so this Peterloo name was an ironic use of Wellington's victory over Napoleon?"

"Exactly. Just four years earlier. And in fact, this Peterloo Massacre became such a powerful working-class symbol for government repression, that even twenty years later, 'Remember the Bloody Deeds of Peterloo' was painted on demonstrators' banners."

"And did the government bring about any changes?"

"Oh, certainly. Several hundred people had their lives changed forever. They were transported to Australia, but as for parliamentary reform, there wasn't any."

"So Grandpa, the whole thing was a waste of time, no?"

"No, not really, because there was a renewed interest in James Watson's ideas, but as usual, he was stony-broke and so he couldn't afford to finance any sort of reform organisation. In the end, he ended up once again in the debtor's prison."

"Poor man."

"Not necessarily. You see, being in prison at the beginning of 1820 probably saved his life."

"Being in prison saved his life?"

"Yes, my dear. You see, it was then that Thistlewood, who was the undisputed Head of the Spencean Society, planned the Cato Street Conspiracy."

"Ah, I was wondering when we would come back to that."

"Now, don't you be so cheeky, young lady. You know that I love telling a good story, and all this…"

"What, you mean Spa Fields and Peterloo?"

"Yes, and all of this has been a good lead up to the final chapter, so to speak."

"OK, Grandpa. Let's have it. The full works about the Cato Street Conspiracy."

"Right-ho. But after tea. All this early nineteenth century history is making me thirsty. So, there's a dear, put on the kettle, find a few of my favourite chocolate biscuits and then we'll get on with the Cato Street Conspiracy, OK?"

It was OK, as half-an-hour later found Grandpa and Sophie back in Grandpa's book-lined room, with the ex-history professor about to launch into 'his good story'.

"All right, Sophie, use your imagination and cast your mind back to the winter of 1820. The general atmosphere in the country is pretty bad. The people, especially the poor people, are cold and angry. They are extremely disappointed with the government and the economy. The government has done nothing in the way of parliamentary reform and the Peterloo Massacre has left a very vivid scar in the public memory, and no one was angrier and more scarred than…"

"Arthur Thistlewood?"

"Exactly. But by this time, Watson was languishing in prison and there were some new men in the Spencean

Society. These included William Davidson, James Ings, Richard Tidd, John Brunt and George Edwards. They…"

"Grandpa, you never cease to amaze me. How is it you always remember all these tiny details, you know, like everybody's names and things like that?"

"Well, I suppose because I find this stuff fascinating, no? I mean, you remember all the words of the pop songs you hear, and I can't tell the difference between the Beatles and any other singers."

"Grandpa, your choice of pop singers is somewhat dated. But, yes, what you said is true. But please continue. I know you're dying to."

"Ah, so here we are. The winter of discontent; the winter of 1820. Is your imagination working? So let it work on a small and dark room as before, in the back room of a pub or in someone's house. The night is cold and wintry, and the Spencean Society members are sitting around a table, complete with a flickering candle or two, debating the events of the day as usual:

Thistlewood: And so, my good friends, where do we go from here? Do we follow James Watson's lead and quietly hand out pamphlets and hope to bring about change like that, or shall we take a more active role?

Brunt: I think that we should be more active. After all you, Arthur, have already had some experience in organising large outdoor meetings, haven't you?

Thistlewood: Aye. That's right.

Tidd: I say, what about that public reception meeting you organised for 'Orator' Hunt after Peterloo? How many people attended that one? Twenty thousand?

Davidson: No. The Times said that thirty thousand people turned up to that one. That surely took some organising.

Brunt: That's true enough. And think about all of the people who came to hear James Watson before he ended up in prison.

Ings: Aye, you're right there.

Davidson: I mean there was John Thelwall, Major Cartwright as well as Sir Francis Burdett. They all came, and no doubt more would have done so, if they'd had the chance.

Edwards: True enough, but how shall I say his? Some people don't want too much to do with us. Y'know, they consider us a dangerous lot and, Arthur, they think that you are much too revolutionary, if you don't mind my saying so.

Thistlewood: I don't mind at all. I'd prefer to be known as a man of deeds rather than someone who just sits around and talks all day but does nowt else.

Davidson: Hear, hear! That's what I like to hear. Deeds, not words!

Edwards: So if that's the case, Arthur, have a look a look at this little article that I saw in yesterday's

428

copy of the New Times.

Thistlewood: (Reads to himself and then aloud) 'London, February 1820. Several members of the British government... blah... blah... blah... going to hold a small dinner party... blah... blah... blah... intimate gathering... blah... blah... blah... at Lord Harrowby's house...'

Brunt: Where?

Thistlewood: Lord Harrowby's. Now where's that? Ah, it says here – thirty-nine Grosvenor Square.

Davidson: Lord Harrowby's you said? Well I'll be blowed! I used to work for him once. You know, I even know some of the blokes who are still working for him, his servants I mean.

Thistlewood: Davidson, you know what, you've just given me an idea. What if we decided to do a Guy Fawkes on those big knobs, y'know, those members of the government. That'd make the authorities listen to us.

Tidd: Aye. They'd have no choice then.

Thistlewood: What do you say, Edwards?

Edwards: Hmm, I'm not exactly sure.

Thistlewood: Why not?

Edwards: What if we fail?

Thistlewood: We fail. That's it. But if we don't try, we're not going to get anywhere, are we?

Edwards: Well, if you put it like that, I suppose you're right.

Davidson: But Arthur, what exactly do you mean, by

doing a Guy Fawkes? Do you mean that we should blow up the place with barrels of gunpowder?

Thistlewood: *No, no. Nothing like that. I'm thinking rather that we burst into their cosy chit-chat supper party and just kill them there and then.*

Tidd: *How? What with? Our bare hands? Guns? Clubs?*

Thistlewood: *Yes. Sabres, guns and pistols. Short and sweet. Just use your imaginations. (And with that he rubs his hands with unconcealed glee).*

Brunt: *You know, Arthur, I think we shouldn't use guns. They're too noisy. A good sabre or sharp pointed awl, you know, like one of my shoemaking tools, would do the job just as well as any gun. Don't you agree, Tiddy?*

Tidd: *I do. You certainly can do a lot of damage with shoemaking tools. I've hurt myself pretty badly at times, accidentally of course, so I should know.*

Thistlewood: *Then it's agreed. No guns, so no noise.*

Ings: *Well, I know what I'm going to take, and that's my butcher's knife. It's been a long time since it's been used to cut up some fresh meat. I know I've been sitting here quietly all evening, but I for one won't be too sad to cut off Castlereagh's head, and also Sidmouth's if it comes to that.*

Davidson: *Er, Lord Sidmouth if you please. (Stands up and makes a mocking bow) No, wait a minute. Let's be serious. As I said before, I used to work for Lord Harrowby in...*

Tidd: What! You with your black face?

Davidson: Richard Tidd, don't you be so rude. Just because I was born in Jamaica doesn't mean that I don't know how to behave. And just you remember this. Despite my black face, I am an educated gentleman.

Brunt: Oh yes?

Davidson: Oh yes, indeed. I once studied law and then I went on to study mathematics in the university in Aberdeen. But anyway, enough of that now. Let's get down to brass tacks. I think that if we're going to go through with this plan, I should be one of the main organisers.

Thistlewood: I agree with Davidson here. So you're saying that you know the house in Grosvenor Square?

Davidson: Every inch of it.

Thistlewood: And the servants there?

Davidson: I don't know if I'll know all of them today, especially as I haven't worked there for some time. But I'm sure there'll still be some there who I'll know. You know, servants don't leave a place like that in a hurry.

Thistlewood: All right then. Let's finish this meeting off here now. Davidson here will try and get us some details about the house and the servants...

Tidd: And try and find out who is going to be at this supper thing.

431

Thistlewood: Exactly, and also when it is going to be held.

Davidson: You mean at what time of the day?

Thistlewood: Yes. (Standing up and blowing out the almost burnt-out candles) So, my friends, I suggest that we meet again at the end of the week, say Friday, and in the meanwhile Davidson will try and find out as much as possible about the Grosvenor Square house and supper-party.

"And so it was that William Davidson, under the guise of friendship, went round to thirty-nine Grosvenor Square the next day and started to chat to one of Lord Harrowby's servants with whom he had worked in the past. To the would-be assassin's surprise, the servant informed him that Lord Harrowby was not in London at the time. He didn't say where he was, but he insisted on telling Davidson that His Lordship would not be at home on the evening in question, and that if Davidson wanted to talk to him about the possibility of future re-employment then he would have to arrange the meeting for another date. As expected, Davidson reported this back to the others at their next meeting.

Davidson: And so I tell you, this servant was quite insistent. He kept telling me that Lord Harrowby wouldn't be at home on the night of the supper-party.

Thistlewood: How reliable is this servant?

Davidson: Oh, he's reliable enough. Works well and so on but...

Thistlewood: Well, I for one don't believe him. What do you others think?

Edwards: I agree with Arthur. I'm sure that he's lying. He's probably been told not to tell anyone about the Cabinet meeting which will be held there.

Ings: But there's no secret about that. It was in the paper. Edwards showed it to Arthur, didn't he? So people must know about it.

Thistlewood: Aye. But it probably wasn't in all the papers. And anyway, it was only a small paragraph hidden away among the more important articles.

Brunt: I agree with Arthur. Despite what this servant says, I say we go ahead with our plan.

Tidd: And so do I.

Thistlewood: Come, let's have a show of hands. All of those who agree we continue with our plan to kill the members of the Cabinet...

Davidson: Especially Castlereagh...

Ings: And Lord Sidmouth...

Thistlewood: Yes, yes, so gentlemen, please raise your hands. (All hands are raised, Edward's first). Right, then that's settled. So I suggest we do the following: I'll ask John Harrison, who can't be with us tonight, to rent a small room near Grosvenor Square, so we'll have a place nearby

> *to work from and where we can store our*
> *weapons and our disguises...*

Davidson: But that'll cost a lot of money.

Thistlewood: No, it won't. First of all, it will be as I said,
> *just a small room and John will tell the landlord*
> *that he'll need it only for a week or, say, two*
> *weeks at most. And then once we've got the*
> *room, we'll meet again there to make the final*
> *arrangements. Are we all agreed?*

"They were. And leaving the building quietly in pairs, they quickly melted into the dark and murky night of a typically drizzling London winter.

"A few days later, Arthur Thistlewood was able to report back to the others that John Harrison had found and located a small place which also included a hayloft and stable in Cato Street, a small side street just off Edgware Road. The surrounding area was pretty run-down and shabby, and so the presence of Thistlewood and Co. would not arouse any suspicion, by their dress and manners. Even the 'Horse and Groom' public house opposite the Cato Street gang's temporary premises looked quite seedy."

"Grandpa, that sounds the perfect background in which to organise and carry out a plot."

"Yes, I suppose you're right. And so, on 23 February 1820, Arthur Thistlewood and the others were sitting in the Cato Street hayloft having what they presumed would be their final planning meeting. No doubt they were discussing the necessary logistics, like which weapons to bring, the timing of the attack, their escape routes and things like that and…"

"Excuse me for interrupting you, Grandpa, but from your tone it sounds like something went wrong."

"It did. But don't rush me. Never rush anyone in the middle of a good story. Ah, where was I? Oh, yes. So there they were, sitting in the hayloft going over the final details. James Ings had been told to wait at the bottom of the stairs, to be on guard. Suddenly he was surprised to find himself surrounded by a few policemen who quickly overpowered him, one of the more burly ones clapping his hand over Ings' mouth in order to prevent him from warning the others."

"But how did the police know about their new place in Cato Street?"

"Elementary, my dear Sophie, elementary. You remember one of the plotters was called Edwards?"

"George Edwards?"

"Yes. Well he, in fact, was a government spy who had wormed his way into the gang or as we say today, infiltrated the gang. After every meeting, he would write down his notes on little strips of paper and then pass them on to his boss, Inspector John Stafford at the Bow Street police station."

"But didn't Thistlewood or any of the others ever suspect him?"

"Well, it seems that one or two of them did, but Thistlewood apparently managed to persuade them that they were wrong and in fact Thistlewood made Edwards his number two man. Actually, it was Edwards who was always pushing Thistlewood to carry out his murderous plan. In fact, if you remember, it was Edwards who first told Thistlewood about the Cabinet meeting in the first place, you know, when he showed him the small notice in the paper."

"So, Grandpa, they all fell for it."

"Yes they did. Hook, line and sinker."

"So what happened next?"

"Oh, the end came quickly enough. After bundling Ings up and getting him out of the way, the chief police officer took a dozen of his men and they promptly climbed up into the hayloft. As soon as he got there, he shouted, 'We are peace officers. Lay down your arms'. Thistlewood and Davidson tried to use their swords while the others went for their pistols. Richard Smithers, one of the officers, tried to make an arrest but Thistlewood stabbed him. It was a fatal move and Smithers died soon after. A couple of the gang tried to fight it out, but the remainder surrendered quietly. Thistlewood and a couple of others managed to escape out of a window, but they didn't get very far and were soon rounded up again by the authorities."

"I bet the government were pleased to catch that lot."

"I'm sure they were, and especially as they had set the trap. In fact, they remind me of the methods Cecil and Walsingham used during the days of Good Queen Bess. And yes, as far as the government were concerned,

Thistlewood and Co. had been a real thorn in their sides for quite some time."

"So what happened to them? Were they hanged? Were they transported? What?"

"Oh, you are impatient, aren't you? Well, I'll put you out of your misery. Eleven members of the Spencean Society were charged with conspiracy and treason. As you can imagine, the government wanted to throw the whole book at them, but this time, Sophie, they were smart and had learned from previous trials."

"What do you mean?"

"In this trial, which took place about two weeks later, Lord Sidmouth, the Home Secretary, decided not to use George Edwards as a witness for the prosecution in court."

"Because he was a spy?"

"Exactly. Instead, the government used other sources for evidence, and they also persuaded Robert Adams and John Monument to give evidence against the other members of the gang. With all this evidence in hand it was plain sailing for the authorities. Two months later, Thistlewood, Davidson, Brunt, Ings and Tidd were all found guilty of high treason and…"

"Given the chop."

"Well, as Shakespeare would phrase it, they 'shuffled off this mortal coil'."

"Were they hanged then?"

"Yes."

"And what about the others? After all, they'd also

437

been involved, no?"

"Yes, they were sentenced to be executed as well, but then their sentences were commuted, and they were transported to Australia instead."

"Even the two who told on the others?"

"Yes, at least that was the case for John Harrison. But I can't really remember if Robert Adams suffered the same punishment."

"So when were the others hanged?"

"Ooh! You are a bloodthirsty little lady, aren't you?"

"Oh no, Grandpa. It's just my healthy interest in history. After all, you have taught me to look out for historical detail."

"All right, you win. So, the five Cato Street plotters were hanged at the beginning of May 1820 outside Newgate prison."

"You mean publicly?"

"Exactly. The government were determined that these men were to be made an example of. You know, justice being seen to be done."

"That sounds pretty nasty."

"It was. But I suppose it was more or less the same as sticking the heads of traitors on spikes on London Bridge or something like that which they used to do two hundred years earlier."

"I suppose so."

"I believe Thistlewood was one of the first to be hanged. But before that happened James Ings started to sing 'Liberty or Death' and Thistlewood shouted at him,

'Be quiet. We can die without all that noise.' And if I remember correctly, I read once that Brunt and Ings really suffered during the hanging."

"How? Don't you always?"

"Of course you do, but in their case the hanging wasn't done properly. Apparently, the knot on the noose must have been in the wrong place and the hangman's assistants had to pull on their legs in order to finish them off and put them out of their agony."

"Ooh, but that's horrible!"

"I know. But it seems that Thistlewood died quickly enough and so did Davidson, the ex-Jamaican, and so did Richard Tidd, who was a big and heavy fellow."

"And so I suppose that was the end of the Cato Street conspiracy?"

"Exactly. But maybe the government had learned something from the experience. Twelve years later, in 1832, the first Reform Bill was passed which was an important step in making this country more democratic. Not that everyone was suddenly given the vote, you understand, but it certainly got the ball rolling."

"By the way, was it Lord Castlereagh who brought in this Reform Bill, you know, after having been influenced by the Cato Street conspiracy, Peterloo and the Spa Fields demonstration?"

"No, Sophie. Actually, he had quite a sad end. Two years later, he went insane and cut his throat with a penknife. He was then buried in Westminster Abbey."

"I see. So the Castlereagh Street where I'm going

tomorrow to get my computer bits is named after him."

"Exactly. But it's the very small side-street called Cato Street which became famous in that area, well, at least in February 1820."

Chapter Nineteen
Nine Plots against Queen Victoria

Queen Victoria

"Grandpa, Queen Victoria was queen for over sixty years. Were there any plots or conspiracies against her?"

"Plots and conspiracies, Sophie? Yes, there was one conspiracy, but that came towards the end of her reign. It was in 1887 and it was supposed to kill her, after she'd been queen for fifty years."

"Who was responsible for that?"

"A group of Irish nationalists and, of course, coming when it did, their plot was called the Jubilee Plot."

"And it failed?"

"Yes, Sophie, it failed. But let me tell you something about some of the other attempts to kill her before I tell you about this Jubilee Plot. Do you have the time?"

"Yes, I was going to read over *Julius Caesar* for my English class tomorrow, but I suppose he can wait."

"Ah, Julius Caesar, another victim of another plot but, as you say, he can wait. So let's get started with Queen Victoria."

"And, Grandpa, before you start, was there only one plot against her? I mean, she was queen for an awfully long time."

"I know and so I'll tell you something about the other attempts to assassinate her before we get to the grand finale."

"Fair enough, but before you start, why weren't there any more plots or conspiracies against her? Why were there only attempts to kill her?"

"I think the reason is that, as a British queen in the nineteenth century, she didn't have that much power."

"You mean that it was Parliament that was the real ruler, not the queen?"

"That's right and, like now, the queen was more or less a figurehead. But let's get started. Here, give me that green book about Queen Victoria on the bottom shelf there and we'll see what happened to Britain's second longest reigning monarch. Ah, here we are, the first time someone tried to kill Queen Victoria was in June 1840. She'd been on the throne for nearly three years and was pregnant at the time of the shooting. The would-be assassin's name was Edward Oxford and he tried to shoot her with two pistols while she was out driving in her carriage with her husband, Prince Albert."

"But, Grandpa, were they all alone? Weren't there any policemen or guards with her?"

"Yes, Sophie, there were two guards, but you must remember, people then, for whatever reason, weren't as scared of terrorists as they are today. And I think that, in general, the authorities' anti-terrorist actions weren't like they are now. But to get back to Edward Oxford. He was only eighteen years old when he tried to kill the queen. He had been a bartender but was now unemployed and living with his mother. Later, Prince Albert, the queen's husband, described him as a 'little mean-looking man'."

"That sounds a good description of a killer."

"Maybe, but fortunately for Her Majesty, even though he was only six paces away from her when he tried to kill her, he missed. Luckily, at that moment, she had turned her head to look at a nearby horse and later she said that she thought the noise of the shot was from someone who was shooting birds in the park."

"And what happened when he tried to use his second pistol?"

"Ah, this time, the queen saw him and ducked. But this time, her would-be assassin wasn't so lucky. The crowd surrounding him grabbed and disarmed him. He seemed to have been quite proud of what he'd done, because he shouted, 'It was I. It was me that did it'. He was arrested and charged with treason. Then the police went to search his room and they found a sword and scabbard there as well as machinery to make more bullets. They also found some literature about an imaginary military group which he called 'Young England'."

"What do you mean by 'imaginary'?"

"What I mean, Sophie is, that such a group did not really exist. It was all in Edward Oxford's head. After the police had finished their investigations, he was tried at the Old Bailey in July and…"

"Found guilty."

"No, Sophie…"

"No? But he had tried to kill the queen. Twice!"

"I know, but in fact he was declared 'not guilty by reason of insanity'."

"And so they let him off?"

"No, my dear, not at all. He was sentenced to be detained 'until Her Majesty's pleasure be known'. In other words, he was sent to an asylum for where he remained a perfect patient for the next twenty-four years."

"What did he do there?"

"He drew pictures, read a lot and learned to play the violin. He also learned to play chess and became very good at it too. Then, after twenty-four years, he was given a conditional release."

"On condition that he wouldn't shoot the queen again?"

"No, Sophie. The condition was that he would move to Australia and if he ever returned to England, he would be put back in prison for the rest of his life."

"And what did he do in Australia?"

"He lived a very respectable life in Melbourne and called himself John Freeman. He became a housepainter and joined the local Mutual Improvement Society. He also married a widow who had two children and then he became a churchwarden."

"So he really did become a reformed character."

"Yes, Sophie, he did, indeed. And in addition to what I've just told you, under the penname of 'Liber', he wrote articles for the local paper, *The Argus*, about the markets, racetracks and slums in the city and later he turned these into a book called *Lights and Shadows of Melbourne Life.* And for the rest of his life he claimed that the reason he had tried to shoot the queen was to try and be famous."

"In other words, to get his fifteen minutes of glory."

"Right. He always claimed that the pistols weren't loaded, and this may have been true as they never found any bullets around at the scene of the shooting."

"And when did he die?"

"He died on 23 April 1900, St. George's Day, aged 78."

"All right, that was number one plot. What was

number two?"

"Number two took place in May 1842, that is, two years after number one."

"By another assassin who later reformed?"

"I don't know if this one was reformed, Sophie, because this man, John Francis, tried to kill the queen twice, on two separate occasions. The first time he tried to shoot her was while she was riding with Prince Albert in their open carriage in the Mall."

"Grandpa, why did you say 'tried to shoot her'?"

"Because his pistol jammed and so he stuck it underneath his coat and ran away before anyone could catch him. The second attempt took place on the following day. The queen and Prince Albert thought that the best way of catching him was to ride out in the park in their carriage again and act as a decoy."

"That was very brave of her."

"Yes, Sophie, you're right. Anyway, the queen and Albert set off again and sure enough John Francis tried again. As luck would have it, and standing almost right next to the royal carriage, his pistol jammed again. The police, who were ready this time, jumped on him and caught him. He was put on trial, found guilty…"

"And hanged."

"No, Sophie, he…"

"What? He was also found to be insane?"

"No, he was sentenced to be hanged and quartered but the queen said that, instead, he was to be banished; transported to Australia and sentenced to 'hard labour' for life."

"Hmm, Grandpa, some people never learn."

"Maybe you're right there, but the authorities did what the police said. Shortly after hearing all the criticism against them and how they had not protected the queen very well, they established their first detective department. And perhaps then they were ready for the next attempt on Her Majesty's life."

"When was that?"

"One month later at the beginning of July – 3 July 1842. The would-be assassin this time was a bitter man, who had a deformed spine – he would have been called a 'hunchback' then. He was very depressed and thought that if he did something dramatic, such as shooting the queen, somehow his life would improve."

"And did it?"

"I'm not sure you'd call what happened an improvement, Sophie, but I'll tell you. This young man, seventeen-year-old John William Bean, was in the crowd outside Buckingham Palace waiting for the queen to come out. When she emerged, he aimed his pistol at her, but it failed to fire. A bystander managed to grab Bean's wrist, but he wriggled free and escaped. That night, the police rounded up every 'hunchback' living in London and found Bean at home. They arrested him and at his trial he claimed that he wasn't really a dangerous assassin…"

"Because his pistol wasn't loaded."

"Exactly. He was sentenced to eighteen months of

hard labour and released. Later, he married, twice, and had a son, but despite that he continued to suffer from depression for the rest of his life. In the end, the fifty-seven-year-old John William Bean committed suicide by taking an overdose of opium."

"And did the queen have a quiet time after this?"

"Yes, Sophie, for about seven years until another unemployed man, a Mr William Hamilton, decided to shoot her near Regent's Park."

"Was she also in her carriage this time?"

"Yes. She was driving through Green Park on her way back to Buckingham Palace with three of her children, including the future Edward VII, when Hamilton fired his pistol at her. Fortunately, he missed, and the park's Head Keeper managed to subdue him. He was handed over to the police. At his trial, Hamilton, an unemployed Irish bricklayer who had been orphaned early in life, told the judge that Her Majesty had never been in danger because his pistol was loaded only with gunpowder…"

"And no bullets?"

"Right, no bullets, and that he had shot at the queen 'for the purpose of getting into prison'. He said that he was tired of being out of work."

"Did this melt the hearts of the judge and jury?"

"No, Sophie. It didn't. He was found guilty and sentenced to spend seven years in the prison colony of Gibraltar. After that he disappeared from history, as he moved to Freemantle in Western Australia and was never heard of again."

"And that, Grandpa, brings us up to assassin number five. Was he another unemployed orphan or so-called 'hunchback'?"

"No, my dear. Robert Pate was an ex-British army officer who was born into a rich family. After he left the Army, he started showing signs of mental instability and, among other things, he became known for goose-stepping like a Nazi soldier around Hyde Park. One day he saw the queen coming out of Cambridge House where she had gone to visit her dying uncle. Her carriage came to a stop just outside her uncle's home and…"

"He shot her."

"No, Sophie. He hit her with his cane – his metal-capped walking stick. Fortunately, it wasn't a fatal blow, but it smashed her bonnet and caused her to bleed. He was immediately arrested and taken to the local police station where he was charged. Of course, he was put on trial after that and charged with three crimes: striking and alarming the queen and disturbing the peace."

"Did he plead insanity, Grandpa?"

"No. His lawyers asked for a lenient sentence saying that Pate had suffered from a momentary lapse caused by a weak mind. He was found guilty and sentenced to seven years hard labour and transportation to Tasmania."

"Wow! That must have been a bit of a blow to someone coming from a rich family, don't you think?"

"Yes, Sophie, I'm sure it was, but it was reported that his father preferred that to having his son imprisoned in England and being birched as well."

"Why?"

"Because then he would have been in the public eye. This way, he was sent abroad, and people soon forgot about him. Also, Pate's father, by pulling some strings, made sure that his son had an easier time than the judge had ordered and, after a year, he was given light duties to perform."

"And did he remain in Tasmania for the rest of his life?"

"No, he returned to England after serving his sentence and marrying a rich heiress there. He lived in south London and died a rich man aged seventy-five."

"So Grandpa, he did well out of hitting Her Majesty. I mean, he met this rich lady out there in Tasmania, came home and lived to a ripe old age, at least for those times."

"Yes, Sophie, perhaps you're right. And what's interesting about this particular attack on Queen Victoria is that Pate was the only one of her assassins who actually harmed her. None of the others did."

"But what about... Wait, wasn't that a knock on the door? Just a minute, Grandpa, I'll go and look."

A few moments later, Sophie was back with another girl.

"Here, Grandpa, here's Jane. Do you remember her? She was here when you were telling us about Lady Jane

Grey."

"Ah, that's right, she was…"

"And Jane, my grandpa is busy telling me about the people who tried to bump off Queen Victoria. Did you know there were eight attempts on her life?"

"No, Sophie," replied Jane. "I didn't know anything about that except that I do know that there was a man with the same surname as my uncle, Jimmy O'Connor, who tried to kill her."

"Very good, Jane. I was just coming to him. He is the next one on my list. On 29 February 1872, that is, on Leap Year's Day, and over twenty years after Pate had hit her with his cane, another seventeen-year-old, an Arthur O'Connor, climbed the fence at Buckingham Palace and sneaked into the courtyard unseen. He rushed up to where Her Majesty was sitting in her carriage, presumably before going out for a ride, and raised his pistol at the queen."

"That's right," Jane said. "But I heard that her faithful servant, John Brown, grabbed O'Connor by the neck and beat him up."

"Exactly, Jane. But what nobody knew then was that O'Connor's pistol was broken and wouldn't have worked in any case."

"But Grandpa, why did he want to shoot the queen? What had she done to him?"

"Well, as you can guess from his name, O'Connor was Irish and he hoped that he would frighten her into signing a document that would release all the Irish political prisoners being held in Her Majesty's prisons. He said that he had never intended really to hurt the queen but just wanted to persuade her to release his fellow Irishmen."

"Which she didn't, of course."

"No, Sophie, she didn't. She awarded a special medal to John Brown, and Arthur O'Connor was sent to prison for a year and given twenty strokes of the lash."

"That's right, Professor," Jane added. "And my father told me that afterwards he was exiled to Australia."

"Like Edward Oxford, William Hamilton and Robert Pate."

"Exactly. And now we come to our last attempt to kill the queen and this one happened five years later, in March 1882. Once again, Her Majesty was sitting in her carriage…"

"Grandpa, I'd have thought that she wouldn't have dared sit in it anymore."

"Well, she did, Sophie, but this time she was in Windsor. She was surrounded by a group of Eton schoolboys when suddenly a shot was fired. The would-be assassin was Roderick Maclean, a shabbily dressed unemployed thirty-year-old clerk. Immediately after firing his pistol, he was set upon by a group of Eton schoolboys and some say that they bashed him up using with their fists and umbrellas. At his trial he was found 'not guilty but insane' and sent to Broadmoor Asylum where he spent the rest of his life."

"Professor Warkworth, how long ago was that?"

"He died in 1921, Jane, so you do the maths."

"That means he was there for thirty-nine years."

"Wow! You are indeed quick at maths. Sophie told me you are the best in your class."

"Thank you, Professor, and was that the last attempt on the queen's life?"

"Yes and no, Jane. You see, there was a more serious plot to kill her some five years later. It was called the Jubilee Plot..."

"Because it was planned to take place during her Golden Jubilee?"

"Yes, Sophie. In 1887. Fifty years after she became queen."

"So this wasn't just the mad attempt of an unemployed clerk or a disgruntled Irishman?"

"Yes and no, Sophie. You see this conspiracy was organised by some Irishmen, but they weren't going to do it simply because they were unemployed. Their aim was to blow up Westminster Abbey where the queen and most of her cabinet ministers would be celebrating her Golden Jubilee."

"Like Guy Fawkes?"

"Exactly."

"But they failed, didn't they?"

"Yes, Jane, they did. One of the plotters was a man called Francis Millen. Some say that he was actually a government agent who kept encouraging the plotters so as to draw them out."

"You mean like that Gifford man who did the same in the Babington Plot against Queen Elizabeth I?"

"Sophie, you surprise me. I never thought you'd remember that one."

"And why not, Grandpa? I also remember you telling me that George Edwards did the same in the Cato Street conspiracy."

"Sophie, I *am* impressed. We'll make a historian out of you yet. But, in June 1887, there were reports in some of the newspapers that a plot to assassinate the queen had been discovered and later, two Irishmen called Harkins and Callan were arrested for importing dynamite into England. They were put on trial and James Monro, the Assistant Commissioner of the Police, said that Francis Millen had been the chief organiser. But then something suspicious happened…"

"Francis Millen was run over by a runway horse."

"No, Sophie, he was …"

"Mysteriously poisoned."

"No, Jane. He was allowed to leave the country. He went to the United States and died in mysterious circumstances."

"And what happened to Callan and Harkins?"

"They were found guilty and sent to prison for fifteen years."

"So, Grandpa, of all the attempts to assassinate Queen Victoria, they all failed, and only one of them, when Robert Pate hit her with his cane, actually hurt the queen, but not seriously."

"Exactly, Sophie. And now I think it's time for us to celebrate Her Majesty's multiple escapes with a good cuppa and some chocolate digestive biscuits."

"As you would say, Grandpa, exactly."

Chapter Twenty
King Edward VIII's Other Problem (1936)

King Edward VIII   *George Macmahon*

"Grandpa, were there any other attempts to kill a British king or queen after those who tried to shoot Queen Victoria?"

"Yes, Sophie, there were, but fortunately not many."

"Why, who else?"

"Well, there were several attempts to kill the present queen and another one to kill her uncle, King Edward VIII."

"So why didn't we hear about the ones who tried to kill the queen?"

"That's because the Secret Service sat on them for many years."

"And Grandpa, when did they happen?"

"I'll tell you later, but as I like my history to be chronologically correct, I'll tell you about the man who tried to kill Edward VIII. The man in the brown suit."

"Why do you call him that?"

"Because, Sophie, that's what the papers called him at the time and also because a book about this would-be assassination was also called that."

"So what happened?"

"Well, let's start this story at the beginning. And the beginning was in Ireland. In County Tyrone, to be exact. Our hero, if you can call him that, was born there in about 1902 and he was called Jerome Bannigan. His father was a delivery man for a bakery and his family, that is, the parents and their three sons, were described as 'people with difficult personalities'."

"Hmm, that doesn't sound like a good start to life, does it?"

"No, Sophie, it doesn't. Anyway, when Jerome was a young lad, the family moved to Glasgow and settled down in Govan, a poor working-class area, the area where they made the ships on Clydeside. Then when he was about twenty-five years old, he was arrested and jailed for embezzlement. After spending some time in prison, he returned to Ireland, to Dublin this time, and changed his name to George Andrew Campbell McMahon. And it was by this name that he became known as the man who tried to assassinate King Edward VIII."

"Did he continue with his criminal career in Ireland?"

"No, Sophie, because he didn't stay there long enough. He crossed 'o'er the water' as the Irish say and moved to Liverpool. There, as a petty criminal, he worked for a nasty character called Harry Longbottom."

"What did he do? Embezzle again, steal?"

"No, Sophie. He was involved in some sort of anti-Catholic and anti-Irish election work for this Longbottom character who was a violent Protestant politician and pastor. He also worked as an informer for Scotland Yard's Special Branch, that's the branch of the police who are responsible for national security and…"

"But, Grandpa, he was a criminal."

"I know that, Sophie, but the police used him. As they say, use a thief to catch a thief. And it was during this period, that is between 1927 and 1936, that he also made money smuggling guns to Ethiopia or, as it was then called, Abyssinia. It was while he was busy doing this that he became involved with the Italian government, as Italy under Mussolini had invaded Abyssinia in October 1935."

"I see, and so what happened next?"

"So while he was working as an informer, he told the police that he had heard about some people who were smuggling guns into Ireland to be used by the IRA. It seems that McMahon used to visit his uncle in Ireland, back in County Tyrone, and as his uncle's farm was on the border between Northern Ireland and Eire, McMahon was able to learn about these smuggling activities. He told his bosses in the Special Branch and they then told the top brass in MI5."

"MI5?"

"Exactly. However, MI5 didn't pay much attention to this and so McMahon presumably continued on his merry way, working for Harry Longbottom, acting as an informer for the Secret Service and smuggling guns to Abyssinia."

"Grandpa, how do you know all this? Wasn't it all hush-hush?"

"I suppose it was at the time but then, later, McMahon wrote a forty-page account of his activities, that is, after he had attempted to kill Edward VIII. He called it *He Was My King.* Later, McMahon told MI5 that there would be an attempt made to kill the king, but they ignored him."

"Why?"

"I suppose that because they'd already had past dealings with him, they considered his information to be unreliable."

"But Grandpa, McMahon *did* make an attempt on the king's life later."

"I know that, Sophie, and so MI5 tried to hush it up. You see, if it had got out that they had known about it earlier and not done anything, then it would have been

459

most embarrassing for them, wouldn't it?"

"Yes, I suppose you are right."

"But then, Sophie, there's another angle to the story. A historian called Alexander Larman wrote a book about this attempted assassination, and he claimed that MI5 didn't cover up this attempt on the king's life in order to hide their incompetence, but that they did so on purpose."

"Why?"

"Larman claims that MI5 may have known all about this planned assassination but that they were willing to let it happen…"

"Do you mean like that conspiracy theory when the CIA allowed Lee Harvey Oswald to kill John Kennedy because he was thinking of stopping the war in Vietnam?"

"Yes, Sophie, something like that. You see, Edward VIII was known to be a Nazi sympathiser and this was something that was very embarrassing for the British government. Remember, this was the summer of 1936 and Hitler had been in power for three years already."

"So if McMahon had succeeded in killing the king, then that would have been the end of the government's embarrassment?"

"Exactly."

"But you haven't told me what happened on the actual day. Did McMahon actually shoot the king?"

"No, Sophie, he didn't. McMahon was standing there in the crowds on 16 July 1936 watching the king ride his horse as part of the Trooping the Colour ceremony. When the king was approaching Buckingham Palace and came near McMahon, McMahon raised his arm in order to shoot the king. However, a woman in the crowd standing next to him grabbed his arm instead. In addition, a policeman who was nearby punched McMahon whose revolver then flew through the air and hit the king's horse…"

"Oh, the poor beast."

"Fear not, Sophie. Nothing happened to it. Then the policeman arrested McMahon and he was taken away. Later he was put on trial at the Old Bailey, and he claimed that he had deliberately made a hash of killing the king even though the Italians had paid him to do so. He also told the court that he had warned MI5 but they had ignored him."

"So was he let off? I mean, no real harm had been done, had it?"

"No, Sophie, but instead of being accused of assassination and treason, he was charged with 'unlawfully possessing a firearm and ammunition to endanger life'. He was, of course, found guilty and he was sentenced to a year's imprisonment with hard labour."

"What? Only one year?"

"Yes, my dear. He was lucky."

"He certainly was. If he'd tried to kill the king six or seven hundred years earlier, they would have hanged, drawn and quartered him."

"Yes, I'm sure you are right."

"What happened to him after that? Did he become a reformed character or a celebrity?"

Professor Warkworth shrugged. "I don't know, Sophie. All I know is that the king abdicated a few months later in December in order to marry his lady-love, Wallis Simpson, and after that they lived for a while in France before moving to Bermuda."

"Well, at least this story has a happy ending, which is more than can be said for most of your stories."

"Exactly, my dear, and now let's have a cup of tea and this time I'll have mine in the mug which has got a picture of Edward VIII's parents on it."

"Ah, you mean George V and Queen Mary."

"Exactly."

Chapter Twenty-One
Kill the Queen – Three Times!

  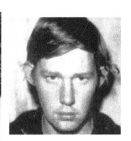

Elizabeth II - Marcus Sarjeant - Christopher Lewis

"Grandpa, before you started telling me about the man in the brown suit who wanted to kill Edward VIII, you said that there had been a few attempts to kill the queen. Can you tell me now what happened?"

"Certainly, Sophie. There have been at least three attempts that we know of…"

"Why do you say, 'that we know of'?"

"Because, Sophie, there may have been more and when you hear what I'm going to tell you, you'll understand."

"Do you mean that one or more may have been

hushed up because some important people would have been embarrassed like they did when McMahon tried to kill Edward VIII?"

"Yes, Sophie. I do. But this is what happened when the first attempt was made on the queen's life in April 1970. This attempt was called the Lithgow Plot."

"The Lithgow Plot. That's a funny name. Where is it from?"

"It's from Lithgow in New South Wales, Australia. The queen was on a train there with her husband on a royal tour in April 1970 when it was discovered that someone had rolled a huge wooden log onto the rails and jammed it into place."

"But that could have killed her!"

"Exactly, and if this plot had succeeded, the train would have been derailed and it would have smashed into the embankment next to the railway track."

"Why did you say, 'if this plot had succeeded'? What happened?"

"Because, luckily for the queen, the train was travelling very slowly at this point and so nothing terrible happened. The train did hit the log as planned but all it did was to make it slide along the rails for about seven hundred yards and that was it. There were no loud noises, and the queen and Prince Philip didn't know anything about it until they were told later."

"Did they find out who was responsible for this?"

Professor Warkworth shook his head. "No, Sophie. They never did, but they suspected that the IRA were responsible. However, no one was ever charged and that, as far as we know, that was the end of it…"

"Unless someone is covering up another embarrassing situation."

"Sophie, what a cynic you've become! Do you really think that after fifty years this incident wouldn't have leaked out to the media or been exposed by a particularly curious historian?"

Sophie shrugged. "Grandpa, you can never know. But tell me, you said that there was more than one attempt made on the queen's life. What happened the next time and when was it?"

"The next time someone attacked the queen took place eleven years later, in June 1981. A seventeen-year-old called Marcus Simon Sarjeant from somewhere near Folkestone fired six shots at the queen when she was riding her horse down the Mall."

"Six shots!"

"Yes, Sophie, but don't worry, nothing happened to her as they were all blanks."

"So why did he do it, Grandpa? It sounds stupid to me."

"As you said, it was, and now I'll tell you what I know about this second assassination that never was. This Sarjeant fellow was what I suppose one could consider as a normal teenager living in the 1980s. His parents were married, he'd been a member of the Boy Scouts and he joined the Air Training Corps when he was fourteen where he won a marksman's badge."

"Ah, this is where the love of guns comes into play."

"Wait a minute, Sophie, and let me continue. Our hero left school in 1980, now aged sixteen, and with seven CSE passes he joined the Royal Marines. He left after three months saying that he kept being bullied by the officers there. After this he tried to join the Army, but nothing came of this. It seems that after two days he'd had enough."

"Well, that's not a very glorious start if you want an exciting career."

"Yes, Sophie, I agree with you. And not only that, but he also failed when he applied to join the fire brigade and also the police. So in contrast to all these macho jobs, he got a job working at a youth centre in Folkestone and also at the zoo. But while he was trying to become famous, he was unemployed and living at home with his mum while his dad was working abroad."

"But where did he get a gun from? Normally, kids of my age don't have access to real guns."

"Well, he was in luck. His dad had an old Webley revolver and so he had to get some bullets for that. However, in order to do so, he had to join a local gun club and also to get a licence. This didn't work out as planned so he bought two replica revolvers by mail and I assume these came with blank bullets. In addition to all this, he wrote a letter to the queen at Buckingham Palace saying, 'Your Majesty. Don't go to the Trooping the Colour ceremony because there is an assassin set up to kill you, waiting just outside the palace' and…"

"Grandpa, he must have been really crazy. Whoever tells the king or whoever that they are going to kill him? It sounds a bit like the warning you told me about when King James I was warned by one of the Gunpowder Plotters four hundred years ago. And besides, I bet the queen receives letters from crackpots like that all the time."

"I agree with you, Sophie, I wouldn't be surprised. But that's what he did. And that wasn't all. He also wrote letters to two magazines and included a picture of himself armed with his father's revolver."

"So what happened in the end?"

"So picture the scene, Sophie. On that sunny June day in 1981, it must have gone something like this:

'Oh, Mabel, isn't this a lovely day for the parade? I hope we won't have to wait too long before we see the queen.'

'Is she coming in a car or will she be riding her horse?'

'On her horse, I would think. That's what she normally does.'

'Oh, good. I do so love to see her on her horse. It looks more regal to me, if you know what I mean. As I was saying to my George yesterday, I hope…'

'Look Mabel, here she is, just coming along on that big black horse of hers. Doesn't she look nice sitting up there?'

"Suddenly six shots, fired in quick succession are heard and the queen's horse leaves its formation and heads off in the direction of the crowds lining the route. The queen leans forward, pats her horse on the side of its neck and quickly calms it down. It then rejoins the parade and continues walking as planned. Just as it does so, a lance corporal in the group of guards standing in front of the two gossiping women leans over and grabbed Sarjeant by his hair and pulls him over the barrier. At the same time, another guardsman, a policeman and a St. John's Ambulance volunteer help the lance corporal wrestle the shooter to the ground before bundling him into a police van and driving him away.

'Mabel, I wonder where they're going to take him?'

'To the nearest cop shop, I suppose. But did you see how I hit that young man with my brolly? I really gave it to him, I did. The cheek of it! Shooting at the queen and scaring her poor horse.'

'Yes, you're right, there. And did you see how quickly she brought him back under control? In seconds, she did. I must say, you can see that she's an experienced rider.'

'I agree but what do you think is going to happen to that young man? I wonder why he did it? He shot all those bullets and yet nothing happened.'

'Yes, and just as those policemen were taking him away, I heard him say, 'I wanted to be famous. I wanted

to be somebody'.'

'Well, he ain't going to be somebody now. He's going to be a nobody. That's for sure.'

"The woman was right. Marcus Sarjeant was charged under the 1842 Treason Act and tried at the Old Bailey in September 1981. After pleading guilty, he was sentenced to five years imprisonment. While he could not be charged with attempting to assassinate the queen as he was using blank bullets, he was charged with 'wilfully discharging at or near Her Majesty the Queen a gun with intent to alarm or distress Her Majesty'. He appealed this sentence, but his appeal was turned down."

"Grandpa, did he get any time off for good behaviour after that?"

"Yes, Sophie. He was released after three years and after that he disappeared into history under a new name."

"Grandpa, apart from him wanting to be famous, what else was found out about him?"

"Well, during his interrogation, they found out that he'd been inspired by the attempt to kill Pope John Paul II and President Reagan. He also thought that it was cool how Mark Chapman had got his fifteen minutes of glory after killing John Lennon in New York. Apparently Sarjeant had told his interrogators that he'd written, 'I am going to stun and mystify the world. I will become the most famous teenager in the world', in his diary, and said while being questioned, 'I would like to be the first one to take a pot shot at the queen'."

"And was that the end of it, Grandpa?"

"Yes, Sophie. As far as I know, after his release from prison, he came out and hasn't been heard of since. However, this wasn't the end of the assassination attempts on the queen. Four months later, another seventeen-year-old, a Christopher John Lewis, tried to shoot the queen while she was on a royal tour in New Zealand. And this time, this would-be assassin was serious. He used a real rifle and real bullets."

"So what happened?"

"You know what, Sophie, I'm thirsty after all this talking. Let's have a break, drink a cuppa and have a slice or two of your mother's apple pie and then I'll tell you how Christopher Lewis tried to assassinate our queen."

"OK. I'll go and put the kettle on."

Half an hour later, after their afternoon tea, Grandpa and Sophie were back in his study. After bringing out a book of cuttings about royal events, he sat down.

"Sophie," he began. "It was like this. Christopher Lewis was born in 1964 in New Zealand. Unlike Marcus Sarjeant, he had a horrible upbringing. His father was extremely strict and, probably as a result of this, Lewis took out his temper at school and beat up another kid there. As a result, he was expelled. He was a very poor pupil and didn't learn to read or write until he was eight. In addition, again I think due to his background, he worshipped Charles Manson, the American cult-leader and murderer and Lewis, together with two friends, wrote nasty letters to the police, stole guns and robbed a post-office of over five thousand dollars. In October 1981, when he was seventeen, he decided to kill the queen…"

"Why?"

Professor Warkworth shrugged. "I don't know, but that's the sort of fellow we're dealing with here. So to continue, the queen and Prince Philip were in New Zealand on a royal tour and they were due to visit a museum in Dunedin, the same city where Lewis was born. While there, he hid in a toilet, five storeys up in a nearby building, and when he saw the queen get out of her car below, he took a shot at her through the toilet window."

"But he didn't hit her, did he?"

"No, Sophie. Fortunately, he missed and later reports noted that the gun he was using, a .22 calibre rifle, was not powerful enough and that he did not have a very good view of the queen."

"Did they catch him afterwards?"

"Yes, they found him with his rifle eight days later. He was arrested and charged, not with assassination, as he hadn't succeeded in killing the queen, but with being in public possession of a firearm and publicly discharging it. He was sent to prison for three years…"

"What, only three years for trying to shoot the queen!"

"Yes, Sophie, and the last part of his sentence was in the prison's psychiatric ward. And just as the earlier attempt in Australia had been covered up by the authorities, so was this one."

"Why?"

"The government there thought that if this assassination attempt were made public, New Zealand would get a bad name. A place where it wouldn't be safe for tourists to visit. In fact, this whole story wasn't released until February 2008, and that was only because of pressure from the media."

"Huh! So they kept it a secret for twenty-seven years!"

"That's right."

"What happened to this Lewis guy when he was released? Had he learned his lesson and decided to walk the straight and narrow?"

Professor Warkworth shook his head. "No, Sophie, no such luck. While still in the psychiatric ward, he tried to escape so that he could shoot Prince Charles who was touring New Zealand at the time with Princess Diana and their baby son, William."

"But he failed?"

"Yes, and when there was another royal tour, the government had him sent to the far north of Australia – to the Great Barrier Reef – so that he would be nowhere near them."

"And Grandpa, was that the end of the story?"

"Unfortunately, no. About thirteen years later, he

murdered Tania Furlan, a young mother, and kidnapped her baby. He was sent to prison before the trial and, while there, he committed suicide by electrocuting himself."

"Well, Grandpa, I know I shouldn't say this, but he doesn't sound a great loss to society."

"Maybe you are right there, but there was a twist to this horrible tale. Lewis' friend, that is, his cell-mate, Travis Burns, told the authorities that Lewis had killed Tania Furlan and so he, Burns, received a reward of $30,000, but in fact, it was he, Burns who had killed her."

"So Burns got off, scot-free?"

"No, Sophie, because a year later, in 1998, Burns killed another young woman called Joanne McCarthy with a hammer, just like he had killed Tania Furlan. He was sent to prison and, as far as I know, he is still there."

"So Lewis, who tried to kill the queen, in a way died for something that he didn't do."

"Exactly, Sophie. Exactly."

The End

About the author

D. Lawrence-Young was an English teacher and lecturer in schools and universities for over forty years until he retired in 2013. He is happiest researching Shakespeare, English and military history or quirky aspects of British history. In addition to editing *Communicating in English*, a best-selling textbook, he has written one crime and over twenty historical novels which have been published in the UK, USA and Israel.

He has been a frequent contributor to *Forum*, a magazine for English language teachers and also to *Skirmish*, a military history journal. He is a member of the local historical club and from 2008-2014 was the Chairman of the Jerusalem Shakespeare Club. He is also a published (USA) and exhibited photographer (UK & Jerusalem). He loves travelling, plays the clarinet (badly) and is married and has two children.

Bibliography

In addition to various Internet sites, I also consulted the following books:

Arthurson, Ian, *The Perkin Warbeck Conspiracy 1491-1499*, Alan Sutton, Stroud, Glosc., 1997

Ashley, Mike, *British Monarchs*, Robinson Publishing Ltd., London, 1998

Baldwin, David, *The Lost Prince: The Survival of Richard of York*, Sutton Publishing, Stroud, Glosc., 2007

Barrie, Charles, *Kill the Queen! The Eight Assassination Attempts on Queen Victoria,* Amberley Publishing, Stroud, Glosc., 2012

Bennett, Michael, *Lambert Simnel and the Battle of Stoke*, Alan Sutton, Stroud, Glosc., 1987

Breverton, Terry, *Richard III: The King in the Car Park*, Amberley, Stroud, Glosc., 2013

Brooke, Christopher, *The Saxon and Norman Kings*, London, Wiley-Blackwell, 2001

Brimacombe, Peter, *Guy Fawkes and the Gunpowder Plot*, Jarrold Publishing, Andover, Hants., 2005

Budiansky, Stephen, *Her Majesty's Spymaster*, Viking, London, 2005

Cheetham, Anthony, *The Life and Times of Richard III*, Weidenfeld & Nicolson, London, 1972

Comte, Suzanne, (Trans from French by David Macrae,) *Everyday Life in the Middle Ages*, Editions Minerva, Geneva, 1978

Cooper, John, *The Queen's Agent: Francis Walsingham at the Court of Elizabeth I*, Faber & Faber, London, 2011,

Davies, Stevie, *A Century of Troubles: England 1600-1700*, Channel 4 Books, London, 2001

Easton, Robert, *Royal dates with Destiny*, Amberley Publishing, Stroud, Glosc., 2010

Fraser, Antonia, *King Charles II*, Weidenfeld & Nicolson, London, 1979

Fraser, Antonia, *King James I of England, VI of Scotland*, Weidenfeld & Nicolson, London, 1974

Green, Dominic, *The Double Life of Doctor Lopez*, Century, London, 2003

Hanrahan, David C., *Colonel Blood: The Man Who Stole the Crown Jewels*, Sutton Publishing, Stroud, Glosc., 2003

Haynes, Allan, *The Elizabethan Secret Services*, Sutton Publishing, Stroud, Glosc., 1992

Hilliam, David, *Kings, Queens, Bones & Bastards*, Sutton Publishing, Stroud, Glosc., 2003

Hutchinson, Robert, *The Audacious Crimes of Colonel Blood*, Weidenfeld & Nicolson, London, 2015

Hutchinson, Robert, *Elizabeth's Spy Master*, Phoenix, London, 1988

Kelly, Michael, *Reminiscences of Michael Kelly of the King's Theatre and the Theatre Royal Drury lane including a Period of Nearly Half a Century. Vol.2*, Nabu Press Reprint, Charleston S.C., USA, 2011

Larman, Alexander, *The Crown in Crisis: Countdown to the Abdication*, Orion Publishing Co., London, 2020

Lewis, Brenda Ralph, *Kings & Queens of England: A Dark History – 1066 to the Present Day*, Barnes & Noble Publishing, NewYork, 2006

Lewis, Matthew, *The Survival of the Princes in the Tower: Murder, Mystery and Myth*, The History Press, Stroud, Glosc., 2017

Miller, Margaret, *The Witch Cult in Western Europe*, Oxford, Oxford University Press, 1962

Murphy, Paul Thomas, *Shooting Victoria: Madness, Mayhem and the Rebirth of the British Monarchy*, Head of Zeus Publishing, London, 2013

Parris, James, *The Man in the Brown Suit: MI5, Edward VIII and an Irish Assassin*, The History Press, Cheltenham, UK, 2020.

Plaidy, Jean, *Mary, Queen of Scots: The Fair Devil of Scotland*, W.H.Allen & Co. Ltd., London, 1975

Pollard, A.J., *Richard III and the Princes in the Tower*, Alan Sutton, Stroud, Glosc., 1991

Ridley, Jaspar, *Elizabeth I: The Shrewdness of Youth*, Fromm International Publishing Corporation, New York, 1989

Sellar , W.C. & Yeatman, R.J., *1066 And All That*, The Folio Society, London, 2001.

Smith, Lacy Baldwin, *Treason in Tudor England: Politics & Paranoia*, Pimlico, London, 2006

Travers, James, *Gunpowder: The Players Behind the Plot*, The National Archives, Richmond, Surrey, 2005

Williams, Brian, *Tudor Secrets & Scandals*, Pitkin Publishing, Stroud, Glosc., 2015

Williamson, David, *Brewers' British Royalty*, Cassel, London, 1996

Williamson, Hugh Ross, *Historical Enigmas*, Michael Joseph, London, 1974

Wilson, Derek, *The Tower of London: A Thousand Years*, Allison & Busby Ltd., London, 2000

Withington, John, *Assassin's Deeds: A History of Assassination from Ancient Egypt to the Present Day*, London, Reaktion Books Ltd., 2020

Wroe, Ann, *The Perfect Prince*, Random House, New York, 2003

If you have enjoyed *Kill the King & Other Conspiracies,* why not read...?

Colonel Blood – Soldier, Robber and Trickster has it all: royalty, love-affairs, lusty wenches, war and fighting. But above all, an incredible robbery. This is the life of self-styled 'Colonel' Thomas Blood, the 17th century dashing Anglo-Irish adventurer who achieved fame by (almost) succeeding in stealing the Crown Jewels in 1671.

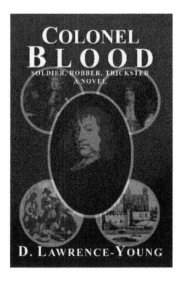

But Blood did much more. He changed sides from being a Royalist to a Roundhead during the Civil War and also became involved in several treasonous plots. He saved a friend from being hanged and twice attempted to kidnap and kill his longtime enemy, the Duke of Osborne. But despite being caught trying to steal the Crown jewels, he was saved by King Charles II. Why was the king so magnanimous? What hold did Blood have over the 'Merry Monarch'?

D. Lawrence-Young has written one crime and over twenty historical novels which have been published in the UK, USA and Israel. He loves writing about Shakespeare and the picturesque characters who make English history so fascinating. When he is not writing, he enjoys checking out the places which feature in his novels.

Take some twenty British villains. Then add their dastardly crimes and their miserable backgrounds. Mix in some nefarious conversations and combine all this to produce this exciting collection of true stories.

This book describes, in an entertaining way through facts and conversations,

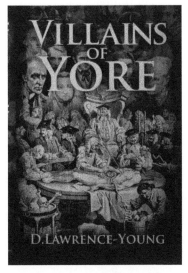

how criminals such as, Richard Pudlicott in 1303 up to the 20th century Elephant Gang operated on the wrong side of the law to make their fortunes. Reading your way through these 700 years, you will meet other well-known characters such as: Dick Turpin, Burke and Hare and Moll Cutpurse, as well as some lesser known but equally nasty villains including: Colonel Blood, Mary Carleton and Jonathan Wild, the 'Thief-taker General.'

D. Lawrence-Young's well researched "*Villains of Yore*" will open your eyes to the criminal world and give you a completely new view on British social history.

CPSIA information can be obtained
at www.ICGtesting.com
Printed in the USA
LVHW030629040322
712532LV00001BA/11